MONTH-BY-MONTH GARDENING
GEORGIA

Inspiring | Educating | Creating | Entertaining

Brimming with creative inspiration, how-to projects, and useful information to enrich your everyday life, Quarto Knows is a favorite destination for those pursuing their interests and passions. Visit our site and dig deeper with our books into your area of interest: Quarto Creates, Quarto Cooks, Quarto Homes, Quarto Lives, Quarto Drives, Quarto Explores, Quarto Gifts, or Quarto Kids.

© 2015 Quarto Publishing Group USA Inc.
Text © 2015 Walter Reeves & Erica Glasener

First published in 2015 by Cool Springs Press, an imprint of The Quarto Group, 401 Second Avenue North, Suite 310, Minneapolis, MN 55401 USA. T (612) 344-8100 F (612) 344-8692 www.QuartoKnows.com

Cool Springs Press titles are also available at discount for retail, wholesale, promotional, and bulk purchase. For details, contact the Special Sales Manager by email at specialsales@quarto.com or by mail at The Quarto Group, Attn: Special Sales Manager, 401 Second Avenue North, Suite 310, Minneapolis, MN 55401 USA.

ISBN: 978-1-59186-628-2

Library of Congress Cataloging-in-Publication Data

Reeves, Walter, author.

  Georgia month-by-month gardening : what to do each month to have a beautiful garden all year / Walter Reeves & Erica Glasener.
      pages cm
  Includes bibliographical references and index.
  ISBN 978-1-59186-628-2 (sc)
  1. Gardening--Georgia. I. Glasener, Erica, author. II. Title.

  SB453.2.G4R433 2015
  635.094758--dc23

                            2014039036

Acquisitions Editor: Billie Brownell
Design Manager: Cindy Samargia Laun
Layout: Danielle Smith-Boldt

MONTH-BY-MONTH GARDENING

GEORGIA

**What to Do Each Month to Have
a Beautiful Garden All Year**

WALTER REEVES & ERICA GLASENER

COOL
SPRINGS
PRESS

Dedication

To my brothers and sisters: Robert, Alan, Carol and Nancy,

for their continued love and support.

—W. R.

To my mother, my best editor.

—E.G.G.

Acknowledgements

We are grateful for the research and information provided by the dedicated county agents, specialists, and Master Gardeners who tirelessly serve the citizens of this state through The University of Georgia Cooperative Extension. Erica especially thanks Daryl and Georgia for their loving support.

Contents

Are you instantly skilled at whatever you try to do? Of course not! You practiced long and hard in your parents' car before you were ready to hit the highway. Professional athletes spend their youth mastering the basics of their sport in order to rise to the top of the sports world. Great cooks don't become great by making macaroni and cheese from a box.

Successful gardeners don't become successful without experience. Maybe in the past they started a few annuals, planted some seeds, pruned a bush, or dug weeds from their lawn. Each completed task gave them confidence to try another. Many say they learned the most from their failures, not from their achievements.

Some folks are convinced their thumbs can never be as green as their neighbors'. They look at a beautiful bed of flowers, a pristine lawn, or a neat landscape and persuade themselves that others have some secret they can never share.

In truth, all they lack is *experience*. A basketball player will practice his jumpshot thousands of times. Some shots will go in; some will bounce off the rim; some will fly over the backboard. Still the ballplayer practices, confident that eventually his successes will outnumber his failures.

To be a good gardener, you have to start somewhere. If you were lucky enough to have a parent or neighbor who taught you the basics, great . . . but you still have lots to learn! If you grew up in a tenth-floor apartment and have never planted a plant, great . . . you can learn the basics without having to get rid of any misconceptions.

Every gardener needs to know the basics. What follows are some of the skills and techniques you should know in order to grow as you garden.

TESTING YOUR SOIL

Plants need adequate nutrients in order to grow properly. They receive the nutrients from the soil and from the fertilizer you add. In order to know how much fertilizer to add, your soil should be tested at least every two years.

Good gardeners notice when they have different soil types in different areas of their landscape. It is possible that you have the same soil throughout. It might be a dark brown, sandy loam; a gray, sticky clay; or common Georgia red clay. If earth grading was done before your home was built, perhaps the front yard is one soil type and the backyard is another.

Separate samples of soil should be collected from each of your soil types. After you have tested the soil, you can decide how to fertilize each area properly.

UNDERSTANDING THE NUMBERS ON A FERTILIZER BAG

There are three major nutrients needed by a plant: nitrogen (N), phosphorus (P), and potassium (K). The numbers on a container of fertilizer denote the percentages of N, P, and K inside. For example, a bag of 24-4-8 has 24 percent nitrogen, 4 percent phosphorus, and 8 percent potassium. Thirty-six percent of the bag's content is plant food; the rest is inert filler, like clay. Nitrogen, phosphorus, and potassium are called macronutrients because plants need them in significant amounts.

HERE'S HOW

TO PERFORM A SOIL TEST

1. Use a clean trowel and bucket. In each area with different soil, take ten plugs (deep, hearty scoops) of soil. A plug should be 4 to 6 inches deep so that soil from the plant root zone will be tested, not the soil on top of the ground. Place the plugs in the bucket.

2. When ten plugs have been collected from an area, mix them together in the bucket. Remove stones, grass, worms, and other materials. Scoop out approximately two 8-ounce cups of soil—this is a representative sample of all the soil in a particular area.

3. Add some science.

   Using a Commercial Kit: Purchase a soil-testing kit from a garden center and read the directions carefully. If you do not understand them, ask a garden center employee or a gardening friend to explain them. Most kits require that you add chemicals to a small sample of soil and water, then wait for a color change. Once the color has developed, it can be compared to a color chart, giving you an estimate of the nutrients available for your plants. Commercial kits are generally easy

1. *What does nitrogen do?*

Nitrogen promotes the growth of roots, stems, and leaves. An appropriate supply of nitrogen gives plants healthy dark green foliage. Too much nitrogen can cause growth to be too rapid, causing the plant to grow tall and fall over. Excess nitrogen can also delay or prevent flower and fruit formation.

2. *What does phosphorus do?*

Plants store energy in their seeds, roots, and bark, and they need adequate phosphorus in order to flower. Phosphorus is essential for flower, fruit, and seed production. Plants lacking sufficient phosphorus usually have purplish leaves, petioles, and stems. They grow slowly and mature very late.

3. *What does potassium do?*

Potassium is important for the manufacturing of carbohydrates (sugar and starch) by plants. When sufficient potassium is available, plants produce stiff, erect stems, and the plants are more disease-resistant. When insufficient or excess potassium is in the soil, plants contain too much water, are susceptible to cold injury, and growth is reduced.

4. *What do micronutrients do?*

Plants also need other chemicals in order to grow and remain healthy. Because smaller amounts of these nutrients are needed, they are called micro-nutrients. Calcium (Ca), magnesium (Mg), iron (Fe), sulfur (S), and many other chemicals are needed in small

to use, but the results might not be as accurate as you would like. It takes a sharp eye to compare colors, a task made more difficult by the orange hue of Georgia red clay.

Using a Laboratory: The most convenient soil-testing laboratory is usually the University of Georgia Soils Laboratory. Look in the phone book under the government listings for your county, under either "Cooperative Extension Service" or "University of Georgia." Your County Extension office can give you details on how to bring a soil sample to them. There is a nominal charge, in the range of $8 to $12, for each sample. The University of Georgia Soils Laboratory will test your soil and send you a written report on the nutrients it contains. The acidity (pH) of the soil will be noted. Fertilizer recommendations are included, along with the amount of lime your soil needs. A single composite sample of soil can be tested for five different plants that

might be growing in that soil type in your landscape. In other words, if you are growing flowers, fescue, azaleas, and a maple tree in your front yard, specify that your soil should be tested, and recommendations given, for each. The single laboratory charge includes up to five individual tests.

4. Interpret the results. The most important soil-test result is the acidity (pH) of the soil. Add the recommended amount of lime to your soil before worrying about fertilizers. The commercial kits will make general recommendations for the amount of fertilizer to use, but the laboratory will recommend specific amounts. Don't worry if you cannot find the exact fertilizer analysis mentioned in a soil-test result. If 10-10-10 fertilizer is recommended, either 8-8-8 or 13-13-13 can be substituted as long as you use a bit more or a bit less, respectively, than the recommended amount of 10-10-10.

amounts. A lack of calcium in tomatoes causes the condition known as blossom end rot. A lack of iron can cause leaves to turn yellow. Most Georgia soils have enough micronutrients to keep plants healthy. If your soil is very sandy or is all clay, additional micronutrients may be needed. The best way to supply micronutrients is by mixing composted manure, homemade compost, or "enriched" fertilizer with your soil.

5. *What does garden lime do?*
Garden lime raises the pH of the soil. Georgia soils tend to be acidic by nature, and regular applications of fertilizer tend to acidify the soil even further. Acid soil ties up many nutrients. They are less available to your plants even though they may be physically present in the soil. For this reason, lime is regularly applied to soil to counteract the soil's acidity and raise its pH.

HERE'S HOW

TO READ A FERTILIZER LABEL

1 **Type of fertilizer**
"Ready to use" means that you can directly apply according to the instructions. Fertilizer marked as "concentrated" has to be mixed with water before spreading on plants.

2 **The fertilizer brand name**
There are different brands of fertilizer, just like there are different brands of clothes.

3 **Intended use**
This tells you which plants the fertilizer is for. Use different fertilizers for grass, vegetables, and flowers.

4 **Fertilizer analysis**
Every fertilizer has three numbers on the bag, separated by dashes. This is called the analysis, or sometimes the N-P-K number. The first number is the percentage of nitrogen in the fertilizer, the second number is the percentage of phosphorus, and the third number is the percentage of potassium. This number is also a ratio. For example, a fertilizer with analysis 10-10-10 has a ratio of 1:1:1; in other words, the same percentage of available nitrogen, phosphorus, and potassium in the fertilizer. A 12-4-8 fertilizer has three parts nitrogen to one part phosphorus and two parts potassium.

1 Ready to Use
2 FERTIFEED
3 *All-Purpose Plant Food*
4 12-4-8

FertiFeed Ready to Use All-Purpose Plant Food
Net Weight 4lb. 12oz. (2.15kg)

GUARANTEED ANALYSIS

5 Total Nitrogen (N)	12%
12.0% Urea Nitrogen	
6 Available Phosphate (P_2O_5)	4%
7 Soluable Potash (K2O)	8%
Manganese (Mn)	0.05%
0.05% Chelated Manganese (Mn)	
8 Zinc (Zn)	0.05%
0.05% Chelated Zinc (Zn)	
9 Inert Ingredients	76%

Information regarding the contents and levels of metals in this product is available on the Internet at www.regulatory-info-sc.com.

KEEP OUT OF REACH OF CHILDREN

5 **Nitrogen content**
This number indicates the percentage of nitrogen in the contents of the package. In this example, a 4-pound bag with 12 percent nitrogen has .48 pounds of nitrogen.

6 **Phosphorus content**
This shows the amount of phosphorus in the fertilizer.

7 **Potassium content**
This number shows the amount of potassium in the fertilizer. This fertilizer example has .32 pounds of potassium in a 4-pound bag. If you need to apply 2 pounds of potassium per 1,000 square feet, you would need 6.25 bags of this fertilizer.

8 **Nutrients other than N-P-K**
These are micronutrients, other nutrients that plants need in smaller amounts than nitrogen, phosphorus, and potassium.

9 **Other ingredients**
Other ingredients make the fertilizer easier to spread.

6. *What is pH?*

The numerical measurement of a soil's acidity is called "pH." The pH number scale ranges from 0 to 14. A number from 0 to 7 indicates acidic conditions. A number from 7 to 14 indicates an alkaline soil. Most plants grow best when the soil pH is between 5.5 and 6.5. Some plants, like azaleas, blueberries, and centipedegrass, tolerate more acidic soil than other plants and usually do not need lime.

PREPARING A BED

Just as newlyweds select a cozy bed to share each night, plants must be given a comfortable bed (of a completely different nature) in which to grow. Preparing the bed is a simple but vital job. If you plant bulbs in hard clay, they will never look like the picture on the garden magazine cover. If you install a hosta in full sunshine and in sandy soil in south Georgia, you'll have nothing but bleached leaves by July.

Preparing a bed requires a bit of work, but it is a chore that will reward you and your plants for years to come. Plant roots need three things: oxygen, moisture, and nutrients. The magic ingredient that provides these three things is organic matter. Whether you use composted pine bark, animal manure, or compost that you make yourself, it is almost always a good idea to mix organic matter into your existing soil before you plant.

Adding the right amount is important too. A dusting of rotten leaves added to a bed does no good. Your goal should be to have a bed that is one-third organic matter and two-thirds existing soil.

There is an alternative to adding only organic matter to the soil. Expanded shale can be added to the soil to keep it loose on a long-term basis. Expanded shale does not hold moisture or nutrients very well, but unlike organic matter, it permanently loosens and does not disappear from your soil. Mix a 2-inch layer of expanded shale plus a 1-inch layer of organic matter into your bed if you use this product.

TO PREPARE A COZY PLANTING BED

1. Use a shovel or rototiller to dig up the soil in the location you've chosen. The soil should be loosened to a depth of 10 inches.

2. Thoroughly break up the big clods of earth. All clumps should be less than 1 inch in diameter.

3. To the area you tilled, add a layer of organic matter 2 inches thick. Mix it deeply and completely with the existing soil.

COMPOSTING

The best source of organic matter for your garden is homemade compost. Why is it better than the store-bought stuff? Because it's alive!

Compost is full of tiny fungi, bacteria, and other creatures. These organisms can digest leaves, grass clippings, lettuce leaves, and wood chips. Euphemistically, we say they "break down" these items. In fact, they eat and then excrete organic materials. As anyone who has changed a baby diaper knows, poop is sticky. The sticky excreta of fungi and bacteria is made that way by a substance called "glomalin." This glomalin glues together the tiny particles of clay in your soil. When tiny grains of soil become big soil granules, the soil becomes soft and loose. Sterilized cow manure can't do that. Composted wood fiber can't do that. Both are valuable soil amendments . . . but compost is best.

Composting is not rocket science! If you have a corner where two fences meet, pile your fall leaves there. In six months, you'll have compost. In fact, there are just two steps to making compost:

1. **Pile it up.** Compost bins can be purchased, or you can simply make one out of stiff welded-wire fencing. Join the ends of a piece of fencing that is 4 feet high and 10 feet long. The hollow barrel you create is a perfect compost bin. Pile leaves and grass clippings in it during the year. Next spring, lift the bin off the pile and scoop out the rich compost underneath the top layer.

2. **Let it rot.** There is no need for "compost helper" products; Mother Nature will make compost without your help. Experienced composters turn their piles a few times a year to make the process go faster. However, organic matter will decompose whether the pile is turned or not. A good spraying with the garden hose while the leaves are being piled will help keep the pile moist. A shovelful of soil sprinkled over each successive bag of leaves will introduce all the fungi needed to make perfect compost by next summer.

Green versus brown. You can also add grass clippings, raw kitchen vegetables, raked leaves, coffee grounds, and many other things. Eventually, compost will happen!

To speed up decomposition in your compost pile it is recommended that you use a ratio of 25 to 30 parts brown to 1 part green. A good rule of thumb is to have a little more brown than green. The brown materials including brown leaves, grass, paper, sawdust, straw, and twigs help the good bacteria and microbes to multiply and slow down the release of nitrogen. Without enough brown, your pile of vegetable scraps and fresh weeds may become smelly and slimy, due to the nitrogen breaking down too quickly. The more diverse your compost is, the healthier the environment for microbes to live in.

Most importantly, experiment and find out what works best for you.

Turn your compost on a regular basis to speed up the process.

REPLACING ORGANIC MATTER

Summer heat and Georgia rainfall will slowly cook away the organic matter in your garden soil. A few years after you worked so hard to make good planting beds, they will need another infusion of rich organic matter. This presents a problem if you have a bed of perennials or shrubs that you don't intend to move. The best way to replenish organic matter is to add a 1-inch layer of composted manure on top of the soil each January. First, rake away any mulch around your plants, add the manure, then cover with fresh mulch. When the soil warms, earthworms will go to work tilling the soil—without any more work on your part!

SUNSHINE VS. SHADE

Jekyll Island is a great place to sit on a sunny beach during the hot summer. Even the hardiest beach bums, though, know to apply lots of sunscreen before they sit down for a noontime picnic. Brasstown Bald is a magnificent mountain, but even locals don't climb it in January without dressing in their warmest clothing. The point is, people can adapt to their surroundings. In general, plants can't. The location you choose for your plants must match their tolerance for sunshine and other weather conditions.

This is not as hard as it seems. Nurseries do a good job of labeling the conditions their plants prefer. Study the plant label before you purchase a plant to make sure it will be happy where you site it.

That said, sometimes nursery labels are less informative than you'd like. What does a sunshine icon on a label mean when it is half darkened? Does it mean the plant prefers constant partial shade or a half-day of full sunshine? Is the label truly accurate for Georgia's intense sunshine conditions? Would the plant be happy in full Ohio sunshine but scorched after a day's worth of Georgia's July heat?

JUDGING LIGHT CONDITIONS

We realize that sunshine intensity differs across Georgia. Compare the noon sunshine in Savannah to noon sunshine in Blairsville: they're radically different! This is how we define sunshine conditions in Georgia:

- Full sunshine in south Georgia is unfiltered sunshine for more than eight hours per day; in north Georgia, it is unfiltered sunshine from morning to night.

- Partial shade (moderate shade) in south Georgia is all-day sunshine filtered through high pine or hardwood (oak, maple, poplar, and so forth) foliage or three hours of direct sunshine between sunrise and noon followed by shade. In north Georgia, it is sunshine filtered through high pine foliage or four hours of direct sunshine between sunrise and noon.

- Shade in south Georgia is all-day sunshine filtered through dense hardwood foliage or direct sunshine that hits the plant for less than two hours per day. In north Georgia, it is all-day sunshine filtered through scattered hardwoods or direct sunshine that hits the plant for less than three hours per day.

- Dense shade means no direct sunshine hits the plant all day; this might be the shade under a southern magnolia, or the shade between two houses whose shadows prevent sunshine from hitting the earth at all.

While we occasionally recommend motorized tools such as lawn mowers, aerators, and rototillers, the following list of basic tools should be adequate for you to start gardening.

Basic tools for the garden or landscape include:

1. **Long-handled, round blade shovel.** The rounded point allows you to push it deeper into the soil than a flat-blade shovel. The long handle gives the leverage needed to lift and turn over the soil.

2. **Handpruners.** The kind with bypass blades usually lasts longer than the type with a blade and anvil.

3. **Spading fork.** It looks like a pitchfork, but the tines are shorter and wider. Great for digging bulbs or potatoes, a spading fork also penetrates clay soil better than a shovel.

4. **Bow rake (also called an iron rake).** It has short tines on one side attached to a steel frame (the bow). Useful for raking the soil smooth.

5. **Hand trowel.** Solid, one-piece models last much longer than those with flimsy handles, which are only slightly less expensive.

6. **Leaf rake.** Plastic or metal, they are quieter and more useful than a leaf blower.

7. **Wheelbarrow.** Every time you have to carry a heavy bag of lime from your car or transport a pile of leaves to your compost pile, you'll be glad you have this handy tool.

As your interest in gardening increases, you will probably want to purchase additional tools, depending on the type of gardening you do. To save money, keep an eye out for tools at flea markets or yard sales.

GARDEN TOOLS

Gardening is not a mental exercise. It requires tools to help you accomplish a task quickly or properly.

PESTS, BUGS, AND CRITTERS

Most gardeners use insecticides with reluctance, knowing that beneficial or harmless insects perish alongside harmful ones. You can minimize the need for insecticides by encouraging beneficial insects to make their home in your garden.

Remember that it takes a few days or weeks for beneficial insects to build their populations enough to control pest insects. One reason we consistently recommend using water to wash aphids from plants is that water does not harm the tiny beneficial wasps that parasitize aphids naturally. Initially allowing a bit of damage to your plants often permits natural controls to strengthen. Common beneficial insects include the following:

- Ladybugs (both adults and larvae) are voracious aphid eaters.

- Green lacewings have larvae that eat spider mites, aphids, and other small insects.

- Ground beetles consume many insects that hide in mulch at night.

- Garden spiders catch whiteflies, ants, beetles, and leafhoppers in their webs.

- Hornets, paper wasps, and yellow jackets may be pests at times, but these insects love to eat leaf-feeding caterpillars.

- Parasitic wasps are tiny insects that are non-threatening to humans. They lay their eggs on aphids and caterpillars, parasitizing and killing them.

The following are some ways to encourage beneficial insects:

- In out-of-the-way corners, plant bronze fennel, Queen Anne's lace, dill, lemon balm, and parsley. Do not remove their flowers, since these provide nectar for adult beneficial insects.

- Plant attractive annual flowers such as alyssum, candytuft, marigolds, and salvias, which are also alluring to beneficial insects.

- Learn to identify beneficial insects and their immature life stages. A lady beetle larva looks

like an orange-and-black alligator. You might think it a pest unless you have learned to recognize it.

WHAT IS A PESTICIDE?

A pesticide is a chemical that is used to kill or control a pest. The chemical can come from organic sources and be called an organic pesticide, or it can come from a chemical manufacturer and be called a synthetic pesticide. In either case, it is still a pesticide.

Pesticides can be classified according to the pests they affect. An insecticide kills insects. A fungicide kills fungi. A herbicide kills plants. Miticides, bactericides, and molluscicides are also used in the garden or landscape, to control mites, bacteria, and slugs and snails respectively.

Organic pesticides usually come from plant, animal, or mineral sources. Pyrethrin is an insecticide that comes from chrysanthemum flowers—pyrethroids are insecticides similar to pyrethrin that have been synthesized in a laboratory. *Bacillus thuringiensis* (B.t.) is a disease spore that is an excellent control for caterpillars. Diatomaceous earth is a mineral that kills crawling insects by drying out their protective body coating. Many organic pesticides are used by commercial farmers and landscapers because they offer superior efficacy or safety.

A synthetic pesticide is manufactured in a laboratory or chemical plant. Synthetic chemistry allows great amounts of a chemical to be manufactured at low cost.

WHICH ONE IS SAFER?

Most of the synthetic and organic pesticides available to gardeners have been tested and studied at length by scientists to make sure they do not present a great risk to the user or to the environment.

Neither organic nor synthetic pesticides can be considered safe in all circumstances. Just because it comes from a laboratory does not mean a synthetic pesticide is more dangerous than an organic one. Before any product may be sold as a pesticide, it must pass extensive tests devised by researchers and the government. The tests help make sure the pesticide is effective and, when used properly, is unlikely to harm humans, animals, other organisms, or unintended targets.

It is important to treat *all* pesticides with caution and to use them properly.

HOW DO PESTICIDES WORK?

Whether synthetic or organic, most pesticides work by interfering with a chemical process in the pest. The synthetic insecticide permethrin interferes with nerve transmission in an insect. Organic insecticidal soap dissolves pest cell walls so they dry out. If you want to know more about how a pesticide works, visit ExToxNet (http://extoxnet.orst.edu/) on the web.

Some pesticides are systemic and some are contact pesticides. A systemic insecticide, like the chemical imidacloprid, is drawn into a plant's leaves and is spread throughout the plant's tissue. An insect feeding on any part of the plant is affected by the chemical. A contact insecticide, like horticultural oil, must touch the insect directly in order to affect it.

READ THE LABEL!

The best way to learn how to use a pesticide safely is to read its label. Government rules mandate that specific information must be included on the label. Signal words such as WARNING, CAUTION, and DANGER must be clearly visible. Usage instructions must be plainly written. The active ingredients must be listed (although the tongue-tangling names of some chemicals are intimidating to all but scientists!). Do not use a pesticide until you have read the label completely and understand how to use the product.

- Emphasize ant control in your garden or landscape. Ants tend aphids, scales, and mealybugs, and they interfere with the natural enemies of these pests.

- Use low-impact insecticides such as insecticidal soap, horticultural oil, and B.t. before reaching for synthetic contact insecticides.

Some gardeners feel they can achieve control of pests by releasing purchased beneficial insects in their landscapes. Researchers caution that it probably doesn't pay to make a mass release. Most will disperse and fly to other yards some distance away. It is usually best to attract beneficials rather than import them.

STORING PESTICIDES

In general, dry fertilizers and pesticides need to be kept dry, and liquid fertilizers and pesticides should be kept from freezing. Dry chemicals need to be protected from humidity as well as rain. A lockable cabinet is the safest place to store pesticides. Failing that, store yours in a large plastic sealable tub. Label the tub and place it where children and pets cannot get to it.

Labels on pesticide containers tend to become tattered over time. Use a rubber band around the bottle to keep the accordion-style directions neat. If the label comes off a container completely, dispose of the chemical according to the directions below.

DISPOSING OF PESTICIDES

It is hard to estimate how much of a pesticide you'll need for some jobs. When spraying dormant oil on an apple tree, will it take a quart or a gallon? When spot-spraying weeds, should you mix a pint or a sprayerful? Sometimes you'll have pesticide left over when you are finished with a job, and what should be done with the excess?

Often the best answer is to save the mixture for a few days and use up what's left. Most pesticides do not deteriorate rapidly and will remain effective for at least a week. If the job at hand doesn't need another application, look for another site. Does a neighbor need the pesticide on his or her lawn? It is not a good idea to simply dump the surplus in one spot; that could lead to surface water contamination.

Most homeowner pesticide products are not manufactured in such a concentrated form that a single accident would pose great harm to the environment. Call your county government for specific directions. Small containers of pesticide concentrate can be disposed of by pouring the liquid into a gallon container of kitty litter, wrapping the container several times with newspaper, and putting it out with your garbage. Municipal landfills are designed to keep chemical contaminants out of the environment.

AND WHAT ABOUT THOSE TONGUE-TWISTING LATIN PLANT NAMES?

Latin plant names help gardeners know exactly which plant they have or want, regardless of the plant's physical appearance. A plant's common name is usually unique, but not always. The plant your neighbor calls wild honeysuckle is likely not the pestiferous vine—it is probably a native azalea. Neither rose-of-Sharon nor moss rose is a true rose. Someone just thought they looked like a rose, and the names have been commonly used through the years.

When we want you to know about a specific plant in this book, we use the scientific name so you'll know exactly which one we are describing. You don't have to know or use Latin plant names, but it does help to know that there is a big difference between a magnificent dogwood *Cornus florida* 'Cherokee Princess' and a sparsely flowering *Cornus florida* 'Transplanted It Out of the Woods Years Ago'!

SUCCESS

Gardening success can be summarized in just three rules:

1. Know your plants.

2. Know your site.

3. Even if you ignore the first two rules, plant anyway!

You might have success in spite of yourself or you might suffer failure. Either way, you'll learn and have fun and you will have started down the road to being *a successful gardener in Georgia!*

HOW TO USE THIS BOOK

Gardening in Georgia is a year-round affair. Gardeners in the northern United States have a long rest each year during their severe winters. Not us! Even in winter there is a day or two each week when something productive can be accomplished in your landscape. Our growing season is such that many different plants can be grown in Georgia, from tropical fruit in Hahira to alpine evergreens in Hiawassee.

With all the gardening opportunities we enjoy, it is natural to feel a bit overwhelmed. There are weeks in April when it seems that everything must be done now! That's why we decided to write this book: to help guide you through your garden tasks all year long.

We have divided the book into twelve chapters, January through December, with suggested tasks for each month, such as planning, planting, care (including pruning), watering, fertilizing, and problem-solving (such as controlling pests).

When possible, we have included lists of plant combinations or plants for special areas, such as groundcovers for shade or annual vines with colorful flowers. In addition, we provide lists of plants recommended for our region. Our soil, heat, and humidity dictate what can be grown and require that you prepare the soil before you plant. Knowing which plants will thrive, and what they need, is half the battle. We also provide information about using (or not using) pesticides.

Gardening in Georgia is, above all, a humbling experience. No one can know everything about every plant. Rosarians might not know rutabagas; fruit growers might not know a ficus from a fothergilla. Each of us will be an amateur at one thing and an expert at something else. Gardeners who have just begun to learn can be discouraged by failure. Every leafless plant or fruitless tomato seems to signify that the gardener did something wrong. Gardeners who have traveled farther down the path, though, think of failure as just one more way to make good compost.

GEORGIA'S HARDINESS ZONES

The United States Department of Agriculture has divided the country into hardiness zones based on the lowest temperatures expected in the region. Georgia spreads across two hardiness zones. The area below a line drawn between Columbus and Augusta is zone 8. The area above that line is zone 7. Colder parts of the country have zones with lower numbers. When purchasing a perennial plant or shrub, you will find its care tag often specifies the hardiness zone for which it is best suited.

Always consult plant tags to determine if plants are suited for your weather. If a plant is listed as "Hardy to zone 6," it is assumed that it can withstand any cold temperatures that zone 7 might present. On the other hand, a plant listed for zones 8 to 9 cannot be expected to survive a winter in the northern part of the state without extremely good care!

We hope this book helps you find an area in your garden in which you can excel. There is no shame in trying small bits at a time, and there is great enjoyment when your efforts succeed. Read closely, work hard, look for miracles . . . and have a great time gardening in Georgia!

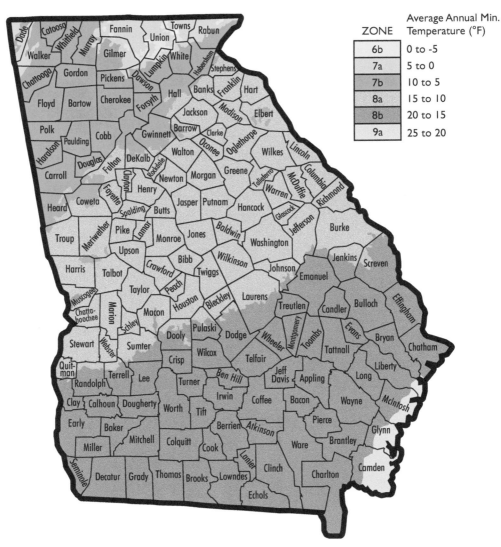

ZONE	Average Annual Min. Temperature (°F)
6b	0 to -5
7a	5 to 0
7b	10 to 5
8a	15 to 10
8b	20 to 15
9a	25 to 20

USDA Plant Hardiness Zone Map, 2012. Agricultural Research Service, U.S. Department of Agriculture. Accessed from http://planthardiness.ars.usda.gov.

January

January is a great time to take a critical look at your garden. If your garden looks good in January, it probably looks great the rest of the year.

Examine the environment in which your existing trees and shrubs are growing to help guide your plant choices. Is it a hot, sunny spot in summer, or is it cool and shady? Determine how much sun you get in a particular area. Start by observing the sun at different times of day, beginning in early morning, then at noon, and again in the afternoon. Record the number of hours of direct sunlight an area receives—in January and at other times during the year. Remember to allow for the difference between winter and summer light, especially in areas with deciduous trees.

If you want sun-loving plants, four to six hours of direct sunlight is ideal. If you're a shade gardener, plants need some light to thrive, perhaps a half-day of bright indirect light. High shade from mature deciduous trees will allow a good bit of light into an otherwise dark area. If there is not enough light and plants are weak and not thriving, you may have to do some selective pruning and open up the canopies of large trees nearby.

Some plants may have outgrown their allotted space, or they may not be thriving because conditions have changed. Where you once had full sun may be shady now because a large tree has matured. Perhaps a natural disaster turned a shade garden into a sunny desert. Whatever the reason for the changes in your garden, you can take action in response to them.

Once you have your basic visual information you can decide where you want to place additional plants. Start with trees and shrubs; later you will add perennials, annuals, vines, and bulbs. Begin a garden journal so you can keep track of what happens in your garden as it develops. Note changes to your original plan as well as make comments on the weather and take notes on how your plantings develop. Photograph your garden now so you will be able to compare how it looks in winter with how it looks during other seasons. And think about the great garden season to come—it's not far away.

PLAN

ANNUALS

Although the weather is a mixture of chilly and cold now, this is an excellent time to plan how you will use annuals in your landscape this year. You don't have to be an artist to sketch out your garden ideas (but do try to keep it in the same scale).

Many annual flowers can be easily grown from seed. This month is a good time to order and purchase seed and to assemble materials needed for seed-starting.

BULBS

Plan for a sequence of bloom in the spring by including bulbs that will bloom early, mid-season, and later, beginning with snowdrops and crocuses, then species tulips and early daffodils; then late daffodils.

■ *Violas will withstand a light frost.*

Sometimes spring bulbs will begin to emerge (2 inches or so), and snowdrops may be blooming now in the northern parts of the state. Gardeners may worry that these flowers might be damaged by the cold. Just cover them with some pine straw and they should be fine.

EDIBLES

Bare-root fruit trees will soon be available at nurseries. Ask the manager when he or she expects the shipments to arrive. If you want to plant a particular variety, ask if it can be special-ordered for you. If you plan to install dwarf trees, do some research to learn the ultimate size of a mature plant— some semi-dwarf varieties grow larger than you might expect. Figs can get quite large, for example.

Having fruit plants is not a simple matter of planting now, then enjoying fruit for years to come. Most fruit trees, especially peaches, require careful management to control insects and diseases. Smaller fruit plants like blueberry, raspberry, and blackberry need much less care. They also take up less room!

LAWNS

Are you spending more time than you would like taking care of your lawn? Do you really need as much lawn as you now have? Consider these lawn-shrinking tips:

- Eliminate the sparsely growing grass in a shady area. Cover the area with mulch, or plant it with a groundcover such as mondo grass, periwinkle, or pachysandra.

- Grass growing in sharp corners is difficult to mow. Round the corners of your lawn with flowerbeds, shrubs, or mulch.

- A grassy walkway between the front lawn and backyard is likely to have so much traffic in the center that it will never look nice, no matter how hard you try. Install walking stones to keep footsteps off the grass.

PERENNIALS

January is the ideal time to plan your perennial garden.

■ Leucojum aestivum, *summer snowflake, is a great bulb for late spring.*

- Begin by making a wish list of the plants you'd like to include, grouping those that have similar cultural (water, sun, and soil) requirements. Include varieties that shine for each season so you can have a progression of blooms and interesting foliage.

- Sketch potential designs on graph paper, remembering that once you begin to plant your plan may change.

- Leave space in your plan to add annual plants for continuous color.

- When you design your garden, remember that several plants of one variety will make more

of an impact than single examples of many different varieties.

- Siting your perennials against a backdrop of evergreens, a hedge, a fence, or a stone wall will help define your garden and provide structure all year long.

ROSES

This is a good time to order roses from a rose catalog. Catalog ordering gives you many more choices of color and ultimate plant size than most neighborhood nurseries can offer. Local rose societies and botanical gardens maintain lists of roses that have performed well for their members. If one of their recommendations meets your needs, a catalog from a specialty rose nursery will help you find it.

HERE'S HOW

TO AVOID PROBLEMS WITH VOLES

Gardeners with sandy soils, beware: Voles love such an environment, and if you grow crocuses or tulips, these animals can be a challenge. To discourage voles, don't apply a layer of mulch that is too thick (2 to 3 inches is plenty), or the soil will become warmer and more inviting to these pests. Keep the mulch 3 to 6 inches away from stems.

To avoid problems with voles, grow different types of narcissus and other members of the Amaryllidaceae family (including *Leucojum* and *Amarcrinum*), which are resistant to rodents and deer. Narcissus bulbs contain a poisonous alkaloid that acts as a natural pest-repellent.

Professional bulb growers Brent and Becky Heath of Gloucester, Virginia, have had success controlling voles using castor oil. To discourage deer they recommend putrescent egg solids. Look for all of these products at your local garden centers.

Rosa 'New Dawn' is a large-flowered climbing rose that can grow 8 to 10 feet tall.

SHRUBS

- Plan to replace shrubs that are not thriving with those better suited to your environment.

- Make a list of possible replacement plants with notes on their cultural requirements, ultimate size, and other features. Collect color photographs from catalogs and develop your own reference guide.

- Locate plant sources. When possible, purchase plants from a local or regional nursery—this will help ensure that they will be best adapted to grow in your Georgia garden. Contact the Georgia Green Industry Association (see Resources, page 221) for a list of nurseries in your area.

TREES

Take an inventory of existing trees, and draw a sketch of where they are located in your garden. Use your house as a point of reference, and indicate which direction is north. How do the shadows of the trees fall? Where are the densest shadows? Sketch where the shadows fall and how

HERE'S HOW

TO DECIDE THE TYPE OF ROSE TO GROW

Roses are grouped by growth and blooming habit. As you choose the roses you'd like to grow, you'll find the following classifications:

Hybrid tea. These traditional one-flower-per-stem roses are used mainly as cut flowers. These roses usually have long pointed buds with high centers. Most hybrid teas have an upright growth habit.

Floribunda. They are similar to hybrid teas but shorter, bushier, and flower in clusters. They provide an abundance of color to any border, hedge, or container.

Grandiflora. Basically, grandifloras are tall floribundas with clusters of hybrid tea-like flowers. This classification can be very confusing, though, because some floribundas grow taller than grandifloras.

Shrub roses. These are colorful roses that are continuously in bloom from spring to late autumn. They provide beautiful flowers with very little care. Shrub roses are excellent to use in borders and as hedges, and some do very well in containers.

Climbers. Climbers are tall, upright, and spreading in growth habit, covering large areas. They are excellent for arbors, fences, and hiding an unattractive view.

far they extend. This will help you determine where you have the most sun or shade and where you need to add trees.

Plan a mix of evergreen and deciduous trees to create maximum interest in your garden all year long. Evergreens planted in groups make an effective backdrop for deciduous trees. Mixing individual evergreens with a planting of deciduous trees will create interest throughout the year.

VINES AND GROUNDCOVERS

January is a good month to begin planning what you will add or take away from your garden. Identify areas where you want to add vines or groundcovers. If your garden looks flat or one-dimensional, vines might be the answer, as they provide instant verticality. If you are running out of space to grow plants, remember that vines grow upwards, and some require only a wall or fence to grab onto and a narrow space to put down some

A well-designed trellis supports climbing plants during the growing season, and it also contributes to the appearance of the yard during the off-season when the plants die back.

roots. Many vines will also grow happily in large containers, trailing over the edge or climbing up onto a trellis.

Add a structure such as an arbor, trellis, pergola, or gazebo. Gather information and ideas about the best structure for your garden; it should be functional and attractive. Scan garden magazines and books for ideas, or consult with a garden designer about which type of structure will work best for your garden style. In addition to providing a place for your vines to climb upon, cling to, or twine on, arbors and other garden structures can serve as key elements in the design of your garden. Placement of the structure is very important. An arbor can lead a visitor from one point to another, invite you to approach, or direct your attention toward a particular view. Positioning an arbor at the end of a path, with a bench placed beneath the arbor, makes a stronger statement than placing one in the middle of your garden.

If you are growing perennial ornamental vines, think about what they will look like throughout the year. What does the foliage look like in autumn? If there are flowers, are they fragrant? Does a particular vine offer attractive bark in winter?

Hire a professional to draw up landscape design plans, or refer to plans in a book. Take time to make sure the scale of whatever structure you build or have built fits into your garden and relates to your house and garden. As a rule of thumb, bigger is usually better. What looks like a massive structure on paper is often just right once it is constructed and standing in the garden. If you don't feel confident about getting the proportions right, and hiring a professional is too expensive, invest in some bamboo poles and construct a temporary arbor. Observe it for a week to determine if the size is appropriate. This is an inexpensive way to learn about scale before you build a permanent structure.

If you have an area of lawn that is thin and patchy because it is beneath large shade trees, think about replacing the lawn with groundcovers. Measure the area so you will know how many plants to purchase in the spring. Mondo grass or liriope are alternatives to turf, and both thrive in the shade.

PLANT

ANNUALS

In south Georgia, colorful annuals can be planted even when the weather is cold. Flowering cool-season plants make an immediate impact in a bare landscape.

In north Georgia, winter annuals can be planted as long as daytime temperatures for a few subsequent days are predicted to be above 40 degrees Fahrenheit accompanied by bright sunshine.

- Plant dianthus, viola, snapdragon, pansy, ornamental kale, English daisy, and parsley. All prefer a sunny spot.

- Plant on sunny days, when the soil is more likely to be warm, and water the plants immediately.

- Purchase plants in 3-inch or larger pots so blooms will continue to appear (plants in smaller containers will stop blooming as they try to establish roots).

BULBS

Once your snowdrops finish blooming, you can divide them. Because these bulbs are so tiny and dry out easily, the best time to divide is while they are still blooming or as soon as the blooms fade. Dig up a clump you want to

HERE'S HOW

TO PREPARE A ROSE BED FOR PLANTING

How to achieve the best planting bed is a topic of much discussion among rose fanciers. Some prefer amending their native soil and giving their roses a "natural" environment. Others construct raised beds, either mounded or lined. Either way has merit; make your choice and get to work before rose planting season arrives.

- Estimate how many roses you plan to grow in an area.
- The bed should be 4 to 8 feet wide. Plan at first on 6 feet between plants. You can make a closer calculation later, after the plants have been purchased.
- Remove all grass from the area. If bermudagrass was growing there, remove and discard all soil to a depth of 6 inches.
- Shovel up the remaining soil to a depth of 10 inches.
- Pour a 2-inch-thick layer of soil amendment over the bed.
- Add 4 pounds of bonemeal and 4 pounds of garden lime per 100 square feet.
- Rototill the soil and amendments together.
- If the bed is not mounded 8 inches above the surrounding soil, add bagged planting soil to the mound. Rototill it completely into the existing bed.

If you choose to line the bed to hold the soil in place, several materials work well:

- Treated lumber (remember to wear gloves when handling)
- Untreated lumber (will last only four to five years)
- Brick (attractive, but mortar joints are beyond the skills of most folks)
- Cinderblock (not very aesthetically appealing; use a cap block to cover the holes)
- Stacked stone (very attractive, but requires a lot of work to build)

TO PLANT BARE-ROOT TREES

Bare-root trees are less expensive and easier to handle, and you can order them through the mail. A bare-root tree is usually up to 10 feet tall with a trunk less than 2 inches in diameter. When you purchase a bare-root tree, you are investing in its root system. If the tree has lots of branches but very few roots, it will take a long time to become established.

1. Make sure roots are healthy. Prune off any broken or dried-up roots. With clean cuts, the roots will heal quickly and there will be less chance of root-disease problems. This should be done when trees are dormant and temperatures are cold or cool (30 to 40 degrees Fahrenheit is ideal—slightly warmer is acceptable).

2. Keep tree roots moist until you plant. If the roots are dry when you receive the tree, soak them in a bucket of cool water for up to eight hours.

3. If you can't plant within a day or two, dig a temporary pit for the tree roots. Water the roots and fill in around them with a mixture of mulch and soil. This will cause the least amount of stress for the tree and help reduce air pockets.

4. When you dig the hole to plant a tree, set the soil aside and use it to fill in around the roots. This way the tree roots will adapt quickly to their soil environment. If needed, adjust the pH by adding lime to your planting hole. It is best to have your soil tested before you plant.

Do not add fertilizer to the planting hole—it could burn the roots, and it's not necessary until the tree is established. If you use a root stimulator, follow directions carefully.

Although it is not necessary to amend the soil before you plant trees, it is important to be sure the soil is well drained. If the spot stays damp, select varieties that will thrive in wet soils, such as the sweet bay magnolia or bald cypress.

To help improve drainage, add soil amendments like ground pine bark or gritty, all-purpose sand, both available at your local home-improvement stores.

If the existing soil is infertile clay subsoil, you should remove it and replace it with soil that has been amended with organic materials.

divide, and gently tease apart the bulbs, making sure each division has bulbs with roots, shoots, and foliage. Replant them as soon as possible in their new location, leaving the foliage intact. Water them in, and next year you should have blooms again.

EDIBLES

Rototill garden beds where you will plant cool-season vegetables. If the soil is ready, you will not have to tend to this task when the early gardening season begins next month. Tilling may also reduce insect pests.

LAWNS

Bermudagrass sod can be successfully laid at any time of year, even if it is brown and dormant. The key to its survival is watering the sod after installation, even when it looks brown and lifeless. Roots are growing into the soil below—they need moisture. In the absence of rainfall, apply ¼-inch of water per week.

■ *Trees and shrubs are packaged three different ways for sale: with a bare root, container-grown, and balled-and-burlapped. Bare-root specimens (left) are the most wallet-friendly, but you must plant them during the dormant season, before growing begins. Container-grown plants (center) are smaller and take years to achieve maturity, but you can plant them any time—preferably during spring or fall. Balled-and-burlapped specimens (right) are mature and immediately fill out a landscape. They are also the most expensive.*

PERENNIALS

In south Georgia, perennials can be planted anytime they are available.

SHRUBS

As long as the ground is not frozen or saturated with water, you can plant shrubs during mild spells at this time of year. In south Georgia, shrubs can be moved to a better spot now.

TREES

This is a good time to plant trees, especially in the most southern parts of the state where winters are mild and the ground is never frozen. Plant balled-and-burlapped, container-grown, or bare-root trees. Before you plant, remove all turfgrass and weeds from the soil surface. A flat shovel works well for this.

VINES AND GROUNDCOVERS

Unless you live in the southernmost part of the state, wait until the weather is a bit milder and the ground is not frozen or soggy before you begin to plant.

CARE

ANNUALS

Don't worry if pansy leaves look pitiful in the morning; they will recuperate by noon as moisture fills the leaves. Pansies protect themselves during cold weather by wilting their leaves. Other plants use a variety of coping mechanisms.

Scatter pine straw loosely over flowerbeds if frigid, windy weather is predicted. When daytime temperatures are above 40 degrees Fahrenheit, lift the straw off the plants and use it for mulch around nearby shrubs.

Remove faded blooms from plants as you notice them. This procedure (deadheading) is particularly important for pansies— these plants produce many more flowers if deadheaded regularly. Hold the plant stems with one hand while tugging on individual flowers with thumb and fingers. Garden scissors can also be used to remove flowers. Snip the blooms with one hand while gathering them with the other.

BULBS

A true bulb may be considered a bud. An onion (a true bulb) sliced lengthwise shows the budlike structure. Pale green leaves in the center are protected by concentric layers of fleshy tissue called "scales." The scales contain stored food and energy for the plant when it is actively growing, and the future flower is protected by the scales and the leaves. At the base of the bulb is a stem to which the scales and small leaves are joined; at the bottom of this is the basal plate, where roots emerge when the bulb is planted. If the basal plate is damaged, there may be fewer and smaller roots. It is for this reason that a healthy basal plate is important. The outer layer on a bulb is dry and papery and keeps the bulb from drying out. This layer is called a "tunic." Daffodils, tulips, and hyacinths all have tunics; a lily bulb has scales that are short and fleshy, and there is no tunic or outer layer to protect them. A bulb is usually underground, but small bulbs called bulbils may appear in leaf axils of a plant like the blackberry lily, or in flowers and on stems of certain bulbous plants.

A corm is a short, enlarged, fleshy underground stem. Like a bulb, it is usually surrounded by a tunic, but the inside is solid. One or more buds give rise to leaves, stems, and flowers aboveground; it roots from the base. Examples of corms are colchicum, crocus, and gladiolus.

A rhizome is a thickened stem that grows completely or partially underground, like rhizomatous iris, which should be planted so the rhizome is barely covered. Growing points initiate at the tip or along the length of the rhizome, and roots develop from the underside. Rhizomes include calla lilies and bearded iris. (Dutch iris grow from bulbs.)

A tuber is a swollen underground branch or rootstock that contains a supply of stored food. It has "eyes" or buds from which stems are produced. Cyclamens, some of the anemones, and caladiums are examples of tubers. When you divide tubers, make sure each section has a growth bud. While cyclamen tubers continue to

get larger over time, they never produce offsets as do caladiums. (Caladiums' offsets can be removed and planted.)

Tuberous roots store nutrients. Daylilies and dahlias are examples of tuberous roots. Their growth is such that the roots grow in clusters, radiating out from a center point, and buds are produced at the bases of old stems. When you divide tuberous-rooted plants, make sure each section has roots and shoots.

EDIBLES

Raspberry and blackberry stems (canes) are not permanent. On most plants, the canes that bore fruit last season will die during the winter to make room for fresh growth. Now is a good time to remove the brown, dead canes from your plants and tie the green canes to your wire trellis.

Prune your muscadine grapes now, removing the long whips that grew last year. Actually, you'll prune back to the first two buds on each long stem, leaving only these to make new growth this year. It is on this new growth that the grapes are produced!

After several years of pruning back to two buds, a series of spur clusters (staghorns) will protrude from the main vine arms. If the clusters crowd each other too much, remove a few to give the rest more room to grow.

Pear and apple trees often suffer broken limbs due to an excess of fruit in August. Shorten long and slender limbs by one-third to one-half. Limbs that cross through the branches in the center of a fruit tree rarely bear fruit. They also shade the leaves of more productive limbs.

Bulb-Daffodil

Corm-Gladiolus

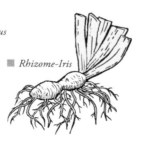

Rhizome-Iris

Tuber-Caladium

This is a good time to examine the structure of your fruiting trees. Remove crossing limbs, dead limbs, and limbs that deviate from the appropriate form.

Fig bushes that have become too large for their space can be severely pruned now. It is best to remove vertical limbs over horizontal limbs.

If the space is small to begin with, consider moving the bush to a spot where it can grow at least 8 feet tall and 8 feet wide.

Leather gloves are a must when working with brambles. Use jute twine to loosely tie up the canes. The twine will rot by the end of the year.

LAWNS

Avoid heavy traffic on dormant lawns in winter; dry grass is easily broken. The living crown of your grass plants may be damaged even though the grass is brown. Since the grass is not growing and able to recover, even a short game of football can cause scars you'll regret in spring.

PERENNIALS

Remove any dead stalks, seedpods, or leaves you missed in the fall. Wait until early spring, just before perennials begin to put out new growth, before you prune plants back hard to a height of several inches. Some perennials don't need to be pruned back hard, but you can tidy them up by removing dead flower stalks.

In south Georgia, cut back clumps of pampas grass and other ornamental grasses to a height of 12 to 24 inches.

ROSES

Existing roses need care during the winter, even during deepest cold.

1. Winter winds can whip climbing rose canes against their trellis, damaging the bark. Use jute twine to tie the loose canes firmly in place.

2. Prune out blackened canes whenever you notice them.

3. Keep a 3-inch-thick layer of pine straw mulch under plants at all times.

SHRUBS

Remove any dead or damaged wood from existing shrubs. Dead wood is dry and brittle—if you are not sure if a branch is dead, scratch it with your fingernail. If the inside is green, then there is still hope, and you can wait until spring to see if any buds form.

Renovate overgrown shrubs by removing one-third of the oldest branches from the base of the plant. The oldest branches are usually the thickest. Remember that many spring-flowering shrubs bloom on old wood (branches that grew the previous season), so you will want to wait until *after* they flower to do any drastic pruning. Examples include forsythia and quince.

TREES

Prune bare-root trees when you plant them. Thin branches that are closely spaced; this will allow better light and air circulation, resulting in better overall growth. Prune any broken roots.

When you prune, make your cut on a slant, just above a bud. On the side branches, make your cut just beyond a bud pointed towards the outside.

VINES AND GROUNDCOVERS

If you have annual vines like moonvine or black-eyed Susan vine that are still clinging to walls, fences, arbors, or other supports, pull them off. It should be easy to pull or prune them off and clean up the surfaces now that they have died. Save any seeds that you missed collecting in the fall. They make easy and inexpensive presents for your gardening friends. Once they drop their leaves, it is easier to see where you want to prune your vines, especially if you want to train them as an espalier (see May).

- Prune to remove dead or damaged stems and twigs from woody vines.

- Prune wisteria vines to reduce or thin side shoots from the main stems. These shoots make flower-producing spurs. For the best blooms, shorten these shoots back to two or three buds. Because it is such an aggressive grower, wisteria needs to be pruned regularly, sometimes two or three times a year.

If you have large areas of evergreen groundcovers like English ivy or vinca, wait until early spring to prune them back close to the ground, and do so only if they need it. Established beds of English ivy or vinca can go for years without being pruned, but if they become overgrown and straggly or start to spread beyond where you want them to, prune away.

WATER

ANNUALS

If the soil is frozen or dry, the roots of winter annuals cannot absorb the moisture they need. Test soil moisture weekly by digging 4 inches into the ground and squeezing a lump of soil in your palm. If it is dry and crumbly, water is needed.

Water your flower beds as needed so moisture is available when plant roots require it after cold nights.

BULBS

Water bulbs as soon as you plant them. Soak the planted area several times, once a week. Apply 2 inches of mulch (pine straw or pine bark) over the planted area.

EDIBLES

In south Georgia, sandy soil loses water rapidly. Plan to add 1 cubic foot of organic material for each foot of hole diameter before planting a fruit or nut tree. The organic particles will act like a sponge during the summer, storing water when it is available and releasing it when dry weather occurs.

Make a habit of mulching plants with shredded leaves each fall. As the leaves break down, earthworms will mix them with the soil beneath.

LAWNS

Water bermudagrass in the absence of rainfall, apply ¼ inch of water per week.

Tall fescue sod installed in the last six months should also be watered regularly (½-inch per week). The green leaves transpire a great deal of moisture on sunny, windy days.

PERENNIALS

If temperatures are mild, plants can dry out. Keep them watered and mulched.

ROSES

Roses cannot tolerate soggy soil—even in winter. If your rose bed is constantly damp, make a mounded bed.

Water any plants you put in last fall. One to 2 gallons of water per plant is sufficient. Remember to drain the hose after every use so it does not freeze and crack.

SHRUBS

Water new plantings. If there is no rain during mild spells, water evergreen shrubs. Don't let them get to the stage where the leaves or needles begin to look crisp and fall off.

Don't allow large shrubs in containers to dry out. When the top 2 inches of the soil in a container are dry to the touch, water until the water rushes out the bottom of the container. If the soil has shrunk away from the sides of the pot you may have to apply water several times, allowing it to soak in after each dousing.

TREES

Water trees immediately after you plant them, and then once a week unless the ground is frozen. Apply 1 gallon per foot of tree height per week.

VINES AND GROUNDCOVERS

If you have areas of groundcovers that have been planted in the past six months, they should be watered weekly (at least 1 inch per week) if there is no rain and if the ground is not frozen. Use a sprinkler, and set out small cans, such as tuna fish cans, to measure how much water the plants receive. Water until the tuna fish can is approximately three-fourths full, which should equal about an inch of water.

FERTILIZE

ANNUALS

Fertilize pansies and other cool-season annuals with a product containing nitrate nitrogen.

EDIBLES

Fruiting plants are deciduous, losing their leaves in winter in most parts of Georgia. Mature plants don't need fertilizer now, since there are no leaves present. New plants, on the other hand, need phosphorus immediately.

Mix 1 tablespoon of 0-46-0 (triple superphosphate) per foot of height into the soil when you plant a fruiting plant. This will give the roots the phosphorus they require when they begin to grow.

LAWNS

You have probably heard of people who "burn off" their bermudagrass lawns in winter: they literally set their lawn afire in the mistaken belief that the ashes contain fertilizer that will feed the grass.

- There is a tiny bit of potassium in ashes, but not nearly enough to risk causing a tragedy in your neighborhood. The flames can easily ignite pine straw islands and cedar siding.

- In most municipalities, outdoor burning is illegal.

There is no need to fertilize any warm-season grass at this time.

PERENNIALS

In south Georgia, you can fertilize newly planted perennials with a half-strength mix of a liquid fertilizer.

In north Georgia, there is no need to fertilize your perennials when they are dormant. Now is a good time to amend soil in new beds so you will be ready to plant in the spring. Spread 2 to 4 inches of compost or manure across an area, and mix it in a good 12 inches deep with the rototiller.

SHRUBS

Topdress shrub beds with 1 to 2 inches of organic amendments such as mushroom compost, cottonseed meal, or cow manure. As the organic material continues to break down, it will be a good source of food for your plants when the roots begin to grow in spring. Be sure you don't pile it up around the stems or trunks of plants.

Apply a 2-inch layer of mulch around new plantings. Use pine straw, bark nuggets, shredded bark, leaves, peanut hulls, or cocoa shells.

PROBLEM-SOLVE

ANNUALS

Visit your flowerbeds each week to look for weeds such as chickweed, bittercress, and henbit. Pull weeds by hand, put them into a container, and remove them from the garden. This will eliminate the possibility of weed seeds being dropped onto the soil. Suppress further weed development by mulching with pine straw or pine bark mini-nuggets.

BULBS

In south Georgia, check for aphids feeding on new foliage and buds of bulbs. Use a strong blast from the hose to try to eradicate these hungry pests.

EDIBLES

Many insects overwinter under the bark of fruit trees. Spray dormant horticultural oil on fruit tree branches and trunks to suffocate dormant insects. Thoroughly cover the entire trunk and all branches with the spray.

LAWNS

If you have a bermudagrass lawn in the northern half of the state, it is easy to spot the green leaves of unwanted tall fescue, chickweed, or wild onion in your brown turf. If you are very careful, you can spray the weeds lightly with a nonselective herbicide now. The weeds will be killed, but if the bermudagrass is dormant, you won't hurt your lawn. It is important to examine your bermudagrass closely to make sure it is fully dormant before attempting this task:

- Get down on your hands and knees. Pull back the dead grass foliage and inspect the stems where they come out of the ground. Do you see any green stems? If so, the grass plant is not dormant.

- Repeat the examination at several spots across the lawn before spraying very lightly.

- Do not attempt this winter weedkilling trick on zoysiagrass, centipedegrass, or St. Augustinegrass lawns. These turfgrasses can be severely harmed by nonselective weedkillers, as can bermudagrass if it is not fully dormant. Hand-weeding is your best option for these turfgrasses.

As winter wears on, the tree leaves you failed to rake last fall can blow across your lawn and build up in piles at the edges:

- Don't let leaves pile up and suffocate your grass. Without sunlight, disease will attack grass crowns and roots.

- Rake up the leaves and add them to your compost pile, or run over the leafy spots with a lawn mower to shred the leaves into tiny pieces.

PERENNIALS

Look for infestations of chickweed, a mat-forming winter annual. The leaves are opposite and densely hairy; the white, notched flowers appear in clusters at the ends of the stems. If a crop appears, pull them out before they set seed.

The best time to weed is the day after a gentle rain when plants are easy to pull up, roots and all.

Remove any dead leaves that have accumulated around perennials. This will help eliminate insects that may be overwintering.

Scale can be white or brown and often look crusty. They appear in clusters on the bark, stems, and

leaves of plants. Use horticultural oil to suffocate insects like scale or other pests.

ROSES

The pine vole is a rodent about the size of a mouse. Voles live under brush piles and in hollow logs; they scurry about, hidden under mulch and groundcovers, looking for plant stems to gnaw on. A vole-damaged rose may suddenly break off at ground level and show clear evidence of gnawing at the soil line.

- Pull back mulch 6 inches from the stem(s) of each plant. Be sure to keep the mulch away from the stems at all times.

- Do not pile brush near your rose garden. Put it at the far edge of your property.

- Keep the weeds at the edge of your property line cut short.

- Voles may be killed with a mousetrap baited with peanut butter. Be sure to cover the trap with an upturned plastic pot so no other animals are harmed. Some gardeners put a slice of apple under the pot to lure the vole to his last lunch.

SHRUBS

Remove debris and dead leaves from planting beds to reduce future insect and disease problems.

TREES

Inspect your trees for pest and disease problems. If you find scale on the bark or in the crotches (where the branches meet the trunk), spray with horticultural oils. Scale is common on Bradford pear trees. Be sure to get good coverage, spraying the branches, trunk, and crotches.

VINES AND GROUNDCOVERS

In south Georgia, check evergreen groundcovers like vinca and euonymus for insect infestations such as scale or spider mites. Scale looks like white and brown specks firmly attached to stems and leaves. The scale—sucking insects that cause leaves to turn yellow and drop—also cause branches to die back. Spray with horticultural oil to control. Read and follow label instructions.

February

February is the ideal month to hire a garden designer to develop a landscape plan for your property or to help you revise your existing plan. Take a good look at your landscape and think about what you would like to add or change. Come up with an overall plan and you will be able to refer to it as you develop your garden over time.

When selecting plants, consider not only the season of bloom and the flower color, but the color of the foliage, the texture of the plant, and what the plant looks like when it is not in bloom. List the attributes of plants you want to grow: flowers, foliage type, and whether or not there are decorative seedheads. Note which plants attract bees and butterflies, and which plants die back after they finish blooming (like the one that seems to disappear soon after its flowers fade). Remember that just one plant of many different varieties will not make an effective display. Think about grouping plants—two or three of the same type will make an impact.

Grouping plants that have flowers with similar colors will also make an effective display. Spring may feature pastel blooms of pink, white, and blue, while summer may be reserved for hot colors like red, orange, and yellow. Remember that green in all its shades is also a color.

Spacing is important too. Do a little research on the cultural requirements and growth rate of the plants you would like to grow before you purchase them. While you don't want to wait three years for your plants to fill in, you don't want your garden to become overgrown in only one year either.

If you draw up your own plans, use graph paper, indicating which plants you would like to include. While you don't have to have a scale drawing, you can use your house as a reference point to help you locate plants in relationship to one another.

PLAN

ANNUALS

Many annual flowers can be easily grown from seed. This month is a good time to purchase seed and to assemble materials needed for seed-starting.

Most homes do not have enough natural light in an appropriate spot to make seedlings prosper. Purchase or build a light stand, which uses fluorescent bulbs above the seed flats. PVC pipe is easily available at home-improvement centers and is quite easy to work with. The pipe fittings allow sturdy connections at the corners of the structure. Special "plant light" fluorescent tubes are not necessary; two cool-white 40-watt tubes will be sufficient.

BULBS

Depending on where you live in the state, early spring bulbs like snowdrops or glory of the snow (*Chionodoxa luciliae*) are beginning to bloom or

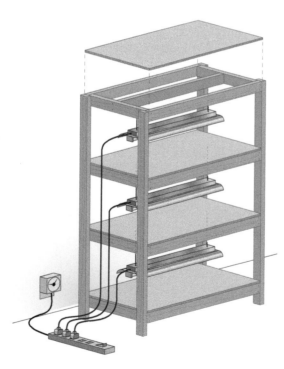

■ *This easy-to-build starter rack holds up to 12 full-size seedling flats or trays and can be located practically anywhere with an accessible electrical outlet. The top shelf offers a handy space for storing extra flats and other supplies.*

are still blooming. Other early bloomers include *Narcissus* 'Rijnveld's Early Sensation', a classic daffodil with a yellow trumpet and petals, and the reliable heirloom daffodil *N.* 'February Gold', which is excellent for forcing and a good variety for coming back reliably.

At the end of the month in the coastal part of the state, expect the old-fashioned *Narcissus jonquilla* to be in bloom. This species of daffodil (called "sweeties" for its sweet perfume), which has rushlike foliage and extremely fragrant flowers, has naturalized throughout the Southeast.

EDIBLES

Asparagus is easy to grow in a permanent bed. The key to success is to prepare the soil properly at the beginning, since you won't be able to improve it for several years. Raised beds, deeply dug and amended with copious amounts of organic matter, will give your asparagus a happy home for years.

- Try to find a hybrid asparagus variety like 'Jersey Giant' or 'Jersey Male'. These hybrids produce twice as many spears as the old-timers' favorite 'Mary Washington'.

- Purchase crowns that are more than one year old; two- or three-year-old crowns are best.

- Avoid harvesting spears the first year. The plant needs at least a year to grow vigorous roots.

LAWNS

When caring for a lawn, there is one basic fact you need to know: how big is it? Application rates for fertilizer and weedkillers are based on applying a certain amount for each 1,000 square feet of lawn.

PERENNIALS

Take a soil sample and have it tested by your local Cooperative Extension Office. You will receive a report that describes the nutrients present in your soil, the amounts in which they are present, and specific recommendations for correct fertilizer use. A soil test will also determine the pH of your soil and the amount of lime it needs.

Wait a year, or even two, after you plant asparagus to harvest the spears.

The pH affects the availability of nutrients and whether they are soluble in the soil. A pH of 7 indicates that the soil is neutral. A pH below 7 indicates acidity, and one above 7 indicates alkalinity. Acid-loving plants like rhododendrons, camellias, and azaleas are happiest in a soil with a pH of less than 5.5. Lime is applied in gardens primarily to raise the pH.

Lime also has a physical effect on soil: in clay soils, it causes particles to form larger units and therefore enables water and air to move more easily through the soil (for information on lime applications refer to page 10). In sandy soils, lime holds particles together so that water is held for a longer time.

As a rule, the rate of application for lime is 4 pounds per 100 square feet. When you apply lime, it is best to make sure that you rototill it in to a depth of 4 to 6 inches. This can be done when you prepare the soil for planting as you add other soil amendments.

ROSES

Roses need at least four to six hours of full sunshine each day. A location that receives morning sunshine and afternoon shade is best because the leaves dry off faster, offering some protection against blackspot and powdery mildew diseases.

SHRUBS

Plan to add at least one shrub with winter blooms or berries to your garden this spring. Winter wonders include winter honeysuckle, evergreen hollies, and deciduous hollies. When you select hollies for your garden, keep in mind that you will need a male plant for pollination in order to guarantee the best fruit production. The female selections display fruit in season, while the male does not. For example, the American holly *Ilex opaca* 'Merry Christmas' needs one male selection of the same species or hybrid; the same is true

HERE'S HOW

TO MEASURE A LAWN AREA

You will need several soft drink cans, a pencil, and a piece of paper; here's how to determine how much fertilizer and/or weedkiller a patch of lawn will require.

- Roughly sketch the lawn and divide it into rectangles.

- Put a can on each corner of each rectangle.

- Walk from can to can; count your paces between each can, and mark the figure on the sketch. Assuming your pace is 2.5 feet long, multiply the number of steps by 2.5 to find the length, in feet, of the sides of each rectangle. If you have a longer or shorter stride, adjust your calculation accordingly.

- For each rectangle, multiply the length of the short side by the length of the long side. This tells you the number of square feet in that rectangle.

- Add the area of all rectangles together to find the total square footage of the lawn.

- Note your measurements in your garden journal.

Remember, we're not trying for "exactly"— just "close"!

of deciduous hollies. Some nurseries sell male selections with the females; one male is sufficient to pollinate a group of females.

TREES

Trees are classed as overstory and understory types. Overstory trees like oak, pine, and hickory form the upper canopy layer in a forest that has more than one layer. Understory trees like redbud, dogwood, and blackgum grow beneath the overstory trees. For the most diverse and interesting landscape, plant a mixture of these two types of trees, as well as evergreen species, for year-round interest.

VINES AND GROUNDCOVERS

This month it's time to peruse catalogs and think about which annual vines you might like to add to the garden in spring. Many are easy to grow from seed that can be started indoors in March. Think about adding some with colorful flowers or interesting fruits. On the facing page is a list of annual vines with a brief description of each. All of these vines are happiest if they receive full sun and are planted in well-drained soil.

If you have a bank where grass won't grow, plant groundcovers to control erosion. One way to get started is to use erosion-control burlap. Put down a layer of pine straw, then put down the burlap.

■ Ilex verticillata *'Winter Gold'*

You can use metal stakes to hold it in place. Plant the groundcovers in the open areas of the burlap netting. Small 4-inch pots or plugs are easy to plant, and if the plants are well rooted, they should establish quickly. The burlap will decompose as the groundcovers grow. Some people put down the mulch before they plant and then dig small holes into the mulch for each plant. Whether you mulch before or after you plant, be sure to water afterwards.

PLANT

ALL

Since individual plants at a garden center cost between $.20 and $2—or more—raising annuals from seed can save a lot of money!

In south Georgia, you can lightly scratch the soil and scatter poppy seed in your flower beds. Since they need light in order to germinate, do not cover with soil. California, Iceland, and corn poppies will sprout when the ground warms up.

The fragrant flowers of sweetpea are a sure harbinger of spring. Most sweetpea varieties are climbing vines. Now is the best time to plant the seed. You can make an informal trellis with three slender pruned branches from your crapemyrtle, apple, or flowering cherry tree. Lean or tie the branches together at the top to make a 4- to 6-foot-high teepee form for the vines to ascend. Make a rich planting soil by mixing bagged manure, sand, and soil in a 1:1:1 ratio. When the seeds sprout, train them up your trellis. Flowers will appear March through May.

BULBS

If you have daffodils or other bulbs that you didn't plant in the fall and the bulbs are still firm, go ahead and plant them. You may not get any blooms this spring, or if you do, they may be shorter than normal, but don't worry! These bulbs should catch up with the rest of your bulbs in a few years. If you don't get your bulbs planted now, they will dry out completely by next fall and there will be nothing to plant.

EDIBLES

Blueberries are among the easiest to grow of the backyard fruit plants. They make a good hedge,

GOOD ANNUAL VINES FOR GEORGIA GARDENS

- *Clitoria* spp.
  Butterfly pea vine produces striking blue flowers.

- *Cobaea scandens*
  Cup-and-saucer vine is a vigorous grower to 25 feet with bell-shaped flowers that open yellow-green and then turn to purple. There is also a white form.

- *Cucurbita* spp.
  Gourd vines come in many different sizes and shapes.

- *Dolichos lablab*
  Hyacinth bean has purple flowers followed by purple pealike pods; it is a perennial in the coastal South.

- *Ipomoea alba*
  Moon vine is known for its fragrant white flowers. Measuring 6 inches across or larger, the flowers open in late afternoon and wither the following morning.

- *Ipomoea batatas*
  Ornamental sweet potato vine is grown for its colorful foliage. There are selections with nearly black foliage and others with leaves that are chartreuse.

- *Ipomoea purpurea*
  Common morning glory is a twining climber with heart-shaped leaves. The funnel-shaped flowers range in color from deep purple to bluish purple or reddish flowers with white throats.

- *Ipomoea quamoclit*
  Cypress vine is a twining vine with delicate ferny foliage and striking scarlet flowers. It's a hummingbird magnet.

- *Mandevilla* 'Alice du Pont'
  A tropical vine that may be root-hardy in the coastal South but should be grown as an annual farther north. This vine is best purchased as a small plant.

- *Mina lobata*
  Firecracker vine has flowers that are scarlet, yellow, and orange. A vigorous climbing vine, it blooms in fall.

- *Podranea ricasoliana*
  Pink trumpet vine is really for coastal gardeners but can be treated as an annual in other parts of the state. It has glossy green foliage and 2- to 3-inch-wide flowers shaped like pink trumpets marked with red veins. You may want to purchase a plant instead of growing it from seed since it is a slow grower.

- *Thunbergia alata*
  Black-eyed Susan vine may survive as a perennial in the coastal parts of Georgia but is an annual in the rest of the state. A twining plant, the flowers are orange, yellow, or white with a purple-black throat.

- *Tropaeolum* spp.
  Climbing nasturtium has flowers that range from orange to yellow to cream. Slightly fragrant, the flowers are also edible.

TO START A LAWN FROM SEED

1. Aerate before seeding.

2. Scatter 3 to 4 pounds of seed per 1,000 square feet if you already have 50 percent grass coverage. Coverage with wheat straw is not needed.

   Scatter 6 to 8 pounds per 1,000 square feet if planting on newly tilled soil. Cover very thinly with wheat straw (one bale per 1,000 square feet).

3. Plan to water each week between now and August.

Do not use weed-preventer products on your lawn for at least six weeks before or after planting tall fescue.

and the leaves are colorful in fall. Blueberry plants should arrive at your nursery any day now.

- Buy the largest blueberry plant you can find, preferably in a 3-gallon pot. A plant this size has a good chance of bearing lightly in its first growing season.

- Dig a 3-foot-wide hole for each blueberry plant, mixing in ½ cubic foot of peat moss for every foot of hole diameter. The peat moss yields the acidic soil that blueberries love.

- Do not fertilize with synthetic fertilizer (10-10-10, and so forth) for one year after planting. Use manure or blood meal instead.

- Plant at least three different varieties for the best production.

LAWNS

If your tall fescue lawn is thin now, late February is a good time to plant seed. The soil is cold, so seed will not germinate quickly. However, you need to get started so the seed can take advantage of any warm days that come along.

PERENNIALS

Start perennials from seed indoors under lights (see Annuals). Some seeds require stratification before they will germinate. Referred to as "after-ripening," they may require either a cold or warm treatment. Leaving seeds in a polyethylene bag in the refrigerator for one to four months at 40 degrees Fahrenheit will accomplish this. Other seeds need to be soaked in hot water and then given the cold treatment described previously. Some seeds need to have their seed coats broken mechanically before they will germinate. Some need light to germinate and should not be covered with soil.

ROSES

Plant potted and bare-root roses now, a few weeks before the last frost. Before planting, prune away any dead or broken branches.

SHRUBS

Prepare the soil for planting shrubs in the spring. Add soil amendments and rototill to a depth of 8 to 12 inches. You have many choices when it comes to soil amendments for your garden. Although peat moss is an option, it is expensive, breaks down quickly, and causes soil to be more acidic. It is better to use a soil amendment like chicken manure, horse manure, or mushroom compost, or a soil conditioner product that loosens and aerates the soil.

Continue planting shrubs as long as the ground is not frozen. Plant container-grown, bare-root, or balled-and-burlapped shrubs. Remove plants from containers.

If you have a balled-and-burlapped shrub and the burlap is a synthetic material, place the plant in the hole and gently pull out the material from around the rootball. This will cause the least amount of stress to the roots.

Dig holes as deep as the size of the container the plant is growing in. For bare-root or balled- and-burlapped shrubs, the hole should be as deep as the roots are long. The width of the hole should be at least twice the width of the container.

This is an ideal time to plant a winter daphne such as *Daphne odora*, an evergreen that should be in full bloom at nurseries now. One whiff of the powerfully fragrant flowers and you'll be hooked. A hardy evergreen shrub, it grows happily in a large pot or in the garden if the soil is slightly moist and extremely well drained.

TREES

In the central and upper parts of the state, plant bare-root trees while they are still dormant. In southern and coastal areas, this is a good time to plant balled-and-burlapped or container-grown trees.

Because the soil in the planting hole settles a bit, plant so the top of the rootball is slightly higher than the ground level. This also helps correct a poorly drained soil situation.

VINES AND GROUNDCOVERS

In the southern parts of the state, this is a good time to plant groundcovers and perennial vines. Wait until soil and air temperatures warm up to plant annual vines.

CARE

ANNUALS & BULBS

Remove faded blooms from plants as they occur.

HERE'S HOW

TO START ANNUALS FROM SEED

1. Fill a plastic nursery flat (or an aluminum pan in which drainholes have been poked) with sterile seed-starting mixture.

2. Make several "furrows," 2 inches apart and ½-inch deep, across the surface of the growing medium with the point of a pencil.

    Read seed packets carefully. Some seed, like impatiens and poppy, need light in order to germinate. They should simply be scattered onto the soil surface. Pat the soil with your hand to press them into good soil contact.

3. For tiny seed, mix ¼-teaspoonful of seed with a tablespoon of dry sand. Fold an index card in half, and pour the seed/sand mixture in the center. Gently tap the card to direct the seeds and sand to drop in the furrows in the growing medium. Large seed can be placed by hand in the furrows. Cover the seed with a thin layer of vermiculite unless directed on the seed pack to expose the seed to light.

4. Spray-mist the growing medium with water to moisten the soil. It should be just slightly moist, *not soggy*.

5. Cover the tray or pan with clear kitchen plastic wrap. Affix masking tape to the ends of the container, and note the name of the seed, the date planted, and the date the seed should germinate.

6. Place the seed-starting trays in bright but indirect sunlight (a south- or west-facing window is ideal), or under the light stand described earlier (the fluorescent tubes should hang just a few inches above the plastic covering).

7. Remove the plastic when most of the seeds in a tray have sprouted. Raise the fluorescent tubes as the plants grow. If the plants become crowded, use a spoon to scoop individuals out of the tray, which can be planted in separate plastic pots.

EDIBLES

It is common to have several days of warm weather in February, followed by a frigid Siberian Express. Fig bushes come out of dormancy readily during warm weather, and they can be frozen to the ground if not protected:

1. Make plans to have ready a sheet of black plastic large enough to cover your plant entirely if icy weather threatens. It is a waste of time to perform this task if you can't cover the entire plant.

2. Anchor the plastic on all sides with stones or limbs.

3. Remove the plastic when the sun comes out the next day. This is especially important if you use clear plastic. Under clear plastic, temperatures rise rapidly!

LAWNS

Notice lawn areas where the shade from a tree has caused grass to grow thinly. Now is a good time to prune out low limbs to allow more sunshine on the grass. Southern magnolia and other densely leaved trees are notorious for severely limiting grass growth. Consider covering the ground under them with mulch.

PERENNIALS

If you didn't clean up your perennial garden last fall, now is a good time to remove dead leaves and cut back plants before new growth begins in spring.

ROSES

If you order roses from a catalog, they will be shipped bare root in order to minimize costs. Bare-root roses are also available at local nurseries; the roots will usually be wrapped in damp wood shavings.

- When your roses arrive home, decide if you can plant immediately or if the plants must be held for awhile.

- If the holding interval will be only twenty-four to forty-eight hours, simply spray water on the roots and rewrap them.

- If you're holding them for several days, plant them in potting soil in 2- or 3-gallon pots. Protect them from freezing while you prepare their new home (see January).

SHRUBS

Continue to prune deciduous shrubs to remove dead wood, rejuvenate them, or keep them from getting too big for the space in which they are growing (as when they block the view from windows or spread out into a pathway). One way to avoid the need to prune constantly is to select the right plant for the right place. Do some research before you plant!

If shrubs have outgrown their original location or have become straggly and spindly in appearance, prune them back severely while they are dormant. Prune back azaleas, spiraea, privet, and *Abelia grandiflora* to a height of about 12 inches.

You may choose to stretch out the pruning over a period of years. Remove one-third of the oldest wood in the first year; in the second year, take

HERE'S HOW

TO PLANT ROSES

Bare root

- Dig a hole 12 inches deep and 18 inches wide in your prepared bed.

- Form a cone of earth in the middle. Spread the rose roots on all sides of the cone.

- Fill the hole with the soil that has been removed, tamping it firmly as you go.

Potted

- Dig a hole 12 inches deep and 24 inches wide in your prepared bed.

- Gently untangle and spread the roots in all directions in the planting hole.

- Fill the hole with soil that has been removed, tamping it firmly as you go.

USING CHEMICALS TO CONTROL WEEDS

It is tempting to consider using a "weed and feed" product to fertilize your grass and kill weeds simultaneously. Consider these points before making your decision, remembering that there are two kinds of "weed and feed" products:

1. A weed and feed that promises to *prevent* weeds contains chemicals that will inhibit all seeds from germinating. If you are planning to plant tall fescue seed now, this type of product cannot be used beforehand. Weed-preventers vary in the length of time the chemical is active in the soil, affecting how long you must wait before planting any seed. If you used one in a previous season, make sure you read the label—if any of the chemical is still present in the soil, you will not be successful when you plant seed.

2. A weed and feed product that promises to *kill existing* weeds can be used on well-established grass. Do not use on newly planted tall fescue or on other turfgrass that is not yet 50 percent green. Read the label of your weed and feed carefully, and follow directions to the letter.

out one-half of the remaining oldest stems and cut back long shoots that grew from the previous season; in the third year, prune out whatever old wood (the oldest wood has the thickest stems) is remaining, and prune new shoots just enough for a pleasing effect.

Prune camellias once they finish flowering. Remove faded blooms and snip back the tips of branches for an overall pleasing effect.

A fungal disease that affects the flowers of *Camellia japonica* and other varieties is spread by spores. Good cultural practices are the best way to control this disease. Refer to the discussion of petal blight in January.

Prune evergreen shrubs like boxwood, holly, anise, leucothoe, and others before new growth begins. Remove dead wood and tip back branches to a desired height.

TREES

This is a good month to prune deciduous trees. Because there are no leaves, you can see the form of the tree and determine where you need to prune.

Sharp, good-quality tools are best; regular maintenance will ensure they last for a long time.

- Handpruners are ideal for heading and thinning stems up to 1½ inches in diameter.

- Loppers are ideal for selective pruning of larger branches.

- Saws are useful for branches that are more than 2 inches thick.

Some saw blades can be sharpened, but others should be replaced periodically. Check the product label for specific information about your blades.

Tips for pruning your newly planted trees:

1. Remove dead or diseased branches.

2. Remove broken branches below the point of injury back to a healthy branch.

■ *Drastic pruning of deciduous shrubs can look alarming, but you'll be rewarded with great growth and blooms in the summer.*

3. Prune to remove branches that are crossing or rubbing. Wounds can develop where branches rub, creating an environment conducive to pest and disease problems.

4. Remove branches that form narrow V-shaped crotches with the main trunk. These crotches are weak and may break in the future. To minimize this problem, select improved varieties of trees with strong branching habits.

VINES AND GROUNDCOVERS

Any plant that effectively covers the ground might be considered a groundcover. Turf or lawn is perhaps the most popular groundcover, but here we will focus on alternatives choices. Groundcovers serve a number of functions. As a living mulch, they not only help conserve soil moisture, but they keep roots of trees and shrubs cool in the summer and warm in the winter. Some groundcovers, like periwinkle, offer handsome evergreen foliage. Others, like green and gold, display attractive flowers in spring, and handsome foliage throughout the growing season. On a steep bank where turf is impractical, groundcovers like monkey grass can be invaluable for controlling erosion.

WATER

ANNUALS

Windowboxes and other outside containers need watering more often than in-ground flower beds. Dig 2 inches into the soil with your fingers. If the soil at that depth is dry, add enough water to the container until water runs out the bottom. Inspect and water flowerbeds as needed.

BULBS

Water bulbs immediately after you plant them, soaking the area thoroughly. Don't water bulbs that you planted last fall until they begin actively growing (the leaves and stems should be several inches high).

Once they start growing, they will need to be watered only if you don't get any rain (at least 1 inch per week). If you have a small area of bulbs

(several square feet), you can use a watering can to water. Apply water to the spot, let it soak in, and repeat. You will want to make sure that water gets to the bulb roots. If you apply 1 inch of water, it should reach roots at a depth of 6 inches in a soil with a moderate amount of clay (30 to 40 percent).

Applying double this amount should be enough for bulbs that are planted as deep as 9 to 10 inches.

HERE'S HOW

TO CALCULATE THE AREA COVERED BY 100 GROUNDCOVER PLANTS

The following chart (reprinted with permission) comes from the publication "Spacing Plant Material: Groundcovers" produced by The University of Georgia Cooperative Extension Service. It predicts the area that will be covered if you use 100 plants at various planting distances.

PLANTING DISTANCE (INCHES)	AREA COVERED (SQUARE FEET)
6	25
12	100
18	225

This information is especially useful when you are trying to figure out how many plants you will need for covering large areas with groundcovers. Remember that starting with small, well-rooted plants is not only easier but it's more cost-efficient.

The chart is intended as a guide, not absolute instructions. In certain places where you want an immediate effect, such as on a steep bank where erosion is a problem, you may want to space plants closer together. Or you may be planting a fast-growing spreader like English ivy * and you can space plants farther apart if you have time before you need the spot to look filled in.

*English ivy can quickly take over an area and become invasive. If it is surrounded by pavement this will help control it from spreading.

EDIBLES

One of the best water-saving investments for a garden is a rubber soaker hose.

- Make a tentative layout of your garden rows and measure the length to determine how much hose to buy.

- A continuous stretch of soaker hose should be no longer than 100 feet.

- You might have to invest in a faucet "splitter valve" so you can send water to each length of soaker hose in its turn.

LAWNS

On a rainy day, notice how water flows or stands on your lawn. Frequent flows of water over one spot will cause erosion. Water that stands for more than a half-day in one spot will drown the grass roots.

- Correct the erosion problem by redirecting the water source, slowing it down, or eliminating it.

- Correct the wet spot problem by eliminating the source of water or making the soil level higher so water does not stand. Plant new grass on the spot.

PERENNIALS

Water containers during mild spells. Water perennials in the ground if the weather is windy for several days. Check them weekly—if there is not adequate rainfall (1 inch or more per week) and the ground is not frozen, plan to water.

Keep the seedlings you're starting indoors moist; a spray bottle of water is an effective way to water seedlings.

ROSES

After planting roses, soak the soil around them thoroughly. This settles the soil and drives out air pockets.

SHRUBS

Keep new plantings well watered (new plantings are those that have been planted in the last six months). Water once a week if you don't get rain.

■ *To determine the rate at which your sprinkler dispenses water to different areas, clean out 8 to 10 tuna cans (or cat food cans, whichever is available) and place them in a random pattern around the sprinkler. Turn on the sprinkler and let it run for 15 minutes. Turn off the sprinkler and measure how much water is in the cans. That number times 4 is the hourly rate of your sprinkler for each different area. If your goal is to spread ½-inch of water in two weekly waterings, determine how long you need to run the sprinkler by dividing .5 by the hourly rate. Supplement the areas that are underwatered as necessary.*

TREES

Water new plantings weekly (new plantings are those that have been in the ground for less than six months). Apply 1 gallon per foot of tree height per week.

VINES AND GROUNDCOVERS

Water groundcover plantings that have been planted within the past six months. A sprinkler is a good way to cover a large area of groundcovers. Place several small cans around the area (tuna fish or cat food cans work well). When the cans are about three-fourths full, the groundcovers are probably watered well enough for the week.

FERTILIZE

ANNUALS

Fertilize pansies.

BULBS

In the southern parts of the state, if your bulbs are actively growing and 2 or more inches of foliage has emerged, you can topdress with a water-soluble formula like 10-10-10. It will get to the roots quickly while the bulb is growing and before it blooms. For daffodils, look for a formula such as 5-11-26.

EDIBLES

Late February is a good time to plant strawberries, if this was not accomplished in the fall.

Once your bed is planted, water it with a high-phosphorus (12-55-6) water-soluble fertilizer at one-quarter strength (usually 1 tablespoon per 4 gallons of water). This will give the strawberry roots the available phosphorus they need without stimulating tender leaf growth.

Fertilize pecan trees in south Georgia with 1 pound of 10-10-10 per inch of trunk diameter (fertilize again in June).

LAWNS

Fertilize tall fescue lawns now (repeat in April, September, and November).

PERENNIALS

Once seedlings germinate and are a few weeks old, fertilize them with a complete liquid fertilizer at half-strength like 20-20-20 or another with a similar ratio.

ROSES

Roses bloom best when the soil has a pH of 6.0 to 6.5. For existing rose beds, have your soil tested,

■ *This is the proper planting depth for a strawberry plant; notice that no portion of the roots is exposed and that the crown is fully aboveground.*

and add garden lime and other nutrients to your beds if recommended.

- Phosphorus and lime do not move rapidly down to the plant root zone; it is best to mix them both with your soil when planting a rose.

- In the absence of a soil test, thoroughly mix ½-cup lime and 2 tablespoons 0-46-0 (triple superphosphate) with the soil you pack around the roots of each rose.

PROBLEM-SOLVE

ANNUALS

It is quite disappointing to observe seedlings suddenly fall over, as if broken at the soil level. A disease called damping off causes this problem; it is due to overwatering, crowding, or poor ventilation of the young plants. To prevent damping off, use fresh, sterile seed-starting medium each time you raise seedlings. Keep the medium moist but never soggy. Increase light and ventilation as soon as symptoms are noticed.

BULBS

If you have problems with voles or chipmunks digging up your bulbs and you did not put down wire mesh when you planted, try this remedy: Mix some liquid dish detergent (a few teaspoons) and water in a quart spray bottle. Add some red pepper powder or hot sauce (a few teaspoons). Spray this around the area where the bulbs are coming up—this should discourage critters from digging up your treasures.

Another approach is to sprinkle red pepper directly on the soil where the bulbs are planted. Keep in mind that rain or dew will make these treatments lose their effectiveness.

EDIBLES

Nematodes are microscopic soil-dwelling worms. Most of them are harmless to plants, but some are parasites of vegetable plant roots. If your tomato or okra roots are infested, it's a good time to remove them.

A RECIPE FOR AMENDING CLAY SOIL

⅓ coarse sand (builders' sand, not play sand—almost like a very small gravel)

⅓ organic material (compost, soil conditioner, or other bagged products)

⅓ existing topsoil (some clay is beneficial but if you have 100 percent clay, remove it and replace it with a quality topsoil)

It the soil is dry enough, this is a good time to work in soil amendments.

Don't prune any fruit tree branches that are within picking distance. The horizontal branches within 6 feet of the ground will bear most of your fruit.

Apple and pear trees are rarely hurt by winter cold. The story is not the same for peach and plum trees. A week of unseasonably warm weather can force the buds of a peach or plum to swell and come out of dormancy. For this reason it is better to wait until mid-March to prune these trees, after the threat of a frigid blast is all but gone.

LAWNS

If your weed problem is minor or your lawn is small, hand-digging weeds is effective and permanent. If you choose to use chemical herbicides, here are some options:

- Spot-spray chickweed with a broadleaf weedkiller. Don't soak the ground—a light spray is best.

- On a warm, windless day, spray wild onions with a herbicide containing 2,4-D, and MCPP. Because many concealed bulblets will remain after spraying, hand-digging wild onions is almost as effective as using a herbicide.

PERENNIALS

During mild spells (when temperatures are such that working outdoors in a long-sleeved shirt is comfortable—in other words, you don't need a hat and gloves), reapply a granular weed preventer (the best time to apply it is in September in established perennial beds to prevent future crops of chickweed and other winter weeds from taking over). Read the label carefully before applying.

In extreme south Georgia, inspect your perennials for signs of aphids or other insects. Use a strong blast from the hose or an insecticidal soap to control them. Horticultural oils are also an option; they work by smothering insects.

SHRUBS

Reapply weed-preventers to prevent any future crops of chickweed from being established. A pre-emergent will prevent weed seeds from germinating.

Pull weeds when they are young, before they set seed. This will reduce future populations of weeds.

Use a hand cultivator to scratch out weeds around shrubs. Apply a fresh layer of mulch to help kill weeds and retain moisture in the soil.

To kill insects that overwinter such as scales, lace bugs, and mites, spray horticultural oil. Scale insects are particularly difficult to control. Closely related to mealybugs and aphids, they have a waxy shell-like covering, either hard or soft, that protects them from natural enemies and insecticides.

TREES

As the weather warms, you might notice small holes in the bark of your maple, pecan, pear, or magnolia trees. The holes are characteristically ¼-inch in diameter and occur in rings around the trunk; often there are several rings in close proximity. The damage is not caused by borers, but by a bird: the yellow-bellied sapsucker. This member of the woodpecker family pecks holes in the bark and licks the sap that oozes out.

Control is nearly impossible. Fortunately, trees are not injured by the annual springtime visit. Hole-pecking will cease for the summer but may briefly recur in late fall.

March

March is a good month to add trees to your garden. They provide a framework, acting like a picture frame for the garden scene. They help create scale, and they set the tone for a particular garden type or style.

Whether deciduous, evergreen, weeping, upright, or columnar, trees come in all sizes, shapes, and forms. Depending on the variety, a tree can provide flowers in spring, shade in summer, and colorful foliage in fall. Trees help to define space, create privacy, provide windbreaks, and reduce the amount of energy needed to cool your home. In addition, they add curb appeal and increase property values. Evergreen trees provide screening or a backdrop for shrubs, perennials, and bulbs. Some trees—like paperbark maple with its glistening cinnamon-colored bark or the coral bark Japanese maple—brighten the winter landscape.

When it comes to choosing a tree for your own garden, be sure you know what the ultimate size of the particular tree will be. This information will help you determine where to site an individual specimen so it won't outgrow its allotted space in a short time or require constant pruning to keep it contained. Be aware too of how close you site trees near your home. River birch trees growing in pots may look to be just right but they will quickly develop into large trees that will require lots of space.

When you design your garden, site your trees before you choose their companion shrubs and herbaceous plants. Where you locate your trees and the types you select can determine the feel of your landscape. Evergreens are often used in more formal gardens, while deciduous trees can be either formal or informal.

Planting a tree is an investment in the future. Choose your trees carefully, and you will reap the rewards for years to come.

PLAN

ANNUALS

It is easy to get caught up in planting fever when you visit a garden center full of spring flowers. Before you visit, make an index card for each bed you'll be planting: Sketch the bed's shape on the card, particularly if it has an irregular instead of rectangular shape. Write down the approximate square footage of the bed. Write down how much sunshine it receives and if parts of the bed are more shady than others. Jot down the flowers you intend to plant and the number you need to buy.

Design ideas for annuals include:

- Choose a spot you want to highlight. Plant enough annuals of one color to draw the eye to that spot. White flowers can lighten a shady spot, but in bright sunshine brilliant red, orange, or yellow flowers are needed to compete with the existing light.

- Don't repeat the same mass of a single color throughout your landscape. One bed of begonias is fine—but six identical beds is as boring as hearing the same piano note repeated endlessly.

- Use beds in the backyard to intrigue viewers from the street. You can enjoy your private view from your kitchen window, but allow part of the bed to be seen through a side gate or around a corner of the house.

- A long bed edged in a single color tires the eyes. Try to make oval or irregular, rounded beds of distinct, single-color annuals that adjoin one another.

- Combine annuals and perennials to have a progression of blooms from spring to fall.

A spot planned to attract butterflies can be the most interesting area of your garden. The butterfly lifecycle requires different plants for the different life stages of the insect—the garden should have plants that feed caterpillars as well as plants whose flowers attract butterflies. Caterpillar-feeding plants include parsley, dill, fennel, milkweed, clover, aster, snapdragon, and sunflower. Butterfly-attracting plants include lantana, butterfly weed, pentas, impatiens, cosmos, salvia, petunia, coreopsis, snapdragon, marigold, Mexican sunflower, aster, and black-eyed Susan.

Another ingredient for attracting butterflies is a source of water. Butterflies will not drink from large, open water areas. Wet sand or mud provides excellent watering holes. A saucer that is designed to fit under a clay or plastic pot makes a good watering hole for butterflies.

- Fill it completely with sand, and add water up to the rim. Make a few shallow depressions with your fingers where water can accumulate.

- A rock in the center of the saucer provides a resting spot for the butterflies.

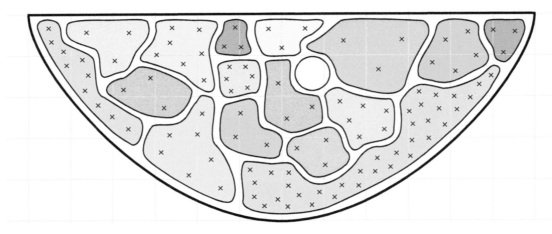

■ *Drawing out where and what you want to plant will help you plan your flower purchases in the spring.*

Wait to plant caladiums until soil temperatures warm.

BULBS

Now that spring bulbs are beginning to bloom, plan ahead for the bulbs you would like to have blooming in summer and fall. Keep in mind that even if summer bulbs like caladiums are available for sale in stores now, you should not plant them until the soil temperature is at least 60 degrees Fahrenheit or warmer and the fear of frost is past. Caladiums require warm soil and air temperatures of 70 degrees or higher during the day and, ideally, not below 60 degrees at night. Depending on where you live in the state, these temperatures could occur in April or May. Purchase a soil thermometer to measure soil temperature. Certain

perennial summer-blooming bulbs like Peruvian lily, *Alstroemeria*, should be planted in the fall.

Following is a list of bulbs that bloom in summer (including rhizomes, tubers, and tuberous roots) with brief descriptions, including whether they prefer sun or shade. While some begin blooming in late spring and continue through summer, others start in summer and continue until frost. There are a number of plants that have striking foliage and insignificant flowers, such as elephant ear and caladium. There are also some types of canna that have fantastic foliage, colorful flowers, or both.

- Elephant ears, *Alocasia* species and hybrids, including upright elephant ear, prefer partial shade to shade. There are many different selections, with large colorful leaves ranging in size from less than 1 foot to 2 feet across or longer and wider.

- Chinese ground orchid, *Bletilla striata*, prefers filtered shade. Plant in early spring. Lavender to magenta miniature orchidlike flowers bloom May to June.

- Caladium hybrids prefer filtered shade to shade. Although some varieties that take sun have been bred, this tropical is indispensable when color is needed in the shade garden. Large (to 1½-foot-long) heart- and arrow-shaped leaves on plants growing 2 to 4 feet tall (depending on the selection) come in a range of colors from almost pure white to dark green. They may be striped, banded, or blotched with rose, pink, silver, green, or bronze.

- Canna species and hybrids prefer full sun to filtered shade. Their dramatic foliage, from dark red to variegated and all the variations, gives your garden a tropical flair. They range in size from 2 to 6 feet tall and can be left in the ground year-round in coastal areas. Plant 5 inches deep and 10 inches apart.

- Taro, *Colocasia esculenta*, prefers filtered shade to shade. This tuberous herb is edible as well as ornamental; in lowland tropical areas, the starchy roots are a staple food. Selections of this plant can grow to 6 feet tall in the garden. Some have huge leaves, 2 feet long and even broader, in one growing season.

- *Dahlia* hybrids prefer full sun. These summer bloomers, usually started from tubers, range from 15 inches to over 6 feet tall. The flowers come in almost every color and form imaginable.

- *Gladiolus* prefer full sun and bloom from spring until fall, depending on when you plant. The dwarf species Byzantine gladiolus, *Gladiolus byzantinus*, has maroon flowers, 1 to 3 inches long, in clusters of six to twelve on 2- to 3-foot stems. Smaller and more refined than some of the larger types of gladiolus, this heirloom is also winter hardy.

- Gloriosa lily, *Gloriosa superba* 'Rothschildiana', prefers sun to filtered shade. Flowers are made up of six bright red segments banded with yellow. Grow in pots. Start tubers indoors in February.

EDIBLES

Start seeds of tomatoes indoors. You'll need six weeks to grow strong plants. They will be ready just in time to plant outdoors when the soil is warm.

LAWNS

The calendar is not a very accurate way to determine when to plant grass or apply a weed-preventer. The timing of many lawn tasks is best determined by the temperature of the soil.

For example:

- Tall fescue or rye seed germinates when the soil temperature is above 55 degrees Fahrenheit.

- Bermudagrass or centipedegrass seed germinates best when the soil temperature is above 70 degrees.

- Crabgrass seed germinates when the soil temperatures are above 55 degrees for seven days in a row.

- Chickweed seed germinates when the soil temperature is 70 degrees and declining.

PERENNIALS

If a scoop of soil holds together but crumbles easily, it is dry enough so you can begin planting hardy perennials. Have a list of plants and a plan ready. Local garden centers and nurseries should have a fresh supply of plants for sale now.

ROSES

Climbing and trailing roses can surprise you with their appetite for space. Study the label that comes with a new rose and space it accordingly.

TREES

Plan to add at least one tree to your garden this spring. Visit your local botanical garden to get an idea of how large a particular variety will be when it matures.

Sweet gum trees have distinctive fall foliage, but the seedpods they drop ("sweet gum balls") can be a tremendous nuisance. There are sprays that cause the flowers to abort so there will be no seedpods, but these are expensive and impractical, as the tree must be sprayed completely every year.

A better solution is to plant the selection known as 'Rotundiloba', which does not form fruit.

VINES AND GROUNDCOVERS

Start annual vine seeds indoors under lights (see page 39). Read seed packages carefully to determine how long it will take until they are ready to plant outdoors. Some require a cold treatment before they will germinate, and others require mechanical abrasion such as nicking the seed coat.

PLANT

ANNUALS

There's still time to start seeds of annual flowers indoors (see February). If you like fragrant flowers, several old-fashioned varieties add spicy scents to

TO START CALADIUMS

If you want to get a jump on the summer season, you can start caladium tubers indoors in March. If you use bottom heat when you start them, their growth will be accelerated (look for a heat mat designed for seedlings). Move them outside in late April or early May once soil temperatures are 60 degrees Fahrenheit or warmer. Use a mix that is equal parts coarse sand, compost, and ground pine bark or peat moss. For tubers that are 2½ inches long or smaller, use a pot that is 5 inches wide and deep. For larger tubers, use a pot that is at least 7 inches wide. You will encourage lots of side shoots if you scoop out the center growing tip. You can plant the tubers directly in a pot with the recommended mix, or scoop out the center growing tips first and then plant them.

1. Fill the pot with 1 inch of potting mix. Place the tuber in the pot. Position the tuber so the roots are at the bottom of the tuber toward the soil.

2. Add 2 inches of potting mix to cover the tuber. Water well until water rushes out of the holes in the bottom of the pot.

3. Keep the pot in bright light (a sunny window). Water when the soil feels dry to the touch.

your garden. Try planting stock, sweet alyssum, sweetpea, flowering tobacco, and annual phlox.

In south Georgia, plant cool-season annuals from six-packs as they become available at garden centers. Viola, snapdragon, pansy, sweet William, and English daisy will bloom in your landscape for the next six weeks or longer.

In north Georgia, you can't expect every plant you installed last fall to make it through the winter. Fill holes in your flowerbeds with new plants. Purchase 3-inch or larger pots; smaller plants will bloom for only a few days.

BULBS

You can start caladium tubers in pots indoors. Start tuberose indoors and plant outside when soil temperatures warm up. Plant the rhizomes 2 inches deep and 4 to 6 inches apart. In coastal areas, they can be left in the ground year-round.

EDIBLES

Plant beet, cauliflower, mustard, radish, and turnip seeds outdoors. Plant strawberries as soon as they become available at your local nursery.

LAWNS

Aerate tall fescue lawns and overseed them if the grass is thin. Wait until soil temperatures are warm, as specified under Plan.

- Listen to the weather forecast to see when a few days of warm weather are predicted. After a couple of days above 50 degrees Fahrenheit, tall fescue seed can be planted in bare spots.

- The seed will germinate as conditions allow. Even if low temperatures occur for a few days, the seedlings will not be harmed.

- Remember that if you are planting tall fescue seed, you can't use a weed-preventer herbicide for six weeks after planting.

Lay tall fescue sod.

PERENNIALS

When you purchase perennials, remember that you are investing in a root system. If you start with a weak plant, it will take twice as long as a strong healthy plant before you can expect a big flowering show, as the plant will put all its energy into developing a strong root system. When you ease a rootball out of the pot, you should see fleshy roots covering at least 50 percent of the soil. If they are dried out and brittle, or if there are only a few, this indicates a weak root system.

This is the time to plant bare-root perennials, while temperatures are mild and many plants are still dormant. Peonies are often sold bare root, as are certain varieties of perennials that are available only by mail-order. Before you plant bare-root perennials, cut off any broken roots or those that

Depth of hole

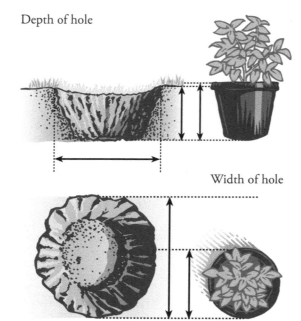

Width of hole

■ *Dig a planting hole that's as deep as the container and twice as wide.*

are dried up; soak the roots in a bucket of water while you prepare the planting hole.

ROSES

If a nearby tree has begun to shade your rose bed, you can either remove the tree or move your roses. Most gardeners prefer the latter.

1. Prune the rose first so you can work without suffering too many wounds.

2. Use a spading fork to lift and explore the soil 2 feet in all directions from the trunk, looking for shallow main roots.

3. When you have identified the main roots, lift them completely from the ground, working from 3 feet away from the plant towards its center. Use handpruners to cut roots that plunge vertically.

4. Thrust a sharp shovel into the soil around the plant, 1 foot from the trunk. Continue in the same manner around the plant, avoiding the previously excavated roots, until you have gone all the way around the plant.

5. With a mighty heave, lever the plant rootball out of the ground. Mist the roots with water and cover with plastic to keep them moist.

6. Plant in a new, sunny bed as soon as possible. See January, page 24 for tips on making a new bed.

SHRUBS

This is an ideal time to plant shrubs, provided the ground is not too wet. The soil should hold some moisture. Try the squeeze test:

Take a handful of soil and squeeze it. If it forms a hard ball, then it is too wet for planting. If it sticks together momentarily but crumbles easily, it is just right.

Remove plants from their containers. (Refer to page 73 for instructions on how to do this.)

If you have heavy clay soils, plant high so the top third of the rootball is out of the ground. This is especially true for shrubs like evergreen rhododendrons, which resent soils that are not well drained. Mound plenty of soil around the rootball and then apply a good layer of mulch, making sure to keep it away from the main trunk.

This will ensure that your plant doesn't dry out too quickly, but the roots won't sit in wet soil.

When you plant, fill in with soil around the rootball and tamp it down with your shoes or a shovel handle. This will remove air pockets and prevent soil from settling.

TREES

Plant balled-and-burlapped or container-grown trees.

Trees are sold as balled-and-burlapped, bare root, or container-grown. Bare-root trees are available for purchase when they are dormant (not actively growing). The best time to plant bare-root trees is as soon as they are dug, or as soon as you receive them.

With balled-and-burlapped and container-grown trees there is more flexibility about what time of year you can plant. Provided the ground is not

HERE'S HOW

TO PLANT TREES

1. Use a garden hose to mark the outline for a hole that is at least two or three times the diameter of the rootball. If you are planting trees with shallow, spreading roots (such as most evergreens) rather than a deep taproot, make the hole wider. Dig no deeper than the height of the rootball.

2. Amend some of the removed soil with hydrated peat moss and return the mixture to build up the sides of the hole, creating a medium that is easy for surface roots to establish in. If necessary (meaning, you dug too deep) add and compact soil at the bottom of the hole so the top of the rootball will be slightly above grade when placed.

3. Place the tree in the hole so the top of root ball is slightly above grade and the branches are oriented in a pleasing manner. Cut back the twine and burlap from around the trunk and let it fall back into the hole. Burlap may be left in the hole—it will degrade quickly. Non-degradable rootball wrappings should be removed.

4. Backfill amended soil around the rootball until the soil mixture crowns the hole slightly. Compress the soil lightly with your hands. Create a shallow well around the edge of the fresh soil to help prevent water from running off. Water deeply initially and continue watering very frequently for several weeks. Staking the tree is wise, but make sure the stake is not damaging the roots.

frozen, container-grown trees can be planted almost anytime, although during the hottest months the trees will sit and wait until soil temperatures cool off before they begin to put out roots.

Balled-and-burlapped trees are dug when trees are dormant, but they may be available from your local nursery throughout the growing season. This means they might have been dug a year ago and have had a chance to recover from any root loss they suffered during the digging process.

When you plant a tree, dig a hole that is wider than it is deep. As a rule of thumb, the planting hole should be at least twice as wide as the rootball. While there may be some controversy about the best way to plant trees, as a general practice it is not necessary to amend the soil in the hole in which the tree will be growing. The sooner the tree adapts to unamended soil, the faster it will become established. If you amend it, you are creating an artificial environment for the tree. It is important, however, that the soil is loose and soft to help root growth.

It is also important to make sure the site where you plant drains easily. If it does not, dig out some of the existing soil and add organic amendments to help improve the texture and drainage.

After you plant, apply a 2- to 3-inch layer of mulch such as pine bark nuggets or pine straw to help keep tree roots cool and conserve moisture.

HERE'S HOW

TO PRUNE FRUIT TREES

Peach and plum trees can be pruned when you are reasonably sure severe cold will not come again. (Shown is an example of an open center pruning pattern.)

- Remove dead limbs or branch stubs.

- Remove limbs that cross through the center or droop too low.

- Remove pencil-sized water sprouts in the center of the tree.

- Try to keep the center of the tree open so sunshine can easily penetrate.

VINES AND GROUNDCOVERS

Plant perennial vines and groundcovers that have been grown in containers and are now available at garden centers.

This is a good time to divide overgrown plantings of monkey grass, creeping liriope, or English ivy. Use a large spading fork and dig up clumps. If you have a large bare area you want to cover, you can divide the clumps into small sections and plant them 12 to 18 inches apart. Make sure each division has an equal ratio of roots to foliage or shoots. Replant the divisions, apply a 2-inch layer of mulch, and water.

Transplant clematis vines before new growth begins. Dig as large a rootball as possible—the more roots, the better. Prepare the new site ahead of time so that the roots are out of the ground for the shortest amount of time. This way fewer will dry out. It is often said that clematis like a hot top (foliage) and cold feet (roots). It is more accurate to say that clematis prefer full sun and plenty of soil moisture. Mulching is very important in conserving soil moisture.

CARE

ANNUALS

Check for the seedlings of annuals you planted last fall. You should be able to see poppy and larkspur seedlings easily. Plants should be 6 to 12 inches apart. Gently transplant to an empty spot any seedlings that are too close. If you have more seedlings than space, remove some of the crowded seedlings by pinching them off at ground level.

BULBS

Remove faded blooms from flowering bulbs, but leave the foliage to ripen.

EDIBLES

If you planted a cover crop on your vegetable garden last fall, mow it first, then till the leaves and stems into the soil.

- On young vines, or on those that did not fruit strongly last year, leave only eight buds per cane.

Finish pruning all grapevines by mid-month. If you wait until later, much bleeding of sap from the cut ends will occur. (Although ominous looking, bleeding does not harm the vine.)

Finish pruning out dead canes of blackberry and raspberry.

Tie green healthy canes to a wire trellis.

Do not delay pruning figs past mid-month. The longer you wait, the more trouble you'll have with rampant, unproductive growth in summer.

It is not necessary in all instances to cut away fruit tree limbs that are growing too close together. Instead, make a spacer from a 12-inch-long (or longer, if needed) piece of 1 × 2 wood.

1. Cut a deep notch in each end of the wood.

2. Force the limbs apart and insert the spacer.

3. Leave it in place for at least two years.

LAWNS

Just as the blades of your bermudagrass, zoysiagrass, and centipedegrass grow and wane over the course of a year, the roots of these grass plants do too. Each plant stores a great deal of energy in its central crown in late fall. As grass blades turn brown, roots also die back. When the weather warms in spring, the crown sends out new, green shoots—and roots begin to grow once again. If anything interferes with root growth or a grass's aboveground green-up this month, your lawn will suffer.

• Avoid using weed-killing chemicals on warm-season grasses in March (occasional spot-sprays are fine). Most weed-preventing chemicals (pre-emergents) can be used without harm to turfgrass.

• Do not fertilize warm-season grasses (see the following paragraph) except in extreme south Georgia.

• Postpone aerating and dethatching until the grass has turned completely green and is growing vigorously.

Spacers

■ *Use spacers or spreaders to encourage fruit tree limbs to grow at 60-degree angles to the trunk.*

A late freeze can wreak havoc on warm-season grasses by killing the lush green growth that has begun to appear. To help your lawn recover from an unexpected freeze:

• Do not fertilize. Wait until April or May to determine which areas have been killed.

• Irrigate the dead spots lightly with ¼-inch of water per week, no more.

• If green grass does not emerge by May, plant sod or large plugs of grass in each dead area.

• Fertilize the lawn on your normal schedule beginning in May.

PERENNIALS

Many perennials with lots of fibrous roots can be dug up with a spade or shovel. Get a big clump—more roots are better than fewer roots. Gently pull

TO DIVIDE PERENNIALS

Some perennials should be divided by hand, not with a sharp spade or digging fork, but by digging up a large clump and then teasing apart the roots, making sure shoots are attached to each section. You can use two pitchforks back to back, or a pitchfork (or digging fork) and a spade to pull apart the rootballs. Try this method with the following plants:

- Columbine, *Aquilegia* spp.
- Epimedium, *Epimedium* hybrids, after they flower
- Blanket flower, *Gaillardia* spp.
- Hardy geranium, *Geranium* spp. and hybrids
- Hellebore, Lenten rose, *Helleborus* hybrids, after they flower
- Coralbells, *Heuchera* hybrids

Other perennials can be divided with the fork or spade technique, in early spring:

- Yarrow, *Achillea filipendulina*
- Japanese anemone, *Anemone × hybrida*
- Aster, *Aster* spp.
- Boltonia, *Boltonia asteroides*
- Chrysanthemum, *Chrysanthemum* spp.
- Coreopsis, *Coreopsis verticillata*
- Pinks, carnations, *Dianthus* spp.
- Coneflower, *Echinacea purpurea* and cvs.
- Daylily, *Hemerocallis* spp. and cvs.
- Hosta, *Hosta* spp. and cvs.
- Beebalm, *Monarda* spp.
- Garden phlox, *Phlox paniculata*
- Black-eyed Susan, *Rudbeckia* spp.

apart the roots by hand. Cut off any damaged or dead roots. Replant divisions at once. Water, and apply a 2-inch layer of mulch.

ROSES

It is important to coat both the tops and the undersides of leaves when applying pesticides. This is difficult to accomplish with dusts but easier with sprays. Spray the undersides of leaves first; follow with a light spray over the top.

Important: Read and follow all label directions when using a pesticide.

SHRUBS

Some evergreen shrubs get overgrown or leggy over time. Now is a good time to renovate boxwoods and other broadleaf evergreens like hollies. Here's what to do:

- Prune back shrubs drastically to a height of 12 inches if they are straggly and have leaves only at the tips of the branches.

Pruning now will give shrubs time to put out new growth that will harden off before hot weather sets in. Pruning tips include:

- If you use electric hedge trimmers to prune your evergreens, follow up with a pair of handpruners, using them to remove stems down to where a branch forks. This will open up the plant and allow light to get in, which will encourage new growth. The result will be fuller, healthier plants.

- In coastal parts of the state, prune spring-flowering shrubs like azaleas and camellias after they finish flowering. If your hybrid azaleas (many ornamental azaleas are hybrids) are getting overgrown or leggy, prune them back to about 12 inches tall. If you keep them watered and fertilized, they should recover and develop into fully leafed plants.

- Native azaleas require little or no pruning unless they are too large for the space in which you have planted them. They should never be sheared (which means cut back to an even height with electric hedge trimmers or hand

■ *Over a period of three years, gradually prune back the oldest stems to rejuvenate the shrub.*

shears), but should be pruned to enhance their natural form. It should be noted that some native azaleas can reach heights of 10 feet or more.

TREES

Prune to remove dead, broken, or diseased branches, and prune out branches that are rubbing or crossing. Both young trees and established mature trees respond to this type of pruning. Pruning large mature trees helps keep them vigorous; such pruning is best done by a professional arborist.

Remove water sprouts (clusters of branches that grow straight up, often from an old pruning wound) regularly. Water sprouts can weaken a tree and can be difficult to get rid of later.

■ *Remove any branches heading into the center of the tree or crossing others.*

Grafted trees (several weeping forms are grafted) may send out tall, straight suckers from the underground rootstock. Prune off these suckers so your tree can use its energy efficiently to produce the desired healthy leaves, branches, and blooms of the cultivar you selected.

Don't prune maples or river birch now. They bleed (produce excess sap) if pruned in late spring. However, although anxiety-producing for the gardener, bleeding does not harm the tree.

Sometimes mature trees create too much shade—even shade-loving plants need light to grow. If your shaded rhododendrons and azaleas are not blooming and lack vigor, they may not be getting enough sunlight. Selectively prune to remove branches; this will open up your tree and allow more light to reach the plants below.

It will also improve air circulation and reduce the potential for disease problems like powdery mildew.

Prune needled evergreens such as pines, cedars, hemlocks, and junipers.

Shearing means that every branch is clipped to an even height at the surface, as with hedges or topiary. The best time to shear needled evergreens is just after they begin to put out new growth in early spring, a time that brings warmer soil and air temperatures.

Pruning now will stimulate dormant buds to begin growing, resulting in a fuller tree.

VINES AND GROUNDCOVERS

Prune back vines that are overgrown, including wisteria, ivy, trumpet creeper, and climbing hydrangea. Wait to prune spring-flowering vines like Carolina jessamine until after they bloom.

Prune back late-flowering clematis to a height of about 2 to 3 feet. Such clematis flower on current-season's growth, which is the top 2 to 3 feet. Plants in this group include *Clematis viticella*, *C. flammula*, *C. tangutica*, *C. × jackmanii*, *C. maximoicziana*, *C.* 'Perle d'Azur', *C.* 'Duchess of Albany', and others.

Prune back large-flowered hybrid clematis such as 'Nelly Moser', 'Duchess of Edinburgh', and 'Marie Boisselot'. These hybrids bloom in mid-June on short stems from the previous season's growth. Prune to remove dead or weak stems, and cut back remaining stems to the first pair of healthy green buds. You can plant other plants under the clematis in this group to conceal the bare stems that develop at the base of the plant as it matures. Perennials like hardy geraniums or small evergreen shrubs make happy companions for clematis.

Wait until after they flower before pruning early-flowering clematis such as *Clematis alpina*, *C. macro-petala*, *C. armandii*, *C. montana*, and *C. chrysocoma*.

WATER

ANNUALS
Check the plastic covering on the flats of seeds you are starting indoors. If a slight haze of condensed moisture isn't present, remove the plastic, and mist the soil until damp.

BULBS
Keep your actively growing and blooming spring bulbs well watered. If you don't get at least an inch of rain per week in your garden, water. Apply 5 gallons of water to a 10-square-foot area.

EDIBLES
Water any fruit trees you planted in the last six months.

- Apply 1 gallon of water per foot of height per week.

- Keep a 2- to 3-inch-thick layer of mulch over the root system.

- Pull the mulch back 3 inches from the trunk in all directions.

LAWNS
Windy days cause grass to dry.

- Water bermudagrass or tall fescue sod that was planted within the last six months.

- Water tall fescue lawns that were recently seeded.

PERENNIALS
Water all new plantings and transplants once a week for the first month after they are planted.

Water established plantings once every two weeks if you don't get an inch or more of rain.

ROSES
Newly planted roses, especially bare-root plants, need regular watering. Give each plant at least 3 gallons of water per week in the absence of rain.

Allow the soil to dry somewhat between waterings.

SHRUBS
Water new plantings "long and slow"—if you use the hose, a pencil-sized trickle is good. Any plants that you have added to your garden within the past six to twelve months will benefit from some extra tender loving care. Depending on the size of the rootball, it may take anywhere from fifteen minutes to an hour with the hose at slow trickle to water an individual shrub.

TREES
Water newly planted trees once a week (unless you get 1 inch of rain) for at least the first six months and up to a year after they are planted. After they are established, check them monthly, and plan to water if there is a drought.

Winter winds can dry out established conifers. Check the soil (feel down several inches), and water if it is dry.

VINES AND GROUNDCOVERS
Water any new plantings of vines and groundcovers as well as existing plantings if there has not been rain (at least 1 inch a week is best).

FERTILIZE

ANNUALS

Fertilize flowering annual plants.

Fertilize the seedlings you have grown indoors with water-soluble houseplant food once the true leaves have appeared (true leaves are the leaves that emerge after the rounded first leaves unfold from the soil). Once plants are a few inches tall, fertilize them every two weeks until they are ready to be planted outdoors.

BULBS

Fertilize spring bulbs after they emerge, before flowering. Topdress with a water-soluble formula like 10-10-10 that will get to the roots quickly while the bulb is growing and before it blooms. For daffodils, look for a formula such as 5-11-26.

EDIBLES

Plants can't use much fertilizer if they don't have leaves. Fertilize established fruit and nut trees when their leaves are expanding. A typical amount is 1 pound of 10-10-10 per inch of tree-trunk thickness. Repeat the feeding in May or June.

The feeder roots of a woody plant may extend twice as far as the tips of its branches. Few feeder roots exist close to a plant's trunk. Be sure to scatter the fertilizer evenly in a "doughnut" around the plant, applying at least half the fertilizer past the branch tips.

LAWNS

Do not fertilize warm-season grasses except in extreme southern Georgia.

Postpone aerating and dethatching until the grass has turned completely green and is growing vigorously.

PERENNIALS

If your perennials are in a healthy soil, it is not necessary to use a commercial fertilizer on a regular basis. Instead, consider topdressing with an organic material such as compost, cow manure, horse manure, or another bagged product. Spread the organic material about 1 inch thick, keeping it away from the stems and crown of the plant (the crown is the center of the plant where stems and buds originate). If you do use a chemical fertilizer, apply 1 pound of a complete fertilizer such as l0-10-10 per 10 × 10-foot square. Water-in the fertilizer. Too little fertilizer is always safer than too much.

ROSES

Roses need regular fertilization in order to grow the leaves and branches that will support new blooms. Follow these steps to fertilize newly planted roses:

- In March, topdress the soil under each plant with 1 cup bonemeal and 1 cup cottonseed meal. Scratch them into the soil, and water with 1 gallon of water in which ¼ cup Epsom salts (magnesium sulfate) has been dissolved.

SHRUBS

Use a balanced granular fertilizer (10-10-10) around shrubs. Determine the amount according to the size of the plants. As a rule of thumb, use 1 tablespoon of 10-10-10 per each foot of shrub

HERE'S HOW

TO FERTILIZE MATURE TREES USING GRANULAR FERTILIZER

1. Estimate the canopy spread of an individual tree in square feet. Apply ¾ pound (1½ cups) of 16-4-8 or 12-4-8 (or a fertilizer with a similar ratio) for each 100 square feet of canopy spread. Reduce the rate applied by half when fertilizing conifers such as pines, hemlocks, and junipers, or when trees are growing in a lawn that receives regular applications of fertilizer.

2. Apply by broadcasting the fertilizer evenly under the tree, as far as the canopy extends and slightly beyond.

3. Water-in the fertilizer—this will wash it off any grass blades and help the fertilizer get to the tree roots more quickly.

4. Repeat this fertilizer application in July.

height. Refer to the product label for specific usage directions.

TREES

Fertilize trees once they leaf out, with a slow-release fertilizer. Read product label directions carefully before applying any fertilizers.

VINES AND GROUNDCOVERS

If groundcovers are planted under trees that are on a regular fertilizing program, they will get plenty of nutrients when the trees are fed. It is not absolutely necessary that you fertilize your groundcovers, but if you think they need it, apply 1 pound (2 cups) of 8-8-8 or 10-10-10 per 100 square feet. Use a broadcast-type spreader to get even distribution over the area. Wash any fertilizer off the foliage when you finish. If you do fertilize, twice a year is adequate, once in March and once in June.

PROBLEM-SOLVE

ANNUALS

Seedlings grown indoors may become infested with whiteflies if your houseplants have them. Spray with insecticidal soap, and use a yellow sticky trap.

BULBS

You may notice that your early-blooming varieties of daffodils have not yet come up and there is no indication that they will, even when you dig down several inches into the soil. They may have root rot. Dig up and discard bulbs. Don't replant without improving the soil drainage.

EDIBLES

Peach and plum fruits are particularly susceptible to a disease called brown rot. It infects the bloom, waiting until the fruit is nearly ripe to exhibit itself. To treat this problem:

1. Spray a fungicide labeled for fruit trees on the tree when almost all the blooms are open.

2. Repeat when 50 percent of the blooms have fallen.

3. Be sure to remove all mummified fruit left on the tree from last season before blooms

■ *Spray seedlings with insecticidal soap if you notice a whitefly infestation.*

appear—this will reduce the chances of infection of this year's fruit.

Spray apple and pear tree blooms with bactericide if you have had problems with fire blight in past years.

LAWNS

It's time for the first application of a weed-preventer for all types of lawns. The next application will be in May.

Remember to irrigate your lawn after applying a weed-preventer herbicide. The water dissolves the chemical, making the top ½-inch of soil inhospitable to weed germination.

On a warm, windless day, kill weeds in your driveway and walks with a nonselective herbicide.

Spot-spray dandelions, curly dock, mugwort, and other perennial weeds with a broadleaf herbicide; you can also dig them out with a dandelion fork.

PERENNIALS

Look for yellow or discolored leaves, stippling (dark tiny spots) on leaves, sticky sap, and other signs of insects.

Treat with horticultural oils or insecticidal soaps as needed. Handweed on a weekly basis to help keep weeds at a minimum.

It's not too late to use a granular weed-preventer in your perennial beds if you didn't use one in February.

ROSES

Our heat and humidity make Georgia a prime site for rose black spot, a fungus disease of rose leaves. Old-fashioned roses tolerate the disease by shedding some, but not all leaves. Many of the newer hybrid tea roses will shed most of their leaves by July if blackspot is not controlled. Here are some organic strategies for blackspot control:

- Plant only roses that are known to have tolerance or resistance to the disease.

- Pick off and discard diseased leaves as soon as you notice them.

- Spray, beginning when leaves appear, with a mixture of 1 tablespoon of baking soda, 2 tablespoons of horticultural oil, and 1 gallon of water. Repeat every seven days. This mixture will not completely protect from disease, but it will delay disease onset.

- Neem oil has shown some promise as a fungicide and may also be used.

- Replace the mulch under your rose every spring.

Chemical strategies for blackspot control include:

- Spray, beginning when leaves appear, with chlorothalonil, or triforine, or myclobutanil. Repeat the spray every two weeks.

- Every month, change the chemical you use. This reduces the possibility of the fungus developing resistance to a single chemical.

Annual weeds can be controlled by applying a weed-preventer to your rose beds now.

SHRUBS

Inspect azaleas for signs of lace bugs: the leaves will have tiny yellow speckles. You will treat for these pests in April or May before adults lay eggs.

Use horticultural oil and insecticidal soap to control insects like aphids, scale, and mites. Read the label carefully. The best time to spray your plants is on a clear day when rain is unlikely for at least six hours—this will give the spray enough time to dry completely. It is best to spray early in the morning when temperatures are coolest. Avoid spraying on windy days when the spray can easily drift to other plants.

TREES

If you see webs in the crotches of your crabapple or ornamental cherry trees, the trees probably have tent caterpillars. The caterpillars leave their nests during the day to feed and can defoliate your tree in no time. Wait until early evening, then remove each nest by piercing it with a long stick and winding the web around the end.

For severe infestations, spray inside the web with a product containing *Bacillus thuringiensis*. Remember that even complete defoliation of a limb will not hurt a healthy tree; it will have plenty of time to grow new leaves after the caterpillars disappear in May.

VINES AND GROUNDCOVERS

If your pachysandra has leaves that are light brown or tan on top, it has leaf scorch. Transplant your pachysandra to a shadier location.

Use a granular weed-preventer twice each year, once now and once in September. An application this month will help cut down on infestations of summer annual weeds. Look for products formulated specifically for groundcovers.

English ivy can be a blessing or a curse; it can definitely become a pest. A rapid spreader, sometimes it leaps from the planting bed and climbs up into the trees. Shading lower branches and collecting litter, rain, or ice, ivy can cause damage to tree limbs.

April

In April, both the native landscape and the cultivated garden are filled with blooms of all types from the tiniest wildflowers to the largest magnolia blossoms. Each day there is a new discovery. While spring is in full swing it's also time to plan ahead for summer and fall.

Even though your tender winter annuals including pansies and violas may still be going strong, this is the month to replace them with summer color. Once the fear of frost has passed, usually around April 15, it's safe to plant. These workhorses provide colorful flowers for months at a time. As their name implies, annual plants live for only one growing season, although some seem to be perennial because they self-seed each year. Summer annuals are planted in spring and die with the first frost. Tuck them into the perennial garden, use them in the shade garden with ferns and shrubs to add spots of color, or combine them with perennials in large decorative containers.

If you have a woodland garden, you can expect to see spring ephemerals now like Virginia bluebells, wood poppies, and trilliums. Ferns are putting up fronds, and spring bulbs including mid-season daffodils and spring beauties are also blooming. Take note of what's blooming in other gardens that you would like to add to your own.

This is also the time to plant warm-season edible crops including tomatoes, eggplants, peppers, and squash. With a little effort you can have a wide variety of vegetables that will produce for months in your garden.

Now through May you can transplant existing shrubs or add those that are container grown. You can also add trees that are container grown or balled-and-burlapped. Make sure to keep them well watered while they become established.

If you are looking for color and fragrance, add a few roses in containers. You can enjoy them when blooms are present, and move them to a less conspicuous spot when the show is over.

Once trees and shrubs leaf out you can begin to fertilize with a slow-release granular fertilizer. Keeping your plants healthy is the best way to ward off pest and disease problems. April is an exciting time in the garden!

PLAN

ANNUALS

One of the hottest landscaping trends in the last few years has been the "Tropical Look." While a year-round tropical landscape might be possible in Brunswick or Savannah, gardeners in other parts of the state usually settle for a tropical corner in the yard.

Two of the most popular plants for the Tropical Look are elephant ear and banana. Common elephant ear produces green leaves that gently sway in the breeze; 'Jet Black Wonder' has dusky black leaves; 'Frydek' sports velvety green leaves

■ Xanthosoma 'Lime Zinger' with Impatiens and Croton

with white veins. Fiber banana (*Musa basjoo*) is reputed to withstand winter temperatures down to 10 degrees Fahrenheit; 'Rojo' displays green leaves with a red stripe. Other annuals with that Tropical Look include amaranth, chenille plant, coleus, dusty miller, perilla mint, polka-dot plant, and purple basil.

BULBS

Photograph your garden as more spring bulbs come into bloom. Make notes in your garden journal about which varieties are fragrant and which make good cut flowers.

After your Easter lily finishes blooming, you can plant it in the garden. Choose a site where the soil is well drained but rich in organic matter. Plant the bulb at the same depth it was in the pot. Let the stems ripen and die down before you remove them. Water the lily after you plant it. Next spring, fertilize with a complete fertilizer like 10-10-10. It may take several years before your lily blooms during its normal midsummer season.

Tulips are a favorite of many gardeners, but not all tulips are created equal, especially when it comes to surviving in our hot, humid climate. While tulips are often treated as annuals in Georgia, there are a few that are good repeat bloomers. (This does not apply to coastal gardeners, whose tulips need to be prechilled before they are planted.) While their flowers are not as large and showy as those of the hybrids, most of the species tulips tolerate the heat better and bloom year after year in the garden. Many of these have graceful, delicate flowers. Low growing and early blooming, species tulips are perfect for the rock garden or for growing in pots. If you're not already growing these tulips, think of adding some to your garden next year.

EDIBLES

If you have never grown vegetables, you might wonder how many you'll have to plant to have fresh produce all summer. The chart on page 66 shows the length the planting rows should be for a family of four to have vegetables all summer long. Remember that some of the vegetables should be planted more than once in order to spread the harvest over the summer. Double the amounts if you plan to freeze or can your vegetables.

REPEAT-BLOOMING SPECIES TULIPS

- *Tulipa bakeri* 'Lilac Wonder', with a sunny yellow heart and lilac-pink petals, reaches 6 to 8 inches at maturity.

- *T. clusiana* var. *chrysantha* has 9-inch stems that produce flowers that are crimson when they're closed. When they open, the inside is bright yellow.

- *T. gregii* has scarlet flowers that measure 6 inches across on 10-inch stems. The foliage is striped or mottled with brown.

- *T. kaufmanniana* is called the waterlily tulip for the flowers that occur on 6-inch stems. They are creamy yellow marked with red on the outside, and yellow in the center.

- *T. tarda* offers bunches of star-shaped tulip flowers of white and yellow, appearing on 6- to 8-inch stems in early spring.

- *T. turkestanica*, 6 to 8 inches tall, has white flowers with orange centers that perfume the air in early spring.

■ Tulipa *'Lady Jane' and* Ipehion

LAWNS

Not all grasses can be grown from seed. Scientists have hybridized some grass species, particularly bermudagrass, to develop superior varieties. Hybridization results in seed that will not germinate. Therefore, sod farmers grow hybrid bermudagrass from sprigs. When the sprigs have grown to cover an area, the grass can be lifted as uniform sod pieces that are shipped to you for planting. Grasses typically installed as sod include the following types:

- **Hybrid bermudagrass** (Tifgreen, Tifway, Tifton 419, Tifton 328, TifSport, and so forth)

- **Zoysiagrass** (Meyer, El Toro, Emerald, Zenith, and so forth)

- **Centipedegrass**

- **St. Augustinegrass** (Floratam, Raleigh, Palmetto, and so forth)

- **Tall fescue** (available only in the northern half of Georgia)

Sod can be ordered from brokers who arrange for it to be shipped to your site. It can be bought in small amounts from garden centers. Don't wait until the day before sod is delivered to prepare the area. Make sure you have plenty of help to lay the sod. Each sod piece may weigh 20 pounds; carrying hundreds of them in one day can lead to exhaustion.

Some lawn grasses grow readily from seed. The key to establishing a lawn from seed is to control weeds while the seeds are germinating. Centipedegrass and zoysiagrass seed do not germinate rapidly. Chemicals that might kill weeds also harm the emerging grass seedlings. Frequent hand-pulling is necessary to keep the weeds at bay. Lawns that can be grown from seed include the following:

- Tall fescue
- Common bermudagrass
- Centipedegrass (somewhat difficult)
- Zoysiagrass (somewhat difficult)

Choosing the right grass for a lawn is initially based on how much sunshine the site receives and how much water you are able to apply in the

SMALL GARDEN PLAN FOR GEORGIA

Proposed garden is 50 feet long and 25 feet wide. Row widths are noted on left side.

2 feet asparagus	*1 Set crowns in March	*1 Buy one-year-old crowns. Do not harvest the first year.
2½ feet cabbage + lettuce	*2 Set cabbage and lettuce March 1	*2 Set leaf lettuce between cabbage plants.
2½ feet onion sets	*3 Set March 10 - 20	*3 Set thick; then thin and eat as needed.
2½ feet parsley (or turnips) + radish + carrot + beets	*4 Around March 20	*4 Seed parsley (or turnips) thick; mix radish seed sparingly with carrots.
2½ feet garden peas + cabbage	*5 Early and late February (for peas)	*5 Sow peas as early as the ground can be prepared. Grow cabbage plants from seed; plants will not be available from commercial sources at this time of year.
2½ feet bush green beans and broccoli	*6 Beans April 1; Broccoli July 10	*6 & *7 Cauliflower plants will need to be grown from seed.
2½ feet southern peas + cauliflower	*7 Peas April 1; Cauliflower July 10	
2½ feet staked tomatoes + bell peppers + eggplant	*8 After frost danger	*8 Prune tomatoes to one stem.
3½ feet staked cucumbers + pole beans	*9 After frost danger	*9 Stake and prune cucumbers and train to climb string or stakes. When apples are in full bloom you can count 150 days forward to determine when to start checking for ripeness.
2 feet potatoes	Late February	

Planting dates are for middle Georgia. South Georgia can plant ten to fourteen days earlier. North Georgia should plant two weeks later in spring.

*Information provided by Wayne J. McLaurin, retired UGA Extension Horticulturist

summer. Consider also the amount of labor you are willing to invest in your lawn

PERENNIALS

If you don't have a plan for your perennial garden, now is the time to create one.

ROSES

Roses do not serve well as foundation plants near a home. They may be covered with blooms and leaves during the warm season, but they are leafless in winter. There are several ways to use them as part of a landscape however:

- Use roses in a mass planting in front of a hedge or in a shrub border.

- Train trailing roses to cover a fence.

- Plant climbing roses on either side of an arbor.

- Install miniature roses in a bed of perennial flowers.

SHRUBS

This is a great time to add shrubs to your garden or to transplant existing shrubs. Make sure you have selected varieties that are suited to the growing conditions in your garden. The advantage of purchasing plants in bloom is that you will know the color of the flowers and will be able to give them your own personal sniff test to determine whether or not they are fragrant.

Photograph your garden as it begins to bloom. In your garden journal, keep track of how long your shrubs bloom, noting perennials that bloom at the same time. This will help you plan pleasing combinations like beautybush, *Kolkwitzia amabilis*, underplanted with *Scabiosa* 'Butterfly Blue'.

TREES

When you consider what happened to the American elm, you can see why you should avoid monoculture, even in your own garden. (Monoculture is planting many plants of only one species in an area.) Years ago, the American elm, *Ulmus americana*, was planted in great numbers throughout the United States. When used as an avenue tree, its graceful vase shape created a dramatic effect. Then the trees were attacked by a fungus known as Dutch elm disease, a fatal disease carried by elm bark beetles that bore into elm limbs. The disease spread from tree to tree very quickly, with devastating effects: whole neighborhoods were denuded.

OUTSTANDING SMALL-TO MEDIUM-SIZED TREES

Gardeners are often overwhelmed with plant selections. Growers and garden designers who have many years of experience growing plants in our Georgia climate can help. Garden designer Jane Bath of Monroe, Georgia, recommends a list of small- to medium-sized trees that she finds outstanding for Georgia gardens:

- Trident maple, *Acer buergeranum*
- Japanese maple, *Acer palmatum*
- Chinese fringe tree, *Chionanthus retusus*
- Yellowwood, *Cladrastis kentukea*
- Flowering dogwood, *Cornus florida*
- Natchez crapemyrtle, *Lagerstroemia indica* 'Natchez'
- Saucer magnolia, *Magnolia* 'Elizabeth'
- Callaway crabapple, *Malus* 'Callaway'
- Sourwood, *Oxydendrum arboretum*
- Chaste tree, *Vitex agnus-castus*

THE BEST PICK PERENNIALS FOR SHADE

Rick Berry, nurseryman and co-owner of Goodness Grows, Lexington, Georgia, has been growing perennials for Georgia gardens for over twenty years. The list below represents some of his top contenders for gardening in the shade.

- Arkansas blue star, *Amsonia hubrichtii*
- Arum, *Arum italicum*
- Hardy ginger, *Asarum* spp.
- Hardy begonia, *Begonia grandis*
- Autumn fern, *Dryopteris erythrosora*
- Barrenwort, *Epimedium* hybrids
- Coralbell, *Heuchera* 'Amethyst Myst'
- Variegated Solomon's seal, *Polygonatum odoratum* 'Variegatum'
- Sacred lily, *Rohdea japonica*
- Strawberry begonia, *Saxifraga stolonifera*
- Toad-lily, *Tricyrtis* spp.

HERE'S HOW

TO DETERMINE THE TYPE OF GRASS TO GROW

Tall fescue is classified as a "cool-season" grass, and it stays green all year long. Bermudagrass, zoysiagrass, centipedegrass, and St. Augustinegrass are all classified as "warm-season" grasses. They are green most of the year, but turn brown (or light green, in the case of St. Augustinegrass) and go dormant in winter. The descriptions below will help you decide which grass will grow in your area, and which ones match your requirements for appearance and maintenance.

Tall fescue grows best when daytime temperatures do not exceed 80 degrees Fahrenheit—at higher summer temperatures, tall fescue has all it can manage just to survive. Best for semi-shade sites or lawns that have a mixture of sunny and shady areas, it can be successful in full sunshine if the soil is tilled properly before planting and you can irrigate in the summer. It is green year-round under proper management and adequate irrigation; it's usually best for the northern half of Georgia. Dozens of new varieties of tall fescue are introduced each year. Proponents of each variety claim theirs is the most shade- and drought-tolerant and the most resistant to disease. Most support these claims by quoting the results of grass-growing trials at research facilities scattered across the country.

- The "turf-type" tall fescues are indeed superior to the "pasture-type" tall fescue that is commonly called Kentucky 31.

- While there are differences between the "turf-type" tall fescue varieties, no one variety surpasses the rest at research facility trials.

- The work you do to prepare the soil before planting is much more likely to produce a great-looking lawn than the tall fescue variety you plant.

Bermudagrass can be planted by seeding or by sodding. Common bermudagrass produces fertile seed, which is sold at most garden centers. Hybrid bermudagrass does not produce fertile seed; the only way to propagate this, and other sodded grasses, is to grow it from sprigs taken from a "mother" plant. On the flat soil of south Georgia, millions of sprigs are planted each spring to become the sod you purchase during the year.

- Common bermudagrass is always grown from seed. It is lighter green in color than hybrid bermudagrass, and its leaves are coarser in texture. Seedheads pop up quickly after mowing, and it invades flowerbeds rapidly.

- Tifgreen (Tifton 328) bermudagrass sod is low-growing and spreads rapidly. It has fine texture and soft leaves.

- TifSport bermudagrass is more cold-hardy than other bermudagrasses. It is dark emerald green, resists drought, and does well in low-maintenance situations.

- Tifway (Tifton 419) bermudagrass sod is darker green than Tifgreen. It is more frost-tolerant, stays green longer in fall, and turns green earlier in spring.

Zoysiagrass is typically installed as sod.

- Emerald zoysiagrass has a very fine leaf texture and good shade tolerance. It is less cold tolerant than other zoysia varieties.

Fortunately for gardeners today, there are a number of disease-resistant selections of the American elm. Look for 'American Liberty' elms, a series of six selections introduced by the Elm Research Institute. Other resistant selections are 'Delaware #2', 'New Harmony', 'Washington', and 'Valley Forge'. Another elm species that exhibits resistance to the Dutch elm disease (but not the elm leaf beetle) is the Chinese or lacebark elm, *Ulmus parvifolia*. The cultivar Allee® ('Emer II') has an upright spreading habit and gray to orange-brown peeling bark; Athena® ('Emer I') is a broad-spreading tree with shiny green leaves, some yellow fall color, and colorful bark in

- Meyer zoysiagrass has a wider leaf than Emerald. It has good cold tolerance but less shade tolerance than Emerald.

- El Toro zoysiagrass sod grows rapidly and has a leaf width similar to that of Meyer.

- Zenith zoysiagrass can be planted from seed, grows rapidly, has a dense growth habit, and tolerates light shade.

Centipedegrass may be established from seed or sod. Its appearance is like that of St. Augustinegrass, but the leaves are smaller and lighter green in color. It requires less mowing than bermudagrass or St. Augustinegrass. It requires no lime and minimal amounts of nitrogen.

St. Augustinegrass is always sodded or sprigged for establishment. It is the most shade-tolerant of the warm-season grasses, but the least winter hardy. Injury is likely if the temperature dips below 10 degrees Fahrenheit. St. Augustine never becomes completely dormant in winter and must begin spring growth from aboveground buds. Newer varieties include Floratam and Seville for south Georgia. Raleigh is suitable for north Georgia up to northern Atlanta.

Seeding versus Sodding – There are two ways to establish a lawn: by planting seed and waiting for it to sprout, or by laying sod and gaining an instant lawn. Some grasses are better planted from seed, while others can only be planted with sod.

shades of gray, green, and orange-brown—both of these are fast-growing and adapt to a range of growing conditions.

Even if you choose these disease-resistant selections, it is still important to plant a diversity of trees in your garden.

VINES AND GROUNDCOVERS

Now that spring is here, daffodils are in bloom. Think about adding some groundcovers to help mask daffodil foliage once the bulbs finish blooming. Remember that you should leave foliage on daffodils, as it is storing energy for next year's flowers. Hellebores and hosta are both well suited as groundcovers for daffodils, hyacinth, Dutch iris, and summer snowflake.

Clematis vines make great companions for roses. You can choose clematis that bloom around the same time that a rose does so that the two flowers will complement each other, or select a clematis that will bloom after the rose is finished. For a winning combination, train *Clematis viticella* 'Etoile Violette', which has purple blooms with yellow stamens, to grow up and through *Rosa* 'New Dawn'. Vigorous and free-flowering, this clematis blooms from midsummer to early autumn, so that even when the rose has finished blooming, you will still have flowers. When you choose a clematis to grow with a rose, select species or hybrids that bloom on current-season's growth so that if you need to prune back the vine early in the spring you will still get blooms that season.

If you have an infestation of Japanese honeysuckle or English ivy that you want to eradicate, this is a good time to get started. Digging out plants, especially the roots, will be easier if you recognize the plants early. Learn to identify the foliage. You can also cut ivy and honeysuckle back to the ground, let them put out new growth, and then spray with a nonselective weedkiller. It may take this twofold approach to get rid of ivy or honeysuckle, as both are tenacious plants.

PLANT

ANNUALS

Soil temperatures determine when you can plant seeds outdoors. When the weather for several days in a row is warm enough to work outside wearing shorts and a T-shirt, it's time to plant! Annuals that are easy to grow from seed outdoors in spring include marigold, cosmos, zinnia, celosia, cleome, sunflower, and nasturtium.

■ *Hellebores and daffodils are good companions in the garden.*

BULBS

Plant Dutch iris now for late-summer blooms. Check with your local Extension office about the last frost date in your area. By mid-April in all but the most northern part of the state, it should be safe to plant many summer-blooming bulbs like canna, elephant ear, dahlia, or gladiolus outside—especially if you are planting them in containers. Before you plant, be sure soil temperatures are 60 degrees Fahrenheit or warmer.

EDIBLES

Plant warm-season garden crops such as tomato, eggplant, pepper, and squash when the soil is quite warm. In south Georgia, this planting time is in late March or early April. Gardeners in the northern half of the state should wait until April 15 to be safe. Of course, some gamblers will plant earlier—but they run the risk of losing everything to a late frost, and even if that doesn't happen, their plants will just sit there, not growing, waiting until the soil is warm.

Fruit trees can be purchased bare-root, balled-and-burlapped, or container-grown. Because the first two types have limited root systems, they are best planted in winter or very early spring. Fruit trees that have been grown in containers have a much more robust root system and can be planted in April and May.

LAWNS

There are two ways to establish a lawn: by planting seed and waiting for it to sprout, or by laying sod and gaining an instant lawn.

PERENNIALS

Divide and transplant perennials.

The best time to divide ornamental grasses is in the spring, just as new growth is beginning. Certain grasses like maiden grass, *Miscanthus* spp., and fountain grass, *Pennisetum* spp., can develop into large clumps and may require a handsaw to divide them. Make sure each division has roots and shoots before you replant it.

Perennials such as bluestar, *Amsonia* spp., and *Astilbe* hybrids can also be divided with a handsaw in the spring; make sure each division has new shoots and roots.

If you want to purchase plants, local nurseries and garden centers should have a good selection of perennials from which to choose.

Space plants to allow enough room for growth. Keep in mind that you may have to move or divide plants next year if they get too large.

HERE'S HOW

TO INSTALL SOD

1. Kill all weeds by spraying the area with a nonselective weedkiller two weeks before planting.

2. Till the soil thoroughly to a depth of 6 inches, mixing in the recommended amount of lime and fertilizer.

3. Rake the area smooth, removing rocks, clumps, and grassy debris.

4. Roll the area with a water-filled roller to reveal low spots. Fill any low spots with soil.

5. Starting along the longest straight edge of the area, lay sod pieces end to end. Make sure each piece is tightly placed next to its neighbor. Stagger pieces in adjacent rows so seams do not line up. Use a small hatchet or sharp shovel to trim pieces to fit around obstructions.

6. Roll the entire area once more, to ensure good sod-to-soil contact.

7. Water the sod thoroughly.

TO HARDEN OFF PERENNIAL SEEDLINGS

1. Take seedlings outside, and place them in a shaded area such as a porch, gradually exposing them to more sun each day.

2. Once they are acclimated to the outside environment, you can plant them in the garden. A week to ten days should be long enough for the acclimation.

If seedlings were sown in individual peat pots, you can plant the pot directly into the ground. A few cuts with your pruners into the bottom of the pot will stimulate roots to become established more quickly. Keep peat pots moist while seeds are germinating and when you transplant them to the garden.

ROSES

Roses make good container plants outside on your patio. You can enjoy them when blooms are present, and move them to a less conspicuous spot when the show is over. Select varieties that don't demand a lot of space.

- To keep the plants upright, use a 24-inch-wide or larger pot, except when planting miniature-sized rose plants. Clay pots or wooden containers "breathe" better than plastic pots.

- Purchase a good-quality potting soil. It should be light and fluffy, not heavy and smelly.

- Place the rose in the sunniest spot possible.

- Check soil moisture every day. Plan to water daily during the heat of summer.

SHRUBS

April is a great month to plant shrubs in your garden.

Soak bare-root plants in a bucket of water before planting, and prune off any dead or badly damaged roots, such as those that are cracked or broken.

When you are transplanting shrubs, dig as large a rootball as possible. The more roots you get, the better success you'll have moving your shrubs. If your shrub is 3 feet across, you should measure 3 feet out from the main stem, all the way around the plant. At this point, take your spade and cut into the roots. Some shrubs, like azaleas, have lots of shallow roots that spread out in every direction, so it is necessary to dig a rootball that is wider than it is deep, looking almost like a thin, wide pancake. Prepare the new location ahead of time. The less time a plant stays out of the ground, the fewer roots will dry out and die. Sometimes a piece of burlap or 4 mil plastic is a useful tool to help drag the rootball to its new home. Place the rootball on the burlap and pull it to where it will be planted.

After planting, tamp down the soil around the roots to remove any air pockets. Fill up the hole halfway with soil, add water, let it settle, and then fill in the remaining soil. Apply a 2-inch layer of mulch, keeping it away from the main trunk. Mulching helps keep the soil cool or warm, depending on the season, and reduces infestations of weeds.

HERE'S HOW

TO PLANT CONTAINER-GROWN SHRUBS

You can plant container-grown shrubs all month long, following these steps:

1. Dig a hole that is as deep as the container and twice as wide.

2. Use a shovel to hit the sides of the container. This will make it easier to slide out the whole rootball.

3. Use a sharp pair of hand pruners to make two or three cuts into the rootball, spacing the distance between cuts equally. This will encourage new roots to sprout and establish more quickly.

4. Trim off any dead topgrowth.

5. Place the rootball in the hole and fill in the soil around it. Don't pile lots of extra soil on top of the top layer of soil—this will suffocate surface roots.

6. Water the shrub well.

7. Apply a 2-inch layer of mulch around newly planted shrubs.

TREES

This is a good time to add container-grown or balled-and-burlapped trees to your garden. Be sure to water them regularly during the first year while they become established.

VINES AND GROUNDCOVERS

Direct-sow seeds of annual vines in spots where you want them to grow. Some vines, like moon flower and hyacinth bean, are easier to establish if you start the seed in peat pots and then, once the seed has germinated, transplant the peat pot directly into the garden.

Plant groundcovers and perennial vines in your garden.

Take the annual vine seedlings you started indoors under lights and transplant to small pots outside. Place the pots in an area that gets lots of bright light but no hot sun. Keep them in this location for a week to ten days before moving them to a spot where they receive full sun.

If there is a threat of frost, move the plants to a garage or a protected area. Wait until the

■ *When planting annuals, plant them at the same depth they were growing in containers.*

frost-free date arrives before planting your new vines in the garden. Check with your local Extension office about the date of the last frost in your region.

CARE

ANNUALS

Though it may be warm during the day, nights are still chilly. The annual plants you have raised from seed for the past weeks can't tolerate cool temperatures. To accustom them to growing outdoors, they should be hardened off.

- If daytime temperatures are above 60 degrees Fahrenheit, take the plants outdoors and place them in a shady spot, for seven days in a row, bringing them indoors at night.

- When nighttime temperatures are 50 degrees or above, you can leave the plants outside both day and night. Bring indoors if temperatures fall below 50 degrees.

- Examine your plants daily to make sure they do not wilt.

- After two weeks outdoors, they are ready to be transplanted into your garden.

Less care will be needed if you select the healthiest plants when purchasing annuals. Be wary of buying a plant fully in flower—nursery techniques that force a plant to flower all at once can leave it weakened and bare in just a few weeks. Choose plants that have just one or two flowers and plenty of unopened flower buds. Gently pull one or two plants from the pot to examine their roots. Soggy soil and brown, jelly-like roots can indicate root rot problems. Evaluate the nursery as a whole. Are most plants in good health, or do they seem to be underwatered or overgrown and floppy? Consider buying plants in 4-inch pots rather than in six-packs. Though they are more expensive, larger plants have more complete root systems and are likely to bloom earlier.

FLOWERING AND FRUITING GROUNDCOVERS

Dwarf plumbago, *Ceratostigma plumbaginoides*
6 to 12 inches high
This hardy perennial may be semi-evergreen in the mildest parts of the state but even where it is deciduous, the indigo-blue phlox-like flowers in late summer to early autumn are reason enough to grow this plant. The foliage is bronzy to dark green and then in autumn it gets tinges of red. Plant this bloomer in full sun or part shade.

Cotoneaster, *Cotoneaster* spp. and cvs.
1 to 16 feet tall
Many different types exist from the very low-growing ground huggers to those with long trailing branches. Many are effective for bank plantings with colorful fruit in shades of red and orange. Some begin to color in summer and provide interest through the winter. Cotoneasters prefer full sun or part shade.

Galax, *Galax urceolata*
6 to 9 inches high
The foliage is 6 to 9 inches high with spikes of white flowers 2½ feet tall. This native perennial grows in tufts and is a slow grower, but in a woodland garden it makes an elegant evergreen groundcover. Up to 5 inches across, the shiny heart-shaped leaves take on shades of bronze in the autumn.

Sweet woodruff, *Galium odoratum*
6 to 12 inches high
Long grown for the fragrant flowers and foliage used to make May wine. Great for the shade or part shade, this perennial likes a moist, well-drained soil. Be warned: this plant is an aggressive spreader. Give this plant full shade in the southernmost part of the state.

Daylily, *Hemerocallis* spp. and cvs.
1 to 6 feet tall
Daylilies make a trouble-free flowering groundcover on a bank, or as part of a mixed planting. The dwarf varieties are well suited for mass plantings. Plant daylilies in full sun or part shade.

Creeping St. John's wort, *Hypericum calycinum*
1 foot tall
This evergreen to semi-evergreen plant is a survivor that can grow and compete with tree roots, tolerate poor soil, or help control erosion on a steep bank. Bright yellow flowers, 3 inches across, occur throughout the summer. If the plant gets overgrown, use the lawn mower or prune it back hard when it is dormant. *Hypericum* prefers full sun or part shade.

Partridgeberry, *Mitchella repens*
3 to 6 inches tall
This creeping native is perfect for the woodland garden with ferns, mosses, and other shade-loving plants. The roundish evergreen leaves are less than 1 inch long. Tiny white flowers appear in late spring to early summer and are followed by bright red berries, less than ¼ inch wide.

Himalayan Sweetbox, *Sarcococca hookerana humilis*
1 to 2 feet high (shown in photo)
This groundcover spreads very slowly by underground runners. The glossy evergreen leaves, 1 to 3 inches long, hide the tiny but powerfully fragrant flowers when they perfume the air in early spring. The flowers are followed by small black fruits. A great groundcover for the shade garden.

BULBS

Remove faded blooms of daffodils before they set seed. Remove the flowers, and leave the stems; the stems help with photosynthesis.

Once the daffodils finish blooming, some gardeners like to tie up their foliage with rubber bands or bunch them up. Not only is this practice unattractive, it prevents sunlight from getting to all the leaves, cuts off air circulation, and increases the chances of fungal problems.

It is important to let bulb foliage ripen. As leaves go through the process of photosynthesis, they store food for next year's blooms. The time to cut off the foliage is when it turns yellow and falls over. Daffodil expert Brent Heath recommends that you wait at least eight to ten weeks after bloom before cutting off bulb foliage.

LAWNS

When you operate a spreader to apply fertilizer or pesticides, avoid casting the materials onto your street. Rainfall will wash these chemicals into municipal water-treatment systems or local waterways. The pollution may harm plants and animals that live near water.

PERENNIALS

Continue handweeding. Spot-spray weeds in perennial beds with a nonselective weedkiller.

Prune back lantana unless you live in south Georgia where it is evergreen. If the plants were overgrown last fall, it is best to prune them now in early spring when they are actively growing. You can cut back one-third to one-half of the total plant, and it will quickly recover.

PROS & CONS OF THE TWO TYPES OF MOWERS

Two types of mowers are generally available: rotary and reel. Here are the pros and cons of each:

Rotary Mower Pros
- Readily available
- Can be used on all types of grasses
- Easy to repair
- Easy to replace blade
- Mulching models recycle grass clippings

Rotary Mower Cons
- Wheel may fall into low spots, yielding half-moon shaped scalped areas
- Blade must be kept sharp to achieve best cut

Reel Mower Pros
- Yields an even, manicured cut on bermudagrass and zoysiagrass lawns
- Less likely to be affected by uneven surface conditions

Reel Mower Cons
- More expensive than rotary mower of comparable width
- Blade must be sharpened by an expert

If you have any perennials that need staking, plan ahead. Right about the time the flower buds begin to show color is the best time to stake. You can use a single stake or a series of stakes for multistemmed plants; bamboo stakes work well. For tying, use green or natural-colored jute twine, which will blend in better than white string.

- Certain perennials like peonies or garden phlox, *Phlox paniculata*, can be staked now with a circular gridded ring placed on top of three stakes. The stakes should be evenly spaced and adjustable. As the plant grows up through the openings, the ring will keep the plant from flopping over when it is in full flower. This type of stake is called a "grow thru" or a metal hoop support.

- For single-stem plants like lilies, place the stake about an inch from the main stem, and tie jute to the stake, leaving 2- to 4-inch loose ends. Bring the lily stem close to the stake, and tie the loose ends around it.

- Another method for staking is to use the twiggy prunings from your trees, cut into various 16- to 20-inch lengths. Stick them into the ground all around young plants when plants are about half their expected height, and in no time the plants will cover the stakes. This works well when there are lots of perennials in one area or for plants like beebalm that have many stems.

If you want to keep the amount of staking to a minimum, plant your garden so that one variety of perennial supports another. Early-blooming Shasta daisies make a good mass to plant in front of salvias, which will bloom later.

ROSES

If you want large, exhibition-quality flowers, you can encourage their formation on hybrid tea roses by disbudding several individual stems. Select a stem that has a small but healthy-looking bud at the tip. Cut off any side buds below it. This directs the plant's energy into producing a large bloom on that stem instead of a few smaller flowers.

SHRUBS

Prune flowering shrubs like forsythia, flowering quince, early-blooming spireas (*Spiraea nipponica* 'Snowmound', *S. thunbergii*), and azaleas as soon as they finish blooming. If shrubs are overgrown and lacking vigor, with very few blooms, pruning can help rejuvenate them. Remove one-third of the

TIPS ON PRUNING ROSES

Many rose plants are produced by grafting a desirable rose onto the stem of a vigorous, but possibly unattractive, rose (the rootstock). The area where the two join is called the graft union. It looks like a swollen knob a few inches above ground level. Don't leave stubs on the graft union when pruning. A fine-toothed saw blade or sharp knife makes clean cuts and permits you to get close to the graft.

Roses that have been grafted onto a rootstock may produce thin sprouts (suckers) arising from the ground around the trunk or below the graft union. The flowers produced on these suckers will not be the same as those on the grafted rose above. Prune away all suckers back to the root or stem from which they come.

Do not simply cut flush with the ground—follow the sucker back to the origination point on the main plant to make your cut.

If the rose is growing on its own roots, flowers on the suckers will be identical to those on the parent.

You may choose to leave these suckers, in order to have a bigger plant, or to remove them.

"Own-root" roses are those that have been propagated by rooting a cutting rather than grafting.

Some rose fanciers believe that own-root roses are more vigorous, more long-lived, and, if the top is frozen, able to sprout back true to the original variety.

oldest wood completely, and cut the remaining stems to a height of 12 inches. Follow this practice for the next few years, and you will create a healthy, vigorous plant.

TREES

There is still time to prune or shear candles on evergreens. Restrict your pruning of deciduous trees to removing dead or diseased branches—wait until winter to do any extreme corrective pruning or to remove any large branches.

VINES AND GROUNDCOVERS

If they need to be tidied up or are getting too rampant for the space they are growing in, prune spring-flowering vines like Carolina jessamine as soon as they finish blooming.

Determine where you'll prune. Here is a list of perennial vines for espalier that produce showy flowers and/or fruit:

- **Akebia,** *Akebia quinata*, has clusters of purple flowers in spring that are often followed by 2- to 4-inch-long, purple, sausage-type fruits in summer to fall.

- **Bougainvillea,** *Bougainvillea* cultivars, offer a long season of bright color for coastal gardens. The colorful parts that surround the tiny flowers are actually bracts.

- **Armand clematis,** *Clematis armandii*, is an evergreen species that has masses of tiny white fragrant flowers in early spring.

- **Firethorn,** *Pyracantha* hybrids, produces red, orange, or red-orange fruit in late summer. The fruit last well into winter.

- **Lady banks rose,** *Rosa banksiae*, an evergreen climber that produces masses of yellow or white flowers in early spring.

- *Wisteria* spp. is an aggressive vine that has beautiful clusters of violet to violet-blue flowers in April to May.

WATER

ANNUALS

April is likely to have several days with temperatures in the 80s. Newly planted annuals can quickly dry out, especially on windy days. Water each plant immediately after planting.

1. Water again twenty-four to forty-eight hours later.

2. Water again four days after the initial planting.

3. Begin weekly watering for all your annuals once they seem adapted to their new homes.

BULBS

Now that spring bulbs are actively growing and blooming, make sure they get plenty of water. Water your bulbs once a week unless you get a good rain, 1 inch or more per week.

EDIBLES

Water newly planted vegetables, herbs, and fruiting plants weekly, providing 1 to 5 cups for small plants, 1 to 2 gallons for shrubs and trees.

Mulching vegetable seedlings immediately after planting is a good practice for three reasons: moisture retention, weed control, and disease control. A thin layer of pine straw or grass clippings works well, or try using newspaper mulch:

1. Unfold a section of the paper, and select a stack of three sheets.

2. Tear the stack halfway down the center, and slip it around the stem of an individual plant.

3. Wet it down to hold in place, then cover with straw or leaves.

LAWNS

After sod has been laid, the lawn must be watered regularly to keep the sod alive while it establishes new roots. Unlike newly seeded lawns, the initial watering of sod should be sufficient to moisten the soil under it to a depth of 6 inches. This will take more than an hour in most cases. Lift a piece of sod and use a trowel to measure the depth of water penetration.

PERENNIALS

For the first few months you may need to water every few days if temperatures are high and plants are planted in full sun. After this initial period, check plants once a week for the first growing

WATERING SODDED & NEWLY SEEDED LAWNS

Water newly planted sod deeply and regularly so the roots will explore the soil beneath the original sod. Use a trowel to check how far water soaks into the soil after an irrigation. Heavy clay soil absorbs water slowly. If water runs off before it is absorbed, split the irrigation into two sessions an hour apart. Sandy soil absorbs water rapidly but dries out quickly. Consider splitting the recommended inch of water per week into two irrigations of ½-inch of water three days apart.

Sod: Here's one example of followup watering after sod has been laid:

- Apply ⅛-inch of water daily for seven days.

- Follow by ¼-inch of water every third day for nine days.

- Follow by ½-inch of water every five days for ten days.

- Follow by 1 inch of water per week for the rest of the growing season.

Seed:

- Apply ⅛-inch of water daily until seedlings are 1½ inches tall.

- Follow by ¼-inch of water every third day for nine days.

- Follow by ½-inch of water every five days for ten days.

- Follow by 1 inch of water per week for the rest of the growing season.

season. If you do not receive 1 inch of rainfall per week, applying 2 gallons of water per 1-gallon-sized perennial should be adequate.

Containers should be checked daily and they may need more frequent watering than plants that are planted in the ground. Water when the soil 1 to 2 inches deep is dry to the touch.

ROSES

Check on roses that you planted earlier this spring.

- Pull back the mulch underneath the plant.

- Make sure the top of the rootball is still at (or slightly below) the surrounding soil surface. If not, pull mulch away completely and add soil to the proper height.

- Replace mulch and water.

SHRUBS

Water newly planted and transplanted shrubs after you plant them and then once a week (unless there is a good rain) for the first month. Place the hose at the base of the shrub and let a slow stream saturate the area. A good rule of thumb is to apply 1 to 2 gallons per foot of plant height. Soaker hoses also work well.

In coastal areas where soils are sandy, shrubs may need watering more frequently. Dig into the top 2 to 3 inches of the soil to determine if it is dry. Established plantings will also benefit from supplemental watering during periods of drought.

TREES

Keep watering new plantings. Apply 1 gallon per foot of tree height per week.

VINES AND GROUNDCOVERS

Water newly planted vines or groundcovers, and water the areas where you sow annual seed. Use a sprinkler to get gentle, even coverage. Keep vines planted in containers watered too. Let the soil get dry to the touch, then water thoroughly, letting the water run out of the bottom of the pot.

TO WATER TREES & SHRUBS

Water your shrubs as soon as you plant or transplant them. Place the hose at the base of a shrub and let a slow stream saturate the area. A good rule of thumb is to apply 1 to 2 gallons per foot of plant height. Water once a week for the first six months unless there is a good rain (1 or more inches per week is a good rain).

- When watering by hand, apply 5 gallons of water per 10 square feet. This is approximately the amount of water delivered by a garden hose operating one minute at medium pressure.

- Soaker hoses are effective too. They can water a swath one foot wide on either side of a hose. Depending on the water pressure, a 50-foot-long soaker hose can water 100 square feet of landscape bed in two or more hours.

- Apply 50 gallons of water per 100 square feet when plants show signs of water stress, such as wilting or leaves that turn blue/gray. In coastal areas where soils are sandy, shrubs may need watering more frequently. Dig down 2 to 3 inches. If the soil is dry at that depth, water.

- During periods of extended drought when it doesn't rain for a month or longer, your shrubs will benefit from supplemental watering.

Water your trees as soon as you plant them; for the first six months, apply 1 gallon per foot of tree height per week unless there is 1 inch or more of rain weekly.

Once they are established, you should have to apply supplemental water only during periods of drought. If there has been no rain for a month or longer, get out the hose. Water is not free, but the money you spend to irrigate a mature tree may save it, which is especially desirable when the tree is a 100 year old oak.

To supply a tree's minimum needs during times of drought, apply 15 gallons of water per inch of trunk diameter once per week. Example: a tree whose trunk is 12 inches thick, 4 feet from the ground, needs 180 gallons of water per week. Attach an inexpensive water timer to your soaker hose and set it to 180 gallons. It will shut off once 180 gallons has soaked out of the hose. Depending on the length of the hose, this could take two to three hours; for this amount of water, the cost will be just a few dollars.

For optimal tree health, apply the amount calculated twice each week during times of drought.

FERTILIZE

ANNUALS

Annuals need nutrients to get off to a good start. Water-soluble fertilizers provide the quickest way to feed plants immediately. Slow-release fertilizers, which come in a granular form, provide nutrients for the entire growing season.

- Use water-soluble fertilizer for the first watering, following label directions.

- Consider placing slow-release fertilizer granules in the bottom of each hole in which you plant an annual, following label directions.

- If you choose not to use slow-release fertilizer, you will need to feed your plants every six weeks with one pound of 10-10-10 for every 100 square feet of flower bed.

Alternatively, use one of the water-soluble products according to label directions.

BULBS

Remember, the ideal time to fertilize bulbs is in the fall when they produce roots that absorb nutrients, but you might choose to fertilize now, too, when spring bulbs are growing and about to bloom. Use a water-soluble fertilizer (10-10-10) that will get to the roots quickly while the bulb is actively growing and before it blooms.

EDIBLES

You can make a simple starter fertilizer solution at home to use on new vegetable transplants:

1. Add 2 tablespoons of 5-10-15 fertilizer to 5 gallons of water.

2. Mix thoroughly and allow it to settle.

3. Pour the solution around new transplants to settle them into the soil.

The jury is still out on the value of commercial root-stimulator solutions for new plants. It is not likely that the products cause harm, so go ahead and use them if you wish.

Fertilize pecans in north Georgia with 1 pound of 10-10-10 per inch of trunk diameter (and again in June).

Do not fertilize blueberries with granular fertilizer during the first year after planting. In later years, fertilize lightly in April, June, and September.

LAWNS

In late April, most warm season grasses can receive their first fertilization, while tall fescue is ready for its last. Any turf fertilizer will suffice unless otherwise noted.

- **Tall fescue:** Fertilize now, but wait until September to fertilize again.

- **Bermudagrass:** Fertilize only when the lawn is 50 percent greened-up.

- **Zoysiagrass:** Fertilize only when the lawn is 50 percent greened-up.

TO CALIBRATE A FERTILIZER SPREADER

It is important to know how much material your spreader is applying when you use it for seeding or fertilizing. Many lawn products list the appropriate spreader setting for several models—but what should you do if your spreader is not listed?

1. Measure an area of 1,000 square feet (10 feet by 100 feet, 20 feet by 50 feet, and so forth) in your lawn.

2. Set your spreader to one-fourth open.

3. Load the spreader with a weighed amount of cat litter. (Ten pounds is usually enough.)

4. Operate the spreader over the 1,000-square-foot-area.

5. Weigh the amount left in the spreader. Subtract from the amount originally in the spreader. The result is the application rate of the spreader for that particular material per 1,000 square feet.

Example: After loading the spreader with 10 pounds of cat litter and operating it over 1,000 square feet, 5 pounds are left. At that setting, and for that material, your spreader dispenses 5 pounds per 1,000 square feet.

- Use a permanent marker to write the results of your calibration on the spreader.

- Each different type of seed or fertilizer will require its own spreader calibration.

- **Centipedegrass:** In south Georgia, fertilize with 6 pounds of 15-0-15 per 1,000 square feet of lawn.

- **St. Augustinegrass:** In south Georgia, fertilize if the lawn is 50 percent greened-up.

PERENNIALS AND SHRUBS

If you haven't fertilized yet, you can apply a complete fertilizer like 10-10-10 at a rate of 1 pound per 100 square feet. If you have soil that has been amended with organic amendments, you won't have to fertilize your perennials every month. If you want to fertilize, three times a year (spring, summer, and fall) is plenty.

ROSES

Fertilize each plant at mid-month with 10-10-10 or water-soluble fertilizer. It is not necessary to remove the mulch before fertilizing; irrigation and rainfall will take the nutrients to the roots.

TREES

Fertilize trees once they leaf out. Use a slow-release fertilizer.

Palms like a fertilizer that is rich in micronutrients, especially magnesium and manganese. Use a slow-release fertilizer that includes micronutrients (refer to the label). A nutrient ratio of 3:1:2, such as 12-4-8, is best.

VINES AND GROUNDCOVERS

To help them get established, fertilize groundcovers that were planted within the last six months. Use ½ pound or 1 cup of 8-8-8 or 10-10-10 per 100 square feet (this is half the recommended rate for established groundcovers).

Fertilize vines only if they need it. If they are healthy and robust, there is no need to fertilize.

Applying a fresh layer of well-composted manure around the base of your vines will provide them with nutrients over a long period of time. Use caution to keep the manure from touching the main stem.

PROBLEM-SOLVE

ANNUALS

Aphids love the lush tips of fast-growing plants. They can suck plant sap easily from stems or leaves and can disfigure the growing tip. Suspect aphids if you see many ants on a particular plant. Examine the undersides of leaves at the branch tips. Aphids may be green, yellow, or black, and they are visible with the naked eye.

If you find aphids, blast them off the plant with a strong stream of water.

BULBS

If you love bulbs but are concerned about the awkward stage they go through when the foliage ripens, try companion planting. Plant your bulbs with companion plants and you can extend the blooming season and provide cover foliage to hide ripening bulb foliage. You can also layer your bulbs so that when one type finishes blooming, another begins. For example, you can plant tulips 10 inches deep, daffodils at 6 inches, and then crocus and dwarf iris on top at 3 inches deep. With this method you will have a long season of spring bloom from your bulbs. Here are some planting combinations:

- Crocus with pansies or lawn grasses

- Daffodils with hellebores and hosta

- Daffodils or surprise lilies with English ivy (use larger-type daffodils, not dwarf varieties, so they are robust enough to compete with the ivy)

- Daffodils with ferns like Japanese painted fern

- Dwarf iris with ajuga or periwinkle

- Daffodils with daylilies in a sunny border (this way you will have blooms in spring and summer in the same spot)

In a shady woodland composed of deciduous trees, bulbs get enough light in the fall, winter, and early spring to ensure good blooms; and when summer arrives, they are protected from the hot afternoon sun.

EDIBLES

Keep a vigilant eye out for chickweed in your garden. Pull it from among your cool-season vegetables, hoe it from the middle of the rows—just don't let it go to seed!

Mulch tomato plants right after you plant them, a practice that will help prevent leaf diseases. Early blight is a fungus that splashes onto leaves from the soil during rainstorms or overhead watering. Once the fungus is on the leaves, it will continue to splash up the plant as it grows.

Control with fungicides is difficult; immediate mulching is much more effective.

Nematodes can greatly limit your harvest. These tips will help minimize their damage to susceptible plants if you have nematodes in your small garden:

- Determine where you will place each plant.

- Shovel the soil out of a 1-foot-diameter hole at each spot.

- Fill the hole with good-quality bagged planting soil.

- Plant seedling plants in the center of the hole.

By the time nematodes have moved from the contaminated soil into the clean planting soil, you'll have harvested plenty of produce. Remove the entire plant and root system from your property.

LAWNS

The presence of big green patches of thin-bladed grass in your bermudagrass or zoysiagrass lawn is usually a sign of annual bluegrass (*Poa annua*). One way to kill it is to soak a foam paintbrush with a nonselective herbicide and carefully wipe it on the weed but not on your grass. (Be sure to wear plastic gloves on your hands.)

Otherwise, make a mental note to use a weed-preventer that is effective on grassy weeds next September; this will prevent the bluegrass seeds from sprouting.

Watch for the bright green leaves of chickweed in your lawn. Spot-spray with broadleaf weedkiller.

PERENNIALS

Check perennials for aphids or other insects; if needed, treat with insecticidal soap.

If 50 percent or more of the plant is infested, it is an option to spray with a contact insecticide.

■ *It's best to put cages on plants while the plants are still small and manageable.*

■ *Create your own support with bamboo stakes and twine.*

Look for signs of slugs or slug damage on plants like hostas: the leaves may be chewed, and often there is a silvery trail on the leaves or on the ground near the plant.

Use a slug bait to control them. You can also put out empty black plastic cellpacks, tucked under leaves and collect them in the morning. Just throw them out with the slugs. Some people swear by beer, just enough to fill the lid of a mayo container. It will also be enough for the slugs to drown if they climb in to investigate.

ROSES

Do not allow winter weeds like chickweed or henbit to grow beneath your roses. Pull them out and sprinkle more mulch in their place to inhibit any sprouts you left behind.

SHRUBS

Check for signs of insect activity or damage. Aphids, scale, or chewing insects may be visible. Try using insecticidal soaps or a strong blast from the hose to control aphids before you resort to using chemical controls. If you notice that azalea leaves are bleached out (silvery and speckled), you may have lace bugs.

Spray with insecticidal soap or an insecticide to treat lace bugs.

Hand-pull any weeds, or use a cultivator to scratch them out. Once an area is free of weeds, apply a pre-emergent and a layer of mulch. This practice will greatly reduce weed infestations.

Some gardeners put down weed fabrics to control weed problems, but newspaper will also work. Apply a layer of newspaper at least three sheets thick and then cover it with mulch. (This technique may not be practical for formal gardens.)

TREES

Dogwood anthracnose (an-THRAK-nose), a fungus, has been attacking dogwoods throughout forests in the eastern United States. The symptoms of this disease, also called *discula*, usually show up in lower limbs first and may spread to the whole tree if not controlled. The

DISEASE-RESISTANT CRABAPPLES

The best way to avoid problems with any plant is to keep it healthy. By choosing varieties that are disease resistant, you are a step ahead of the game. Many crabapples are susceptible to scab, fireblight, cedar-apple rust, and powdery mildew. Some crabapple selections have been hybridized for improved disease resistance.

- 'Centurion' grows to 25 feet high and wide at maturity. Red buds open to rose-red flowers.

- 'Donald Wyman' grows to 25 feet high, with a large rounded habit. It has white flowers and persistent red fruits in winter.

- 'Harvest Gold' offers flowers that are pink in bud and white in flower. Its habit is upright and spreading, growing 25 feet high and 25 feet wide. Its golden fruits look good well into December.

- 'Indian Summer' has rose-red flowers and red fruit. It grows to 18 feet high and 19 feet wide.

- 'Jewelberry' is a small tree, growing 8 to 12 feet high. Pink buds open to white flowers and are followed by masses of glossy red fruits.

disease affects dogwood trees whose leaves do not dry off during the day. Leaves will exhibit spots with tan or brown blotches, bordered in purple, and the leaves will become severely distorted. Infected leaves cling to the tree, even after other leaves drop normally in the fall, and cankers form on the main trunk at the junction of each stem. (Cankers are swollen protrusions that can surround a twig or stem, girdling it and causing the branch to die). Trees in a weakened condition are more susceptible to *discula*—a healthy tree is the best defense against disease and insect problems. Most home landscape dogwoods have plenty of air circulation around them, which protects the leaves from infection. *Discula* is not expected to cause problems for Georgia dogwoods, except those growing in cool mountain valleys. To help prevent dogwood diseases:

- Plant dogwoods in moist, fertile soil, in light shade or full sun.

- Remove and destroy any leaves infected with fungus as soon as you notice them. Rake up leaves as soon as they fall, and burn them or dispose of them. Do not add them to your compost pile.

- Prune out any dead twigs or branches. Prune only during dry weather since fungus problems are usually worse in wet weather.

- Spray trees that you place a high value on with a fungicide in early spring.

- Keep trees watered during periods of drought.

- Plant disease-resistant dogwood hybrids such as 'Aurora', 'Galaxy', and 'Constellation'.

Kousa dogwood, *Cornus kousa*, blooms later and is also less susceptible to diseases than common dogwood, *Cornus florida*. Its flowers appear on the tops of the branches above the foliage and are more starlike in appearance. The large, red, strawberry-like fruits hang down and put on a show in late summer to fall. In winter, the colorful peeling bark adds color to the landscape.

VINES AND GROUNDCOVERS

New growth on some of your vines may look puckered and may be covered with tiny lime green bugs. Aphids voraciously feed on the new growth of vines like clematis and honeysuckle. Try blasting them off with a jet of cold water from the hose. If this doesn't do the trick, use an insecticidal soap.

HERE'S HOW

TO DEAL WITH CLEMATIS WILT

Clematis wilt is caused by a fungus. Present in the soil and on the plant, the spores become active when a specific combination of temperature and humidity occurs. The stems appear to wilt suddenly, often just when the flowers are beginning to open, and the leaves and stems are discolored. The fungus works itself around the stem of the clematis, cutting off the flow of sap. As soon as you notice that a stem is wilted, prune it off until you reach healthy tissue. Sometimes this means you will have to prune a stem to below ground level. Discard all prunings and dead material. Do not add them to your compost pile.

- Clematis are usually more susceptible to attacks by fungus during the first two years of growth. Once they develop woody stems the fungus has a harder time penetrating the bark.

- Pinch back your clematis on a regular basis during the first two years to encourage side shoots. This reduces foliage and therefore the stress on the roots.

- Plant clematis deeply. If a shoot is killed to ground level, new shoots may appear from a node below the soil surface.

May

April showers bring May flowers, and weeds too. Remember, a little weeding each week will help you keep weeds from crowding out the plants you are trying to cultivate.

Spring is bursting with blooms including perennials, roses, shrubs, and trees.

From the familiar azaleas to the less common Chinese fringe tree, flowers are *everywhere*. Pick a bouquet of flowers from your favorite shrubs. Arrange the flowers in a vase and note the color combinations. This may help you decide what colors to add to your garden in the future.

This is a popular month for garden tours and with good reason. Visiting other people's gardens in your region is a great way to find out which plants or combinations of plants will do well in your own garden. You can also get design ideas for garden structures like arbors, pergolas or walls, and walkways. Be sure to take your camera and capture elements and combinations that appeal to you. Take notes on the materials and construction. Adapt design concepts to suit your own unique style.

There's still time to add plants to your garden, including shrubs, trees, perennials, and annuals. Even if you only have a balcony or patio, you can grow many plants in containers including roses, dwarf conifers, and even small trees. Edible plants like blueberries and dwarf peach tree are also candidates for containers. If you are choosing plants with fragrant flowers take your own personal sniff test before you purchase them. It's also a good month to add summer blooming bulbs such as caladiums, cannas, dahlias, elephant ear, gladiolus, and tuberose. Make sure the soil temperatures are warmed up before you plant caladiums. Mulching after you plant will help reduce weeds and keep plants from drying out so quickly.

Whatever tasks you need to do in the garden, May is a glorious month to take care of them.

PLAN

ANNUALS

Plant labels are quite useful in a garden. They help you remember the names of particular flowers, and they can remind you of a plant's source and special care. If you include a plant's scientific name, you can teach yourself the rudiments of botanical Latin! Labels can be made from plastic picnic knives, medical tongue depressors, aluminum window blind slats, strips of plastic cut from recycled non-dairy topping containers, or strips of aluminum cut from recycled aluminum pie pans. Most garden centers sell more attractive and permanent labels: fired clay markers for herbs, rectangular metal tags attached to steel hairpin legs, and copper tags that attach loosely to woody plant stems with wire.

BULBS

Spring bulbs are finished, and summer will soon be here. Plan on adding at least a few summer bloomers to brighten the garden scene. You can easily grow summer bulbs in pots or in the ground. Think about combinations of different bulbs or bulbs and perennials.

One canna with dark or variegated foliage can make a dramatic statement in the perennial border. A combination that promises to light up the shade garden is made of caladiums, cannas, elephant ears, and impatiens. For sun, try combining dahlias with ornamental grasses, butterfly ginger, and one large elephant ear.

EDIBLES

Kiwifruit is delicious, but the vines are not very cold hardy. The fruit can be grown in south Georgia, but plants are not reliably hardy north of Macon. The vine is grown on a double-wire trellis identical to a grape trellis.

- Yearly pruning in March is required because the vine grows so fast. The technique is the same as for muscadine grapevines.

- A male vine is needed to provide pollen for one to five female vines.

- Don't expect fruit for the first two years after you plant. The vine needs at least this long to establish itself.

- Make plans to protect the vine with a plastic sheet whenever temperatures fall below 30 degrees Fahrenheit.

LAWNS

It is possible to purchase seed for warm-season grasses like centipedegrass, bermudagrass, and zoysiagrass, but establishing these lawns is not as easy as establishing a tall fescue lawn from seed. Before deciding to plant warm-season grass from seed, carefully consider whether you are willing to spend weeks babying your lawn. These grasses have tiny seed, which may take many days to germinate even under the best conditions; weeds will sprout as the seedlings struggle to grow, and they may overpower the grass seed.

PERENNIALS

Many perennials are now in bloom or beginning to bloom. Think about the rest of the season and what the garden will look like. Incorporating perennials that have interesting foliage and distinctive forms will help the garden have interest even when there aren't any flowers. When you plant your perennials, remember to leave space for colorful annuals. And remember that white flowers combine well with most other colors in the garden or help to separate one area of color from another.

Photograph the garden at least once in spring, and write the names of the spring bloomers in your garden journal.

ROSES

Notice that roses have compound leaves composed of three to seven small leaflets. Whether cutting roses for display indoors or just to remove old flowers, make your cut just above a five-leaflet leaf. Buds growing at the base of five-leaflet leaves will produce long stems and healthy flowers. Buds growing at the base of three-leaflet leaves are more likely to produce weak stems and flowers. If you prune down to a seven-leaflet leaf, you will remove too much of the plant.

SHRUBS

Now that spring is in full bloom, it is a good time to evaluate individual shrubs and decide if you have the right plants in the right places. Pick a bouquet of flowers from your favorite shrubs.

SHRUBS FOR SPRING BLOOMS

- Deutzia, *Deutzia gracilis* (white flowers)

- Beautybush, *Kolkwitzia amabilis* (pink flowers)

- Mock orange, *Philadelphus coronarius* (white flowers)

- Azalea and Rhododendron, *Rhododendron* species and hybrids (many colors)

- Spirea, *Spiraea* (many species and colors)

- Viburnum, *Viburnum* (many cultivars and hybrids)

Arrange the flowers in a vase and note the various color combinations. This can help you decide which colors to add to your garden.

TREES

Take notes in your garden journal on spring-blooming trees. Record the color of their flowers and how long they bloom, the trees' overall appearance, any pest or disease problems, and whether faded blossoms persist or if they drop off and disappear. Use this information to help guide you in your decisions about adding or deleting trees in your garden.

Keep track of varieties that are successful. Knowing the scientific name is the best way to ensure that you get the plant you want.

VINES AND GROUNDCOVERS

Groundcovers can help you solve problems in the garden. For example, the area between steppingstones is the perfect place to use groundcovers instead of turf. If the site is sunny, try some of the creeping thymes or blue star, *Laurentia*, which has beautiful, tiny blue flowers. For shade, dwarf mondo grass, ajuga, or lesser periwinkle, *Vinca minor*, provide evergreen foliage all year long and require a minimum of upkeep.

In addition to training vines to grow on arbors and pergolas, you may find they are great for covering concrete walls and chain-link fences or framing doors, windows, or garages. Selecting the right vine for the right location will help ensure success.

Self-clinging vines such as English ivy, Virginia creeper, crossvine, and trumpet creeper are ideal for a concrete wall. You may have to help them get started by tying up a few vines and attaching them to the wall until they take hold.

PLANT

ANNUALS

Good gardeners use planting tricks to avoid later chores. Here is the technique Dr. Gary Wade, Extension Horticulturist, uses to combat weeds, conserve water, and get rid of old newspapers:

- Thoroughly till the soil for your bed of annuals. You should have soft soil 6 inches deep.

- Unfold the Sunday newspaper, making a stack of all the sheets. Place near your planting spot.

- Fill a 5-gallon bucket with water; station it near the bed.

- Soak a group of three sheets of newspaper momentarily in the water. Spread them in a single stack over your tilled soil.

- Repeat this process, laying each group adjacent to the previous one, until the entire bed is covered with newspaper.

- Pour pine bark mini-nuggets in a layer 1 inch thick over the newspapers.

- Use a sharp trowel to stab through the mulch and wet paper, making a planting hole for each of your plants.

- Continue planting until the bed is completed.

Caution: Do not use the comics for this process. If you do, your plants will grow funny!

BULBS

Plant cannas, caladiums, dahlias, elephant ear, and gladiolus. Transplant tuberose that you started indoors to the garden. Dahlias are usually planted as tubers but can also be grown from seed; they range in size from only 15 inches to over 6 feet tall. For dwarf types, sow the seed directly in the spot where the dahlias will grow. Start seed for taller varieties indoors in February or March.

Plant summer-flowering garden gladiolus at 1- to 2-week intervals to give you a long season of bloom, up to six weeks. Before planting, treat them with bulb dust, an insecticide-fungicide. Some of the hybrids grow 5 feet high and don't require staking. They offer spikes of flowers with twelve to fourteen blooms at one time. For the most productive corms, select those that are 1½ to 2 inches wide.

EDIBLES

Select bush-type or cherry tomatoes for patio planting. A huge pot is a must! Five gallons of soil for one plant is a bare minimum. Use light-colored pots; dark ones absorb sunshine and cause the soil to become too hot.

Plant rosemary, dill, oregano, mint, and basil for savory summer meals.

The soil has to be very warm (above 65 degrees Fahrenheit) to encourage corn, squash, bean, and field pea seeds to germinate. Plant by mid-April in south Georgia and by mid-May in the northern part of the state. Make another planting in two weeks to spread out your harvest.

LAWNS

Warm soil temperatures usher in the very best months for planting all warm-season grasses. Seeding is less expensive, but you must nurture the seed for several weeks before it makes a respectable lawn. Sodding is more expensive, but you will have the satisfaction of an instant lawn (see April for sod planting procedures).

The seeds of bermudagrass, zoysiagrass, and centipedegrass are tiny. In order to spread them evenly, they can be mixed with sand:

1. Use very dry sand. A large bucket or a wheelbarrow makes a good container in which to mix.

2. Mix one part (by volume) of seed to ten or twenty parts of sand. In other words, mix 1 cup of seed with 10 to 20 cups of sand.

HERE'S HOW

TO PLANT DAHLIA TUBERS

Before you plant dahlia tubers, make sure the soil has been amended with organic materials like compost or ground bark. Here are a few tips for planting the tubers:

- Space the largest types 4 to 5 feet apart, and make sure the hole is 1 foot deep.

- Space medium-sized tubers 3 feet apart and 1 foot deep.

- Space small tubers 1 to 2 feet apart and 1 foot deep.

- If you use fertilizer, use a complete fertilizer like 10-10-10. Thoroughly mix in ¼ cup with the soil in the planting hole, then add another 4 inches of soil over this before you plant.

- With large tubers, it is a good idea to put the stake in the hole when you are planting. This way you won't risk damaging the tuber later with the stake. After you place the tuber horizontally, position the stake a few inches from the eye (growing point). Fill in and cover the tuber with 3 inches of soil. Water thoroughly. Gradually fill the hole with soil as the shoots grow.

3. Apply half the recommended rate traveling back and forth in one direction, and the other half traveling at right angles to the first.

PERENNIALS

Continue adding perennials to the garden, including varieties that will bloom in summer and fall like salvias, asters, chrysanthemums, and common sneezeweed (*Helenium autumnale*). Start with healthy plants that have clean foliage and a good root system.

Gently ease the plant out of the pot before you purchase it. If the rootball is covered with roots that are white and fleshy, then the roots are healthy. If there are more roots than soil, the root system may be stressed. If you have purchased a plant that has been grown in the same container for a long period of time it may be "potbound."

If it is potbound, cut the container down one side and ease out the plant. Make two or three clean cuts into the rootball at various points around the ball to loosen the roots. Gently pull them apart, and spread them out in the planting hole. The plant should adjust and begin to grow where you plant it.

ROSES

Container-grown roses have been in your local nursery for months by this time. When you remove one from the pot prior to planting, you may find a thick mat of encircling roots. Here's what to do:

- Use pruners to cut off any thick roots on the rootball surface. (You could choose to untangle them instead, but this would be time-consuming.)

- Shake the rootball vigorously to loosen roots and remove potting soil from the surface. Roots will now be more likely to explore the surrounding soil when you plant.

- Spread the roots in the planting hole as much as possible before filling with native soil (that is, not amended soil).

- Water thoroughly. Check back the next day and add soil if the earth has settled too much.

SHRUBS

Continue adding shrubs to your garden. Container-grown plants can be planted throughout the year as long as you water properly after planting.

If you transplant a shrub while it is in bloom, cutting it back by one-third will reduce the transplant shock, and the plant will recover more quickly. In the warm coastal parts of the state you will have better success if you transplant shrubs during the cooler months of March or November.

TREES

Plant container-grown trees. Apply 2 to 3 inches of mulch, making sure to keep it away from the trunk. (You can also grow trees in containers on a permanent basis. Japanese maples make lovely specimens when planted in a decorative pot.)

Before you purchase a container-grown tree (or shrub), make sure the plant has healthy roots.

1. One way to check the roots is to lift up the plant by gently tugging on the trunk. If it pulls easily away from the soil, then the plant may have root rot. If it holds firm, it probably has enough healthy roots.

2. Another way to check the health of the whole root system is to gently ease the rootball out of the container. If the upper half of the rootball has lots of healthy roots, you can remove any roots on the lower half that look unhealthy, and your tree should thrive.

VINES AND GROUNDCOVERS

Plant groundcovers and vines throughout the month.

There is still time to direct-sow seeds of annual vines like purple hyacinth bean, moon vine, and others in spots where you want them to grow. Check seed packages for more information about how long specific varieties of vines take to germinate.

CARE

ANNUALS

Annual vines give lots of vertical interest and beautiful blooms to a flower garden, but they must be supported on a trellis, fence, or wall. Good annual vines include moonvine, morning glory, purple hyacinth bean, scarlet runner bean, cypress vine, sweetpea, and thunbergia. A few trellis possibilities include bamboo canes; long, limber branches pruned from your crapemyrtle, or flowering cherry, pear, or apple trees; tuteurs (ornamental towers made from metal or wood, purchased at a garden center); and wire or strings attached to a wooden fence.

BULBS

Keep plants groomed. You can prevent diseases from spreading by removing diseased or dead leaves as soon as you notice them.

Stake lilies before they get too tall and the task becomes more difficult.

When cutting dahlias from the garden, cut them in early morning or evening. Remove any leaves below the top 2 inches of the stem. Place the base of the cut stems in 2 to 3 inches of hot water. Let the water cool for several hours or overnight. Once the water has cooled, fill the remainder of the container with water up to where the leaves begin on the stem.

Cut flowers will last longer if you use a container that is clean and free of dirt and bacteria. Changing the water daily will also help keep flowers fresh.

EDIBLES

A weekly inspection of your fruit plants can reveal problems that need attention.

1. Prune out any dead limbs or twigs.

2. Add mulch if needed. Make sure to keep it pulled back 6 inches from the trunk in all directions.

3. Look for insect or disease damage. Determine if the problem merits control before automatically reaching for a pesticide.

LAWNS

Tall fescue lawns that were heavily seeded in the past six months may have large patches of straw-brown dead grass. This is caused by too many seedlings growing in a small space. When dead patches appear, rake out the dead grass and sprinkle seed very lightly over the spot. Irrigate evenly, and nurture it until the spot matches the rest of your lawn.

When planting in the future remember to use the correct amount of seed per 1,000 square feet.

PERENNIALS

The perennials listed below should be divided in spring after they finish blooming:

- Bleeding heart, *Dicentra* spp. (divide by hand)

HERE'S HOW

TO GROW BIGGER AND BETTER DAHLIAS

Dahlias are great for growing in the border, for cut flowers, or in containers. With pinching and thinning you can increase the number or size of the flowers. For tall varieties, remove all but one or two of the strongest shoots. When the shoots develop three sets of leaves, pinch off tips just above the top set. This should lead to the development of two side shoots from each pair of leaves, and more flowers. If you want to have large flowers, remove all but the terminal flower buds on the side shoots. This will encourage the plant to put its energy into making fewer but larger flowers.

Iris tectorum, *Japanese roof iris*

- Japanese iris, *Iris sibirica* (use a spade or hand saw to divide)

- Japanese roof iris, *Iris tectorum* (use a spade or handsaw to divide)

Depending on the type of plant, deadheading (removing spent blossoms from flowers) can encourage perennials to produce more flowers. Experiment with your favorite plants. Plants that send up more flowers if you deadhead include:

- Blanket flower, *Gaillardia grandiflora*
- Butterfly gaura, *Gaura lindheimeri*
- Pinchusion flower, *Scabiosa* 'Butterfly Blue'
- Vervain, *Verbena bonariensis*
- Speedwell, *Veronica* 'Sunny Border Blue'

Cut or pinch back fall-blooming chrysanthemums and asters by one-third and you will have fuller plants in the fall.

Cutting back certain perennials will often delay their flowering by a few weeks and prevent them from flopping over when they finally do bloom. This type of pruning should be done about eight weeks before plants are expected to bloom. Plants that respond to this procedure include garden phlox, *Phlox paniculata*, and asters.

Experiment with pruning. If you have a group of one type of plant such as beebalm, cut back some of the plants and let the others progress naturally. This method will give you staggered bloom times, which means you will have flowers over a longer period of time.

ROSES

As the first flowers on your shrub roses fade, remove them regularly. This will allow new flowers to form.

When tying a rose to a supporting structure, the attachment should be strong enough to hold the rose in place but not so tight that the stem is damaged. Many rosarians use a "figure-eight" knot. Use biodegradable jute twine or special green rose tape sold for this purpose.

1. Cut a length sufficient to go around the support once and still have 12 inches left over.

2. Tie the material around the support, using a square knot. Two 6-inch lengths should dangle next to the rose stem.

3. Pull the cane gently to the support, and tie another square knot around it. Don't strangle the stem. The tie should be loose enough to allow the cane to slip freely within it.

4. Clip off any excess tying material.

Do not let faded blossoms remain on your roses. Remove and discard them regularly, unless you want rose hips (seedpods) to develop. These are often quite attractive.

SHRUBS

Prune shrubs like viburnum, rhododendron, and mock orange after they finish flowering.

Remove spent blossoms before they set seed on evergreen rhododendrons and mountain laurel. This helps with overall vigor. The plant will be able to put its energy into forming next year's flower buds and new growth instead of seeds.

TO PROPAGATE SHRUBS BY SOIL-LAYERING

1. Choose a limb close to the ground. Press it downward until the stem touches the ground.

2. At the point where the branch touches the ground, scratch the stem (wound it) to expose the inner bark. This is where the roots will develop. You will get even better results if the point of contact also has a node (the part of the stem where shoots, leaves, or buds emerge).

3. Cover the wound (not the entire limb) with soil—the richer the soil, the better the results you can expect.

4. Place a brick or rock on top to hold the branch in place. At least 6 inches of branch tip and leaves should be showing beyond the brick.

5. Keep it watered—don't let it dry out.

6. In two months, tug gently to see if roots have formed. If there are substantial roots, cut the new plant from the mother plant. If there are only a few roots, recover with soil and check again in another month.

A simple method for propagating hydrangeas and certain other shrubs is by soil-layering, a method that can be used from April through autumn.

TREES

No matter what the season, trees with a weeping habit make a dramatic statement in the landscape, whether planted in a container or in the ground. The trees at right have a weeping growth habit or arching branches.

VINES AND GROUNDCOVERS

Make sure vines are tied in place, firmly but not tightly, where you want them to be. If they are woody vines like akebia, make sure the stems are not girdled by the wire or cord you used to tie them to a trellis, arbor, or fence. Wisteria is an aggressive vine. After it blooms, cut back long twining new growth before it forms a tangled mess with the main vine. Save those stems that you want to use to extend the height or width of the vine. Tie them to supports. Use plastic tape so you won't girdle the stems. Many wisterias are grafted and have a swollen area, the graft union. Prune to remove any suckers that occur below this union, as they will not produce the strong growth that the grafted plant does.

Developed by gardeners in Europe during the 16th and 17th centuries, the term *espalier* was applied to fruit trees that were trained in the open, either as a permanent feature or in preparation for placing them on walls or against a trellis. Although they were trained in many shapes, the most common was a tier of horizontal branches on either side of

GOOD WEEPING TREES FOR GEORGIA

- **Japanese maple,** *Acer palmatum* var. *dissectum*

- **Weeping katsura,** *Cercidiphyllum magnificum* 'Pendulum'

- **Weeping redbud,** *Cercis canadensis* 'Covey' (also known as 'Lavender Twist')

- **Weeping redbud,** *Cercis canadensis* ssp. 'Traveller'

- **Weeping blue atlas cedar,** *Cedrus atlantica* 'Glauca Pendula'

- **Weeping Florida dogwood,** *Cornus florida* 'Pendula'

- **Weeping European beech,** *Fagus sylvatica* 'Pendula'

- **Weeping crabapple,** *Malus* 'Red Jade'

- **Weeping Higan cherry,** *Prunus subhirtella* 'Pendula'

- **Weeping Japanese pink snowbell,** *Styrax japonicas* 'Pink Cascade'

- **Weeping winged elm,** *Ulmus alata,* 'Lace Parasol'

■ *Vines like this clematis can be espaliered directly onto a brick wall.*

the main stem. When trained on posts and wires, they were not only productive in a small space, they screened views and acted as walls between one section of garden and another. Today, espalier is also practiced to train plants for pure ornament, in both traditional and irregular patterns, depending on the growth habit of the individual plant.

When you grow vines on a wall, there are several approaches. You can attach panels of lattice to an existing wall and then train the vines on the lattice. This forms a flat trellis. To give the trellis more depth, attach the lattice to the wall on top of 2 × 4 spacers. Use 1 × 4 boards to cover up where two sections of lattice join. Plantings at the base of the lattice will help cover up the fact that the trellis is not attached at ground level.

On wooden fences or walls, you can create a framework using screw eyes threaded with galvanized wire (12 to 14 gauge). The wires should be about 1½ feet apart.

For masonry walls, use anchors with screws or lag screws, threaded rod, nuts, and washers.

The goal is to provide firm support, good air circulation for the plants, and an appealing design. Be patient—it will take a few years of pruning and training to achieve a desired design. For formal designs, any branches that obscure the design can be pruned away. For informal designs, let the natural growth habit of the plant determine where you prune.

WATER

ANNUALS

Nearly every year brings a drought to part or all of Georgia. You can prepare for water shortages by adhering to the principles of xeriscaping (dry-weather landscaping).

1. **Planning and Design:** Establish low-, moderate-, and high-water-use zones. Group plants with similar water needs in the same zone.

2. **Soil Analysis:** Have your soil tested by your local Extension office to determine what is needed for your plants to develop drought-tolerant root systems.

ORNAMENTAL PERENNIAL VINES FOR ESPALIER

These perennial vines are great for espalier and they also produce showy flowers and/or fruits.

- Akebia, *Akebia quinata*, has clusters of purple flowers in spring that are often followed by 2- to 4-inch-long, purple, sausage-type fruits in summer to fall.

- Bougainvillea, *Bougainvillea* cultivars, offers a long season of bright color for coastal gardens. The colorful parts that surround the tiny flowers are actually bracts.

- Armand clematis, *Clematis armandii*, is an evergreen species that has masses of tiny white fragrant flowers in early spring.

- Firethorn, *Pyracantha* hybrids, produce red, orange, or red-orange fruit in late summer. The fruit last well into winter.

- Lady banks rose, *Rosa banksiae*, is an evergreen climber that produces masses of yellow or white flowers in early spring.

- Wisteria, *Wisteria* spp., is an aggressive vine that has beautiful clusters of violet to violet-blue flowers in April to May.

3. **Appropriate Plant Selection:** Choose the plants that thrive naturally in your local environment.

4. **Practical Turf Areas:** Plan to have turf only in small areas near your home's entrance, in recreation areas, or on slopes where other plants would be impractical.

5. **Efficient Irrigation:** Zone your irrigation system to separately water plants with different needs.

6. **Use of Mulches:** Use mulch to prevent evaporation and to maintain even soil moisture.

7. **Appropriate Maintenance:** Water after midnight and before noon. Less water will be lost to evaporation and it will have more time to soak into cool soil.

BULBS

Keep bulbs watered while they are growing and blooming. One inch per week should keep them happy.

EDIBLES

Georgia summers are famous for prolonged dry periods. The best time to prepare for a drought is before it occurs.

- Lay a soaker hose alongside your blueberry, grape, or raspberry plants.

- Place a soaker hose on the ground under the branch tips of fruit and nut trees.

- Consider using drip irrigation to water individual plants.

LAWNS

Lawns need approximately 1 inch of water per week. An inch of water is the amount of rainfall or irrigation it takes to fill a rain gauge or a soup can to a depth of 1 inch.

PERENNIALS

Continue watering new plantings on a weekly schedule. If you have an automatic irrigation system, you will need to adjust its schedule according to the amount of rainfall.

- It is better for your plants if the system comes on once a week or every few days rather than every day.

- Keep track of how much water plants receive. Note this in your garden journal.

- Long, slow, thorough watering is best. Allow the soil to dry out between waterings.

Too much water can be as harmful as too little. When perennials are newly planted, they will benefit from regular watering if there is not adequate rainfall (one inch per week—measure this by using a tuna fish can).

To determine watering time, dig down 2 inches, and if the soil is dry to the touch, it's time to water. Sandy soils may need watering more frequently than those that have a high clay content. Container gardens may need more frequent watering than perennials that are planted in the ground.

ROSES

Rose standards (those trained to have a single upright stem topped by foliage and flowers) are sometimes used as potted patio plants. Check the soil's moisture in the pots daily until you have a good feel for how often they need to be watered. When the top inch of soil is dry, water until the water runs from the bottom of the pot. If the soil is dry every day, the container is too small. Repot the rose into a container that is double the size of the present one.

Check on roses you planted within the last six months. They will not yet have enough roots to easily survive the summer. Water them deeply each week. Use a trowel to check how far the water penetrates (6 inches is a good depth). Two gallons of water are usually sufficient.

SHRUBS

Water all new plantings once a week unless you have regular long, soaking rains (more than a quick thunderstorm). Keep this practice up until plants are well established, or at least for the first growing season. If you use a sprinkler to water a shrub bed, make sure that all parts of the bed receive good coverage.

One way to measure water application is to use shallow cans like tuna fish cans, placing them in several different areas. When they average ¾-inch full, you have probably watered a shrub area long enough for that week.

TREES
Water all new plantings. Thereafter, if there is not adequate rainfall (1 inch per week), apply 1 gallon per foot of tree height per week. Check established trees (trees that have been in the ground for a full year or longer) once a month to make sure they are getting enough water.

VINES AND GROUNDCOVERS
Water new plantings of vines and groundcovers.

FERTILIZE

ANNUALS
One of the advantages of feeding annuals with slow-release fertilizer at planting is that you don't have to rack your brain to remember if you fertilized recently. If you didn't use a slow-release fertilizer, you have two choices for applying nutrients: balanced, granular fertilizers (10-10-10, 8-8-8) and water-soluble products.

If you use a granular product:

- Note how often the product must be applied—usually every four to six weeks.

- Note, and follow, the application rate recommended on the bag.

- Determine how you will spread the granules evenly. Garden centers sell small "whirly bird" spreaders for this purpose.

If you use a water-soluble fertilizer:

- Note how often the product must be applied—usually every two weeks.

- Mix at the recommended rate for the plants (annuals, perennials, shrubs, and so forth) you are tending.

- Since these nutrients can be absorbed by plant leaves as well as roots, use a sprinkling can to get the best coverage. Otherwise, use a bucket and a comfortable dipper to pour the recommended amount beside each plant.

If you have a large area to fertilize, a special device called a siphoning mixer is very useful. This brass gadget attaches to your hose and injects concentrated liquid fertilizer into the water flowing through the hose. A water wand screwed onto the end of the hose allows you to sprinkle the enriched water quickly onto dozens of plants.

BULBS
Keep fertilizer out of direct contact with gladiolus corms. Instead, thoroughly mix a complete fertilizer into the soil before planting, or use superphosphate 0-46-0 (4 pounds per 100 square feet).

EDIBLES
Fertilize vegetables when they have grown enough to demonstrate that the root system has firmly established itself. This is generally two weeks after planting, or when the plant has grown 3 to 6 inches.

Fertilize small fruit trees with 1 cup of 10-10-10 per foot of height; large trees, 1 pound of 10-10-10 per inch of trunk thickness.

LAWNS
Don't apply fertilizer when the grass is wet. The granules will stick to the grass blades and burn them temporarily. Use a drop or a broadcast spreader to apply fertilizer to dry grass. Handcasting results in streaks of under- and overfertilization. Try to fertilize just before it rains, or be sure to irrigate the lawn afterwards.

- **Tall fescue:** If the lawn has not been fed in the past eight weeks, fertilize again, preferably before the middle of the month. Otherwise, wait until September.

- **Bermudagrass:** Fertilize now (and again in June, July, August, and September).

- **Zoysiagrass:** Fertilize now (and again in June and August).

- **Centipedegrass:** in north Georgia is usually green enough to fertilize by now. Use 6 pounds of 15-0-15 per 1,000 square feet of lawn. Centipedegrass grows best at a pH of 4.5 to 5.5. Lime is rarely needed.

- **St. Augustinegrass:** Fertilize now (and again in June, July, and August).

PERENNIALS

Applying a dilute solution of a liquid fertilizer such as 15-30-15 directly to the foliage of new plantings will give them an added boost. Young leaves absorb the fertilizer quickly. It is best to apply foliar feeds early in the day before the intense heat sets in.

ROSES

Fertilize each rose plant in mid-month with 10-10-10 or a water-soluble fertilizer.

Roses growing in containers need more frequent feeding than those growing outdoors (constant watering leaches fertilizer out of the potting soil). Use a slow-release granular fertilizer that dispenses fertilizer each time the plant is watered, or use a liquid fertilizer: cut the recommended dosage in half, but use it twice as often as the label indicates.

SHRUBS

It's still not too late to fertilize your shrubs for the spring if you haven't already done so. Your plants still have time to use fertilizer while they are actively growing. Once it gets hot, growth slows down and plants don't require as much fertilizer. Use a complete balanced fertilizer like 10-10-10. As a general rule, apply 1 tablespoon per foot of plant height. Refer to the product label for detailed information.

TREES

When you plant new trees, mix some root stimulator into the existing soil. This will help plants get established more quickly.

If you want to give new trees (those you planted during the past six months) an extra boost, fertilize them with a complete slow-release fertilizer that has a ratio like 10-10-10. This should only be done twice a year—March and July are recommended. (See March for more information and application suggestions.)

Generally, established trees don't need to be fertilized.

VINES AND GROUNDCOVERS

Fertilize annual vines with half the recommended rate (on the label) of a complete liquid fertilizer with a ratio like 20-20-20.

Fertilize newly planted groundcovers (planted within the last six months) to help them get established at a rate of ½ pound or 1 cup of 8-8-8 or 10-10-10 per 100 square feet. This is half the recommended rate for established groundcovers. Remember, you need only fertilize your groundcovers twice a year. The recommended times are March and June.

If you add organic material to the soil when you plant, you won't have to fertilize your vines, but topdressing with composted manure will give them extra nutrients.

PROBLEM-SOLVE

ANNUALS

Spider mites attack many plants and are common pests of foxglove, verbena, and butterfly bush. Symptoms include yellow-speckled leaves and wilted foliage. The key to their control is regular inspection of your plants and sprays with horticultural oil if warranted. Prune nearby butterfly bushes down to 12 inches tall in March. Be vigilant about pulling weeds whenever you see them. If you can remove them before they drop seed, you'll save many headaches during the summer.

BULBS

Look for aphids on lilies, dahlias, and gladiolus. Spray them with insecticidal soap or a synthetic pesticide. Aphids spread mosaic virus, which attacks lily foliage and for which there is no cure. If any of your lilies exhibit mottled leaves or stunted growth, they may have mosaic. Dig and destroy the bulbs. The best way to avoid this infection is to buy only healthy bulbs and remove injured portions before planting.

You may notice that your bearded iris have notches in the leaf margins, about ⅛-inch wide, and there is also a dark trail in the leaves. This means leaf borers. While you can use an insecticide to control these pests, you can also kill the borers by squeezing the infested leaves between your thumb and forefinger in the areas where you notice them feeding (the dark, water-soaked areas).

EDIBLES

Watch for blackened leaves at the ends of apple or pear limbs. This could be fireblight disease.

- Spray with a bactericide before every rain to protect new leaves.

- Prune out diseased branches. Sterilize your pruner between every cut with a 1:10 mixture of alcohol or bleach in water.

- Mark your calendar to spray again next year when the tree is blooming. Fireblight is spread by honeybees as they travel from flower to flower.

Apply *Bacillus thuringiensis* to cabbage, broccoli, and cauliflower to ward off cabbage looper caterpillars.

To prevent leaf diseases, place a newspaper mulch three sheets thick under tomato plants immediately upon planting. Cover the paper with pine straw.

Rabbits are cute, but they can be a real nuisance when they visit your garden. A short (18 inches tall) fence will keep them at bay while allowing you to easily step over it.

1. Purchase a roll of 1-inch mesh chicken wire 2 feet wide and long enough to encircle your garden. Purchase 2-feet-long sharpened surveyor's stakes onto which you can staple the wire.

2. Dig a shallow trench 4 to 6 inches deep around the garden. Drive the stakes into the trench at 4-foot intervals around your garden.

3. Use heavy-duty staples to fasten the wire to the wooden stakes.

4. If you like, slip the bottom 6 inches of the wire into the trench and cover with soil. This will prevent the bunnies from digging under your fence.

LAWNS

After a few days of rain, mushrooms may sprout in your lawn overnight. Mushrooms can be thought of as the "flowers" of a fungus. These "toadstools" are nothing more than the reproductive portion of a fungus that has quietly been consuming organic debris underground. With warm soil and a bit of rain, the fungus decides the time is ripe to reproduce. It is impossible to eliminate fungi from the soil. The best treatment for mushrooms is to simply pick them and discard them. They are not edible. Use a five-iron on the largest ones to improve your golf game!

Fire ant mounds are quite visible now. Several months of control can be gained by using the "Georgia Two-Step" method:

1. Treat the area with a fire ant bait. The best time to treat is on a warm day, after 10:00 a.m.

2. Apply a powdered or liquid insecticide to individual mounds forty-eight hours later.

Repeat the procedure again in September.

■ *A short fence can keep rabbits out of your garden.*

PERENNIALS

Use insecticidal soap to control insects like aphids, spider mites, thrips, and whiteflies. Spray during the early morning before temperatures get too hot (check the label for recommendations).

Spray the plant to the point where the spray is dripping, being sure to cover the undersides of the leaves.

Continue to handweed. Pulling weeds before they flower or set seeds will help reduce future weed infestations.

Spot-spray with a nonselective weedkiller to control weeds, using extreme caution around perennials and other desirable plants.

If the leaves of your columbine are discolored and have a series of silver trails running through them, the problem is leaf miners. The best and easiest treatment is to shear off plants to the ground and destroy the infected foliage after the columbine finishes flowering. A new flush of growth will quickly replace the old leaves.

Although it is not immune to pests, the native columbine, *Aquilegia canadensis*, is less susceptible to leaf miners.

ROSES

Powdery mildew is a leaf disease whose name perfectly describes its appearance: White powder covering individual leaves and flower buds. It is common in spring and fall when days are warm and humid and nights are cool. Roses that have been planted too close together or where the air remains still are easy victims.

- Plant roses where they have plenty of room between adjacent plants.

- Do not plant roses close to a wall or solid fence.

- If you have had a powdery mildew problem before, select resistant varieties for planting.

- A fungicide spray can be used to control the disease.

The fungi that cause rose diseases can become resistant to a chemical if it is used over and over. To prevent resistance, change to a different fungicide chemical each month.

Read the product label to make sure you are purchasing a different chemical, not just a different brand.

Rose thrips are tiny yellowish insects that damage rose petals by scraping the cells with their mouth parts in order to suck plant juice. Though they are barely visible to the naked eye, their damage is easy to see: brown edges on rose flower petals. If you suspect thrips are present, cut a damaged rose bloom and slap it against a page of white paper. You'll be able to see the thrips scurrying for cover. Many beneficial insects (lacewings, ladybugs, and so forth) feed on thrips. Avoid using contact insecticide sprays. They not only harm the beneficials, but they do a poor job of killing thrips.

Pick off and discard infested blooms. Make a thrips trap by coating a bright yellow card with sticky oil. If the problem is severe, use a systemic insecticide.

SHRUBS

Leaves on azaleas or camellias may become distorted and pale green; as they thicken, they turn brown, then white. These are symptoms of leaf gall. While the disease doesn't kill the plant, they are unsightly. Handpick the galls and destroy them before they turn white.

Continue to examine shrubs for signs of damage from insects or diseases. Spider mites and aphids will be more active as the weather gets warmer.

If the leaves on your crapemyrtle have a grayish coating, you probably have powdery mildew. Cool nights followed by warm days, poor air circulation, and not enough sun all contribute to an environment that favors powdery mildew. This fungus can affect crapemyrtle, lilac, hydrangea, and other plants. For severe infestations, use a fungicide. For an organic alternative to a synthetic fungicide, try spraying a mixture of 4 teaspoons baking soda in 1 gallon of water on the plants. Apply this spray once a week. Be sure to cover the tops and bottoms of the leaves with whatever spray you use.

Spot-spray weeds in shrub beds with a nonselective herbicide. Use extreme caution: Do not apply on windy days, since nonselective herbicides kill everything they touch. You can hold a piece of cardboard in front of a shrub to protect it from damage while you spray the surrounding weeds with the herbicide. If the weeds are close to stems or foliage on shrubs, dip a small paintbrush in the diluted chemical and carefully "paint" the chemical on the weeds. Another, similar method is to don two rubber gloves—to ensure safety—on one hand. Dip that hand in the herbicide and swipe the foliage with the chemical. Discard the paintbrush or gloves after use.

TREES

A bagworm is a wingless moth that forms a protective mass of brown twigs in a cocoon around its body. From a distance the bagworms look almost like tiny cones hanging from a tree. The moths consume great numbers of needles from evergreen plants like juniper, arborvitae, and Leyland cypress. Pick off and destroy the bags whenever you find them. Be sure to wear gloves to protect your fingers from the tree needles.

If you choose to use a contact insecticide, April and May are the months when the moths are most susceptible.

If you notice that the leaves on your sycamore tree have irregular brown dead spots and leaf stems are black at the base, you may have sycamore anthracnose. This leaf blight is caused by several fungi. The fungus first appears on the leaves, then spreads through the veins and down into the stem and branch. The spores that spread the fungus overwinter in the cankers on the branches and in diseased leaves. A lack of overall vigor, heavy rainfall, and low temperatures exacerbate the effects of this disease, which can include total defoliation. Fungicides are effective only if they are applied before the disease appears in the spring. To control the disease:

- Prune out any dead or infected leaves, twigs, and branches.

- Rake up and burn infected leaves to reduce infections in the future.

- Fertilize in spring to increase tree vigor.

- Water trees during a prolonged dry spell (a month or longer without rain).

You may notice that leaves on your red maple, oak, hickory, or pecan are disfigured and deformed by small growths—bumplike swellings—that cover the leaves. In the worst cases, leaves turn yellow and drop prematurely. These are leaf galls, which are caused when insects like mites, midges, and tiny wasps lay their eggs on tree leaves. These curiosities of nature will not go away even if the larvae in the leaves are killed. There are two approaches to dealing with galls:

1. Learn to live with this oddity.

2. Rake and dispose of the leaves each fall to reduce insect populations.

Remove dead or diseased leaves and limbs on trees. Don't put them in your compost pile or they may introduce problems into your garden in the future.

Prune Leyland cypress to control seridium canker. The symptoms include: Older foliage, especially the interior foliage, turns yellow and then brown; branches and twigs die; sunken reddish, dark brown, or purple areas (the cankers) form on the bark; and sap oozes. The sunken areas are the cankers. Often the infection starts on the lower branches of the tree and moves up.

Prune out diseased limbs, being sure to cut 6 inches below where the infection occurs. This will ensure that you prune where healthy wood is growing. Prune branches that are broken or torn from the main trunk. Sterilize your pruner between each cut with a 1:10 ratio of a bleach-water mixture.

VINES AND GROUNDCOVERS

New growth on some of your vines may look puckered and may be covered with tiny lime green bugs. Aphids voraciously feed on new growth of vines like clematis and honeysuckles. Try blasting them off with a jet of cold water from the hose. If this doesn't do the trick, use an insecticidal soap.

June is a lovely month to enjoy the colors and scents that your garden offers. While azaleas, dogwoods, and other spring bloomers have mostly finished blooming, summer color begins to appear in the form of annuals, perennials, bulbs, and shrubs that attract butterflies and humans too. Once your spring-blooming shrubs have flowered, prune to remove any long wild shoots or to maintain a pleasing shape. This way new growth will have time to harden off before the "dog days of summer" set in. Some perennials will put out another flush of flowers if you cut off spent blossoms. You can also cut back chrysanthemums that will bloom in the autumn. This will keep them bushy and full and there will be less chance that they will flop over and lay on the ground once they begin to flower. Prune them back every few weeks until the Fourth of July.

If you haven't added any annual color for summer, there is still time. A mass planting of one variety makes more of an impact than one or two plants dotted here and there. Consider adding some night bloomers and white flowers including moonvine, the garden phlox 'David,' calamintha, and 'Casa Blanca' lilies.

For perennials that will bloom in fall and may need staking, you can use twigs stuck in the ground around the plants as a natural way to stake. In a few months the plants will grow up through the stakes and they will be invisible but supportive.

If you like to use fresh herbs for cooking, make sure you are growing plants like basil, rosemary, and thyme. You can never have too much basil! If your in-ground space is limited you can grow herbs in window boxes or large decorative containers.

PLAN

ANNUALS

There is still time to add annual color to your garden. Decide where and what you want to plant.

BULBS

Gardeners agree that there is really no such thing as "low-maintenance gardening," but there are some bulbs that are proven winners in the low-maintenance quest. Daylilies are at the top of the list for choice summer-blooming bulbs (although not true bulbs, these members of the lily family have tuberous fleshy roots). Lily-like flowers appear above clumps of arching, sword-shaped leaves. One or two divisions (a division is also called a fan, as the foliage looks similar to a fan) can quickly multiply and fill an area of your garden. Daylilies come in a wide range of colors and shades of red, orange, yellow, pink, purple, and more.

With just a minimum of care, daylilies reward you every year with a long season of bloom and lush healthy plants. Plant them in full sun or light shade in a soil that is well drained. There are numerous selections, including types that bloom only once a season and those that bloom for weeks, rest, and then produce more blooms. Combine daylilies in the same planting bed with spring-blooming bulbs and you will have a succession of blooms.

For maximum impact, plant early, midseason, and late-blooming varieties. Modern daylily hybrids range in size from the dwarf, at 1 foot tall, to the giant at 6 feet tall with flowers 3 to 8 inches across. The flower types are diverse, too, from spidery to ruffled. Some of the species and older varieties have flowers that are not only colorful but fragrant as well. Following are a couple daylilies to consider for your Georgia garden. For more information about daylilies, contact The American Hemerocallis Society. Their website (www.daylilies.org) lists daylily groups and display gardens in Georgia under a link for regional activities (Georgia is Region 5).

- *Hemerocallis fulva,* Orange daylily is a deciduous species that is also called ditch lily because it is commonly seen in roadside ditches or old gardens. A tough plant, it grows to 6 feet high and has leaves that are 2 feet or longer. The orange-red flowers, 3 to 5 inches wide, appear in summer and look great in combination with the old-fashioned blue "mophead" hydrangeas. Although it is not as refined as many of the hybrids offered for sale, this tough "doer" is still a good choice for a carefree perennial bulb.

- *H.* 'Happy Returns', a long-blooming daylily hybrid, offers yellow flowers at about 2 to 3 feet high for months, beginning in May and continuing until frost. Its compact size, about 18 inches high by 18 inches wide, makes it ideal for small gardens, containers, or masses.

EDIBLES

The different varieties of sweet corn each require a fixed number of days between planting and harvest. Unless you want a great deal of corn all at once, plant sweet corn seed every two weeks. As the different plantings mature, your corn season will be much longer.

- Plant corn through mid-July.

- Try a different variety of corn each year. You might like the "super-sweet" types ('Kandy Korn', 'Seneca Sweet', and so forth) better than the old standards ('Silver Queen' and 'Truckers Favorite').

Though it is not as critical as with corn, it is also beneficial to make successive plantings of other vegetables: summer squash, lima beans, pole beans, and field peas can be planted every three weeks.

LAWNS

A sharp border on a lawn can make all the difference in its appearance. Whether it is a straight edge next to the sidewalk or a gentle curve next to a flowerbed, the observer's eye finds comfort in a neatly defined edge. Make sure the edges of your lawn do not include sharp angles or dead-end corridors—both are difficult to mow. Before constructing a new edge, push your mower along the boundary of your lawn to gain a feel for how easy or difficult it will be to mow.

Climbing roses are often grown as vines, but they are not true vines. These plants have long canes, or stems, that must be tied and trained into place to encourage them to grow upward. Use twine or twist ties if stems are light; insulated wire or rubber strips if they are woody.

PERENNIALS

Use perennials that complement the existing shrubs and trees in your garden. For example, golden locust, *Robinia pseudoacacia* 'Frisia', has golden yellow leaves, and so does *Spiraea* 'Ogon'; two perennials that complement a planting of these two are the variegated Solomon's seal (green leaves with white edges) and the white-flowered fleabane called *Erigeron karvinskianus* 'Profusion'.

ROSES

There are many kinds of structures onto which climbing roses can be trained. The size of the structure should be in keeping with the eventual size of your rose. Roses do not twine around a support; they must be trained to it. This can be done by tying the canes in place or by resting the canes on supportive parts of the structure. Don't weave the canes in and out of narrow spaces on a trellis. They will be impossible to remove when you prune. When training a rose up a pillar, curve it around the post, barber-pole fashion.

TREES

If you only have trees that bloom in the spring, now is the time to think about planting some that offer blooms in summer. Many of our southeastern natives offer beautiful blooms and interesting forms. Some consider the southern magnolia, *Magnolia grandiflora*, the quintessential southern landscape plant, with its large, white, delicious lemon-scented flowers and glossy evergreen leaves. In recent years, a number of meritorious hybrids have been introduced into cultivation.

- 'Bracken's Brown Beauty' is a selection with a dense, compact habit. It grows to 30 feet high.

- 'Edith Bogue' is a cultivar that has a pyramidal habit and leaves that are narrower than those of the species, often with wavy margins.

- 'Hasse' is a selection that offers an upright growth habit and small, very glossy leaves.

- 'Little Gem' is a cultivar that flowers when it is young, and the undersides of the small leaves

FABULOUS SUMMER-BLOOMING SHRUBS FOR GEORGIA

- **Bottlebrush buckeye,** *Aesculus parviflora*

- **Butterfly bush,** *Buddleia davidii*

- **Summersweet,** *Clethra alnifolia*

- **Gardenia,** *Gardenia jasminoides*, many cultivars—'Kleim's Hardy' is hardy to 0 degrees Fahrenheit

- **Rose-of-Sharon,** *Hibiscus syriacus* 'Diana,' white flowered selection

- **Panicle hydrangea,** *Hydrangea paniculata* 'Tardiva'

- **Oakleaf hydrangea,** *Hydrangea quercifolia*

- **Golden St. John's wort,** *Hypericum frondosum* 'Sunburst'

- **Lantana,** *Lantana camara* 'Miss Huff'

are rust-colored. It reaches only 15 to 20 feet at maturity. Great for a container or small garden, it flowers most of the summer.

If you see attractive summer-blooming trees that you like, make notes so you will be ready to purchase and plant them in the fall or next spring.

VINES AND GROUNDCOVERS

Make notes in your garden journal about the performance of vines and groundcovers in your landscape. Which ones are thriving, and which ones have pest or disease problems? If an area of groundcover is not successful, think about which plants you will use to replace them. Visit your local botanical garden and see what's blooming.

If you have an area that's infested with poison ivy or English ivy that you want to eradicate, spray with a nonselective weedkiller, and then come back in two to four weeks and spray again, or dig out the roots. (Use extreme caution when working around poison ivy if you are allergic to it.) When fall arrives, you can amend the soil and plant something new!

PLANT

ANNUALS

There's still lots of time to set out annual flowers for summer color. Try 'Wave' petunias, narrow-leaf zinnia (*Zinnia linearis*), Mexican heather, and portulaca in sunny spots.

BULBS

Plant caladiums, dahlias, daylilies, and gladiolus.

EDIBLES

Corn is pollinated by wind currents, not by insects. Plant your seeds in several parallel rows side by side (a block) instead of in one long row.

Vegetable transplants are still available at garden centers, but they might not always be the best quality:

- Examine each plant to make sure it does not have leaf disease.

■ *Many vegetables need support to grow upright and produce food. Peppers and eggplants do well when individually staked. Place the stake in the ground next to the plant stem and loosely tie the stem to the stake.*

- Short, stocky plants are better than the stretched-out ones that have flopped over one another.

- Try to purchase freshly delivered transplants rather than those that have been on display for several days.

Many vegetable plants can be grown on a trellis to minimize the space they need. Use strips of cloth or jute twine to tie vines to the trellis.

Tomatoes can be caged or staked to hold the vine off the ground:

- Purchased tomato cages are good for bush and patio tomatoes, but they are usually too small for other varieties.

- A homemade tomato cage may be made from a 6-foot-high section of heavy-duty fence wire 7 feet long. Join the ends of the fence wire to form a tube 6 feet high and 2 feet in diameter. Slip the tube over a plant. Attach the cage to a sturdy stake driven into the ground to keep it from blowing over.

- To stake tomatoes, drive a long wooden stake next to each plant; tie the vine loosely to the stake as it grows longer. Pinch the tips of limbs that sprout from the main stem when they have grown 12 inches. Fruit will then be produced close to the stake.

Watermelon, winter squash, and pumpkin can also be trellised. Follow these steps to build a structure that will serve one plant:

1. Drive two sturdy posts into the ground 6 feet apart.

2. Stretch a 6-foot-long and 6-foot-wide piece of wire fencing between the posts; nail it to the post securely at both ends.

3. When fruits form, use a large square of cloth to cradle each one; tie the diagonal corners of the cloth to the trellis.

■ *Get melons off the ground with a string support structure.*

Do not attempt this trellising technique with large-fruited varieties.

LAWNS
When the soil has warmed above 65 degrees Fahrenheit, you can plant sprigs (small plugs) of bermudagrass, centipedegrass, zoysiagrass, and St. Augustinegrass.

Sprigging saves money because you can divide a sod piece into hundreds of individual sprigs. On the other hand, sprigging is labor intensive, and you must water and weed your newly sprigged lawn frequently. Sprigging is best done on a small lawn:

1. Till the soil 6 inches deep, adding organic matter, starter fertilizer, and lime as recommended by a soil test.

2. Level the area and roll it with a heavy roller to highlight any low spots. Fill low spots with soil before you begin sprigging.

3. Run a motorized core aerator over the lawn twice. This will make hundreds of small holes. The holes should be 3 to 6 inches apart.

4. Soak a piece of sod in a tub of water. Pull apart the sod into as many pieces as possible. Make sure each sprig has roots attached.

5. Keep the sprigs damp in a bucket, and insert them individually into the aerator holes.

6. Water thoroughly and regularly until sprigs take root. Remove weeds by hand.

This is the very best month to plant centipedegrass or zoysiagrass seed. Don't go on vacation—you will need to water the lawn daily and pull weeds conscientiously for four weeks to ensure success.

PERENNIALS
Continue adding container-grown perennials to your garden. Make sure the soil is prepared before you plant. Water and mulch as soon as you get new plants in the ground; this will help keep soil temperatures cooler.

Late spring or early summer is a good time to propagate certain perennials by division, including creeping Jenny, *Lysimachia nummularia*, and astilbe—you may have fewer blooms for one season, but the plants will be robust next year.

ROSES

Roses that remain unsold at nurseries are often put on sale in June. Use extreme caution when purchasing sale roses.

- Do not buy a plant with light yellow foliage—it may be weak from lack of fertilizer.

- Examine each leaf for blackspot disease. If blackspot is found, do not purchase.

- Pull the rose from its pot and examine the roots. If they are brown, smelly, or non-existent, do not bring that plant into your garden.

SHRUBS

Add container-grown plants to your garden as long as the temperatures are not too hot. If temperatures are in the 90-degree Fahrenheit range, the plants will be slow to put out roots.

Rototill and add soil amendments to areas in which you will plant shrubs in the future.

If you have time, hand-digging is another option. You can work on one area at a time, making sure to mix in organic materials to a depth of 12 to 18 inches.

Mulch new plantings with a 2- to 3-inch layer. Keep mulch away from the main stems; when it is piled up around stems it can create an environment that is attractive to insects and pests.

TREES

Plant container-grown trees, and be sure to keep them watered regularly. Mulch the area around a tree immediately after planting.

VINES AND GROUNDCOVERS

You can still add vines and groundcovers to your garden. Annual vines like the cypress vine, mandevilla, and passionflower add a tropical flair

SUMMER-BLOOMING TREES

- Harlequin glory bower, *Clerodendrum trichotomum*
- Franklinia, *Franklinia alatamaha*
- Golden raintree, *Koelreuteria paniculata*
- Crapemyrtle, *Lagerstroemia indica* cvs.
- Southern magnolia, *Magnolia grandiflora*
- Sweetbay magnolia, *Magnolia virginiana*
- Scholar tree, *Sophora japonica*
- Stewartia, *Stewartia* spp.
- Chaste tree, *Vitex agnus-castus*

to the summer garden. They can be trained on a structure or a trellis, or combined with lots of colorful annuals in a large decorative pot. When you add a clematis to your garden, apply 2 inches of mulch over the soil, keeping it away from the main stem. This will help retain soil moisture. As an alternative, you can plant groundcovers or herbaceous perennials over the root area of the clematis and then lightly mulch the groundcovers. Lesser vinca, *Vinca minor*, plants or some of the hardy geraniums make good groundcovers for clematis.

CARE

ANNUALS

When planting transplants, don't just dig a small hole and shove the root system into it. Try to gently untangle some of the roots so they will quickly explore the soil around them. Firm the soil around each plant with your fingers to eliminate air pockets in the soil. Once a bed is finished, water each plant thoroughly. Do not allow transplants to dry out.

BULBS

Cut off the yellowing foliage of daffodils that bloomed in early spring. If it is mostly yellow and lying on the ground, it is safe to cut it off. A rule of thumb is that one-third of the foliage should be yellow.

EDIBLES

Remove stakes from fruit trees that have been planted for several months. They are now strong enough to stand on their own.

LAWNS

It may take weeks for the seed of warm-season grasses to sprout and show green leaves. Keep the soil moist and pull any weeds by hand during this time.

ROSES

Perhaps you have a particularly beautiful rose that all your friends admire. Now is a fine time to propagate your rose from cuttings in order to have a nice gift for your friends next spring. Examine stems in mid-June to find those that began growing in April and have now begun to turn from green to brown.

WATER

ANNUALS

Now that your plants are coming along well, it's time to think about how to water them, with the least effort, for the rest of the summer.

1. Black soaker hoses can be laid in a bed or down a row of flowers, and later covered with pine straw.

2. Drip irrigation systems are available at large garden centers. Though they are a bit more complicated to set up, you can be assured that plants will get the exact amount of water they need.

3. Some lawn and landscape irrigation systems can be adapted to water flower beds. The beds should always be on a different zone from the lawn—the water demands of flowers are completely different from those of lawn grass.

4. A water wand is indispensable for watering garden plants. The stream from a hose blasts plant leaves and scatters soil, but the gentle waterfall from the nozzle of a wand soaks the ground around a plant without disturbing it.

Both metal and plastic wands work well. An easy-to-operate valve is essential. Spend the money to buy a wand that has a valve with a long handle. Your fingers will thank you every time you turn the water on and off.

BULBS

Keep summer-blooming bulbs watered. Check containers daily; feel the top 1 to 2 inches of soil and if it is dry to the touch, water until the water runs out the bottom of the pot. Check bulbs planted in the ground weekly. If you haven't received at least 1 inch of rain per week, water well.

Mulching your bulb plantings not only helps cut down on weed infestations but conserve moisture too. Apply 1 to 2 inches of mulch on top of the soil in areas where you plant bulbs.

EDIBLES

A drip irrigation system uses emitters that slowly drip water wherever you want it to be applied. The emitters are inserted into a plastic pipe that carries water from your faucet throughout your garden.

The best way to learn about drip irrigation is to purchase a starter kit that contains the components needed to water a small area. It can be expanded as necessary.

Soaker hoses laid down the row beside your vegetable plants will water them well without waste.

Water cucumbers regularly to prevent a bitter taste.

■ *When hand-watering, water deeply at the base of the plant.*

LAWNS

Water hoses will leak if stepped on or driven over too often when you're mowing:

- Buy a hose reel to wind up your hose after use.

- Inspect the rubber washer and replace if necessary.

PERENNIALS

Water new plantings once a week if there is no rain. As a rule of thumb, apply 2 gallons of water for a 1-gallon-sized plant; if plants are smaller, they will need a bit less water. If you use a sprinkler, set out a couple of shallow cans (tuna fish cans work great) to measure the water. You will have applied enough water as soon as the cans contain ¾-inch of water.

ROSES

Regularly water any roses planted in the last nine months. Avoid wetting the foliage when you water. A water wand is very handy. It causes a shower of water to cascade over the mulch at the base of the plant without dislodging it.

Check your soaker hoses to make sure they are working properly before the summer heat sets in.

SHRUBS

Summer can arrive quickly. Keep new plantings well watered. Don't wait until plants look wilted before you water; check them once a week. If the top 2 to 3 inches of soil are dry to the touch, it is time to water. When you water, do so thoroughly once or twice a week rather than a little every day. This will help your shrubs develop strong, deep roots. If you use a hose, place it near the center of the shrub and let a small stream of water soak in for at least a half hour. If you use a sprinkler, place some shallow tuna fish or cat food cans around the plants, and water until the cans are ¾-inch full.

Established shrubs benefit from supplemental water during periods of drought. Place the hose at soil level near the center of the plant, and saturate the root area.

TREES

The summer months can be stressful for plants and people. If you don't have an irrigation system, soaker hoses are one way to water your plants thoroughly. Sprinklers are also an option, but make sure you get uniform coverage. Water newly planted trees once a week unless you get 1 or more inches of rain.

Japanese maples with finely divided leaves are quite susceptible to moisture stress during the heat of the summer. The first sign of stress is browning and scorching of the leaves. When planting, consider

HERE'S HOW

TO PROPAGATE ROSES FROM CUTTINGS

A good cutting for rooting is 8 inches long and has brown bark at the base. The stem should not be limber, but should be hard enough to snap when bent.

1. Fill a 6-inch pot with a 50:50 mixture of perlite and peat moss that has been soaked and allowed to drain completely.

2. Dip the severed end of a cutting into a powdered rooting hormone.

3. Poke a 3-inch-deep hole in the perlite-peat moss mixture with a pencil.

4. Insert the base of the cutting 3 inches into the hole. Firm the soil around it.

5. Insert a pencil or wooden chopstick beside the cutting. The top of the stick should be 2 inches taller than the leaves of the cutting.

6. Slip a clear plastic bag over the pot and cutting. The plastic should minimally touch the leaves. Adjust the wooden stake to keep the plastic from touching the leaves.

7. Place the pot, cutting, and bag in a bright but shady spot. Check the soil every three days to make sure it is moist.

The cutting should be well rooted in six weeks. It can be transplanted to a gallon pot for further growth during the summer.

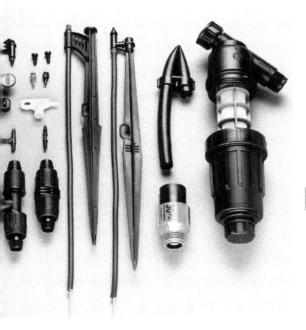

Basic drip irrigation kits come with only a few components, but can be augmented with pieces purchased "a la carte." You'll also need a punch for piercing the tubing and "goof plugs" for repairing errant punches.

Tubing for drip irrigation is thin-wall flexible polyethylene or polyvinyl, typically ¼-inch or ½-inch in diameter. Internal diameters can vary from manufacturer to manufacturer, so it's a good idea to purchase pipe and fittings from a single source.

that Japanese maples prefer a location where they will receive light shade during the hottest part of the day. Spread a 2-inch layer of pine bark mulch under Japanese maple trees to help conserve moisture. Water trees weekly, allowing the soil to dry slightly between waterings.

VINES AND GROUNDCOVERS

With the arrival of warmer weather, plants dry out more quickly. Be sure to check new plantings of vines and groundcovers weekly to see if they need water. If the soil feels dry to the touch when you push your finger into it 2 inches, it's time to water. Clematis vines like plenty of moisture, so be sure to check them regularly. Plants growing in pots will need to be checked daily.

FERTILIZE

ANNUALS

Continue to fertilize at two- to six-week intervals. When you're using granular products, be sure to water afterwards to carry the nutrients down to plant roots.

BULBS

Once they're planted, dahlias don't need supplemental fertilizer unless they are growing in poor soil. If this is the case, you can sidedress when first flowerbuds appear. Apply the fertilizer in rows between the plants with a fertilizer that is high in phosphates and potash, like 5-10-15.

Fertilize caladiums with a complete water-soluble fertilizer like 20-20-20 once a month during the growing season.

EDIBLES

Sidedressing is the practice of applying fertilizer to the ground beside plants as they grow. If your garden vegetables are growing in a row, it is simple to sprinkle fertilizer on the ground as you walk between rows.

You may also choose to fertilize in a circle around individual plants or broadcast it over the whole plot.

It's a common complaint of tomato growers that they have huge vines but few fruit. This condition might be caused by overfeeding with liquid fertilizer.

Once your tomatoes have grown to 2 feet tall, stop fertilizing until blooms appear.

■ *Apply a side dressing of compost, manure, or granular fertilizer to give vegetables and herbs a boost.*

LAWNS

Lawn fertilizers are usually labeled as such. Typically the first number (nitrogen) is the highest among the three fertilizer analysis numbers on the front of the bag. Though the fertilizer numbers differ among brands, any of them can be used successfully if you follow the directions on the bag.

- **Tall fescue:** Do not fertilize this month.

- **Bermudagrass:** Fertilize now (and again in July, August, and September).

- **Zoysiagrass:** Fertilize now (and again in August).

- **Centipedegrass:** Do not fertilize unless you skipped the feeding in May.

- **St. Augustinegrass:** Fertilize now (and again in July and August).

PERENNIALS

Apply a foliar fertilizer to newly planted perennials for a quick boost. Use a dilute solution of a water-soluble fertilizer, following the label directions for half the recommended rate or less. Wait until fall to fertilize established plants.

ROSES

Follow the fertilization schedule described in March.

SHRUBS

If you haven't fertilized shrubs yet, apply some 10-10-10. A granular slow-release fertilizer persists longer than a liquid feed, but both are effective. As a general rule, when using granular fertilizers, apply 1 tablespoon per foot of plant height.

VINES AND GROUNDCOVERS

To help them get established, fertilize new plantings of vines and groundcovers that have been planted in the last six months.

If groundcovers are not planted under trees or shrubs that are fertilized on a regular basis, apply 1 pound (2 cups) of 8-8-8 or 10-10-10 per 100 square feet. Use a broadcast-type spreader to get even distribution over the area. Wash any fertilizer off the foliage when you finish.

During the growing season, clematis vines will benefit from monthly feeding with a complete liquid fertilizer (a ratio like 20-20-20) at half the recommended rate on the label.

PROBLEM-SOLVE

ANNUALS

A great advantage of soaker hose and drip systems is that water is applied only to the roots of plants. By keeping the foliage dry, leaf diseases are reduced.

Annuals produce flowers not for our enjoyment but to make seed to ensure their reproduction. On many plants, the flowering process stops if the flowers are allowed to fade as the seeds are maturing. It is therefore important to regularly remove withered flowers from your annuals. Deadhead ageratum, calendula, cosmos, marigold, pansy, rudbeckia, scabiosa, verbena, and zinnia each week. Remove the yellow flowers from dusty miller as they are produced in late June.

BULBS

Check dahlias for thrips; new growth and buds will look distorted and flowers will fail to open normally. Leaf surfaces may look silvery or bronze. Black specks on the leaves are another indication that thrips are present. Use a strong blast from the hose and wash them off. If you have a severe infestation, you may have to use a systemic insecticide.

Your dahlia leaves may have tiny dark specks and a silvery cast, and the undersides of the leaves may have a fine webbing. This means spider mites. Spray with horticultural oil, insecticidal soap, or a synthetic miticide.

EDIBLES

Blossom end rot is a common disorder of tomato fruit. It is caused by a lack of calcium in the fruit when it is small.

- Add 2 tablespoons of lime to the soil when planting individual tomatoes.

- Keep soil moisture levels constant; avoid wide fluctuations of water around the roots. Use mulch under the tomatoes.

- If you notice the fruit has a rotten bottom (the blossom end), spray immediately with a product containing calcium chloride.

LAWNS

Check your lawn for circular dead spots. It could be "brown patch" but correct your watering and fertilization practices before reaching for a fungicide.

Use a broadleaf weedkiller to spot-spray for violets, wild strawberry, and dandelions in your lawn.

PERENNIALS

During hot, humid weather, problems like powdery mildew on phlox, beebalm, and other perennials may be a problem.

To make an organic spray for powdery mildew, combine 1 tablespoon of baking soda and 1 tablespoon of horticultural oil in 1 gallon of water.

■ *Use your scissors, snips, or hand pruners to snip off dead flowers. Always cut and remove the flower stem at the place where it meets the main plant stem. If you only cut off the flower, you'll have ugly stems hanging around. New growth only sprouts from buds along the main stem.*

Mix well, and spray the plants completely, being sure to wet both tops and undersides of the leaves.

Apply spray early in the day before temperatures get too hot. Avoid spraying when temperatures get above 90 degrees Fahrenheit, as this may burn the plants.

Check for insects, and treat as needed, using insecticidal soaps whenever possible to control problems like aphids, spider mites, and whiteflies.

■ *Avoid overfertilizing tomatoes, which inhibits calcium uptake and can lead to blossom end rot.*

If you have small infestations of Japanese beetles on hollyhocks or other plants, approach them slowly, handpick, and drop them into a jar of soapy water.

Spot-spray weeds in your perennial beds with a nonselective weedkiller.

Hand-pull weeds that are immediately next to desirable plants that might be harmed by chemical controls.

ROSES

Japanese beetles love no plant better than rose leaves and flowers. Nothing is more disheartening than seeing the backsides of a half-dozen beetles merrily feeding on a beautiful blossom. If not controlled, rose leaves will be lace, and the flowers will be disfigured.

NON-CHEMICAL CONTROL

- In early morning, grab an empty soup can and pour an inch of soapy water in the bottom.

- Quietly approach your plants and observe where the cold, slow-moving creatures are resting.

- Gently place the can under a leaf and tap the leaf.

- The beetles will fall off the leaf into the water, and will drown.

- Repeat every morning until the population is decreased.

- Spray leaves with an anti-feedant product containing Neem oil. Neem is not 100 percent effective, but beetles seem to avoid eating leaves where it has been applied.

Make a note to apply milky spore disease powder to your lawn in spring. The disease is deadly to Japanese beetle grubs but harmless to animals and birds.

CHEMICAL CONTROL

- Spray leaves thoroughly with a contact insecticide every three to four days.

- Do not worry if the insects don't immediately fall from the plant—if they come in contact with the insecticide, they will die in a few hours.

Grub-control granules for your lawn are rarely effective in reducing beetle numbers. Japanese beetles can fly from neighboring untreated lawns, and the poison will be for naught.

SHRUBS

Good cultural practices will help reduce pest and disease problems:

- Clean up any leaf litter that accumulates under or around shrubs.

- Destroy infected leaves to prevent the spread of diseases.

- Keep shrubs watered and mulched.

- Keep weeds out of shrub beds.

- You can add groundcovers under your shrubs and trees to help keep roots cool as well as add interest to the garden.

Examine your shrubs for signs of damage by insects or disease. If you have Japanese beetles in small numbers, try handpicking them and drowning them in soapy water (described under Roses). This is best done in the early morning when they are less active. If infestations are severe, you may want to consider using an insecticide.

Check shrubs for signs of aphids or spider mites. Use insecticidal soaps to control these pest problems before resorting to chemical controls. Spray early in the day before temperatures are too hot. When you spray, be sure to cover both the tops and undersides of the leaves and the stems; spray to the point where it drips off the plant.

TREES

Trees are also weakened by a low soil pH. Raise the pH quickly by dissolving 1 pound of hydrated lime in 5 gallons of water. Sprinkle on the soil under the tree branches.

Maintain the pH by scattering 1 pound of garden lime per inch of trunk diameter evenly under the branches of the tree. Wait one year, then have the soil tested to determine if additional lime is needed.

Hand-pull weeds that are right next to tree trunks. A nonselective weedkiller can be used under and around trees if you make sure not to spray it on foliage, bark, or exposed roots.

Most diseases are detected with your eyes. Oak trees, however, sometimes contract a disease that is perceived with your nose. Sap dripping down the trunk of an oak, a few feet from the ground, may indicate a slime flux infection. Also called "wet wood," slime flux is caused by fermentation of the sap under the tree's bark. The oozing sap may smell like vinegar or beer. Wasps, bees, and butterflies are drawn to the smell.

Wash the ooze and slime off the trunk to prevent bark damage. Water the tree regularly during the summer to help it fight off the infection internally.

A silvery sheen on dogwood leaves usually signifies the presence of a fungus called powdery mildew. The fungus sucks moisture from the leaves and causes them to yellow and fall prematurely. It can be prevented by spraying leaves with a fungicide in early May and continuing through mid-June. Fungicide applied now will not cure the infected leaves. Once you see the fungus on the leaves, all that can be done is to protect new leaves.

If the infection is severe, the dogwood may lose up to half its leaves in July. Water infected trees regularly to help them withstand moisture stress.

Crapemyrtle leaves may be covered with grayish white powder, which indicates they are affected by powdery mildew. Spray leaves with a synthetic fungicide before plants bloom. Neem oil may be helpful in minimizing symptoms. The National Arboretum developed mildew-resistant hybrid crapemyrtles by crossing *Lagerstroemia indica* with *L. fauriei* (native to Japan, *L. fauriei* has beautiful bark, is cold hardy, and exhibits a high resistance to powdery mildew).

MILDEW-RESISTANT CRAPEMYRTLES

- 'Acoma' (white flowers)
- 'Biloxi' (light pink flowers)
- 'Comanche' (coral pink flowers)
- 'Hopi' (orange-red to dark red flowers)
- 'Lipan' (medium lavender flowers)
- 'Miami' (medium pink flowers)
- 'Muskogee' (light lavender flowers)
- 'Natchez' (white flowers)
- 'Osage' (clear, light pink flowers)
- 'Sioux' (bright pink, fragrant flowers)
- 'Tuskegee' (deep pink to red flowers)
- 'Yuma' (medium lavender flowers)
- 'Zuni' (medium lavender flowers)

July

July in Georgia is a hot month, a time when you should plan to accomplish any garden chores early in the morning before the heat of the day sets in. Hot weather can stress plants and gardeners too. But it's also a time to reap the rewards of your hard work. Harvest edibles like tomatoes, green beans, squash, and blueberries. Cut flowers to bring indoors for arrangements or to share with friends. If you planted lots of basil, you can make pesto to eat now and then freeze some for later. Herbs like basil produce more foliage if you cut them back regularly and certain perennials will continue to flower if you remove their spent blossoms.

Take inventory of how your plants are doing and make sure that they are all getting enough water. And remember, too much water can be as harmful as too little. If you're not sure, dig down a few inches and check the soil. Don't just go by the calendar when watering. Mature trees will benefit from long, slow watering during extended periods of drought. This small investment will pay off in helping to ensure that your trees are healthy and long-lived.

Plants may be more susceptible to pest and disease problems. Examine them regularly for signs of damage. Use insecticidal soap or horticultural oils to control these problems before resorting to chemical controls. Sometimes a blast of cold water from the hose will eradicate aphids. If you have plants with diseased leaves, collect any leaf litter and dispose of it in the garbage—not the compost pile. This will help reduce the chances of insects or diseases overwintering in your garden and wreaking havoc next spring.

Did you plant any summer bulbs? If so, you will enjoy types like the surprise lilies, *Lycoris squamigera*, when their pink trumpets shoot out of the ground in late summer on naked stems. You'll spot the intense red clumps of spider lily, *Lycoris radiata*, which also bloom on naked stems. If you don't have them, order online now and add some to your garden for a surprise next year.

But most of all, enjoy your summer garden!

PLAN

ANNUALS

Beds of annual flowers should be planned not only for beauty but also for ease of maintenance. A garden designed for a young or vigorous gardener is different from a garden designed for a less vigorous gardener. Easy access gardens should have:

- narrow beds that are more easily reached from the lawn or a solid path.

- raised beds that demand less bending.

- flat, wide paths in the garden that allow wheelchairs or walkers to maneuver easily.

- tools designed for easy grasping.

BULBS

If you have large clumps of daffodils that are healthy but have produced very few blooms in the spring, it is time to divide them. While daffodils welcome the sun in winter and early spring, they benefit from some shade in the summer. If you need to divide them, the best time is after the foliage has turned yellow and fallen over. Late-blooming varieties may still have foliage that is visible in July.

If there is still a bit of foliage to mark where the daffodils are growing, it makes it easier to divide them. When you dig up a clump, dig around and under it with a digging fork or spade. Use caution so as not to cut off roots or slice into the bulbs. Shake soil off the bulbs, and gently untangle the roots. Do not break apart bulbs that are firmly attached to one another or you may injure them, which makes them more susceptible to disease. They will split apart in their own time once they are replanted. If you are moving your bulbs, have the new planting site prepared ahead of time.

EDIBLES

Early this month is the time to plant pumpkins for Halloween. Most varieties need at least 100 days of growth to make a suitable jack-o-lantern. Varieties that produce "baby" pumpkins are often more successful. Varieties with shorter vines take up less space. If you are still short on space, build a heavy-duty trellis on which to train the vine.

LAWNS

Lawns may need watering now, but there's no sense wasting water. If you have an irrigation system, use a sunny afternoon to systematically run through your irrigation zones, noting if any of them are broken or if they spray into the street. All systems should have a rain sensor that cuts off the water when it rains. They are inexpensive and easy to install.

ROSES

Most hybrid roses produce a single flush of blooms in spring or early summer. Some may bloom again in fall. But some species of rose are able to bloom throughout the growing season. Good repeat bloomers are:

- 'Nearly Wild'
- 'Old Blush'
- 'Archduke Charles'
- Butterfly rose
- Knockout™

PERENNIALS

During these hot months, early morning or evening is the coolest time to work in the garden.

This is a good time to edge your flower beds and think about planting projects for the fall. It's amazing how edging beds with stone or brick can give your

■ *To edge a bed, use a sharpened spade, stand on the outside of your garden or landscape bed and hold the spade at the edge of the bed at a 90-degree angle with the spade handle leaning back into the bed. Chop an angle with the spade along the entire bed.*

garden a more refined look, setting it off from lawn areas. Here are some ideas for edging flower beds:

- Use a straight-edge shovel to dig into the soil at a slight angle toward the flower bed; be sure to dig down at least 4 inches. Fill the trench you have created with the same mulch you use on your flower beds—this will delineate the bed line and separate it from the lawn.

- If you use brick or stone for edging, be sure to start with a level area if the bricks are upright, making sure one-third is buried in the soil; sand is a good base and will help the bricks settle.

- Other materials to use for edging include treated wood strips, metal, or plastic buried several inches in the soil.

SHRUBS

Evaluate the shrubs in your garden. Do they look attractive even when they are not fruiting or in bloom? Do they provide a background or complement for your perennials and annuals? Do you have a mix of evergreen and deciduous shrubs, including those with colorful flowers, foliage, and fruits?

There may be gaps in your garden where shrubs would help fill the void. Think about which shrubs you would like to add or eliminate so you can develop a plan for the fall. Note which plants still look good during the hot summer months.

TREES

It is tempting to transplant small dogwood or magnolia trees from the woods into your landscape, but this is usually not a good idea. The roots may be tangled with the larger roots of nearby trees, making transplant shock likely. Only small seedlings can be transplanted successfully—a tree taller than 4 feet is not likely to survive. Because the parentage of the tree isn't known, the seedling may never produce the number of flowers you anticipate. Named, improved selections of trees are more robust, easier to plant, and more likely to bloom regularly.

Are there places in your garden where trees can be added? Think about what size and type of tree would best suit your needs. A medium to large deciduous shade tree can help keep your house cool in the

■ *Ginkgo*

summer and warm in the winter when sunlight is more welcome. When it comes to selecting shade trees, there are many choices. Here is a list of medium to large trees well suited to provide shade:

- Red maple, *Acer rubrum* (there are many good selections)

- Heritage birch, *Betula nigra* 'Heritage'

- Yellowwood, *Cladrastis kentukea*

- American beech, *Fagus grandifolia* (there are many selections)

- Ginkgo, *Ginkgo biloba*

- Black tupelo, *Nyssa sylvatica*

- Yoshino cherry, *Prunus yedoensis*

- Live oak, *Quercus virginiana*

- Black locust, *Robinia pseudoacacia* (there are several varieties)

- Lacebark elm, *Ulmus parvifolia*

VINES AND GROUNDCOVERS

Monkey grass, English ivy, and mondo grass are familiar evergreen groundcovers for shade. There are even some groundcovers that bloom in shade, as shown below. Think about adding some of these to your garden this fall. They will brighten up the woodland and add interest under a shrub. You can also plant these groundcovers as a carpet for spring bulbs, as with some of the early-blooming miniature daffodils or giant crocus. Plant the groundcovers in fall at the same time you plant your bulbs. This way you'll know where your bulbs are, even when they're not blooming.

- Bugleweed (ajuga) has 4- to 5-inch spikes of blue flowers in spring to early summer.

- Green and gold has yellow flowers in spring, some in summer, and then a few in fall.

- Mazus has purplish blue snapdragon-like flowers with yellow markings in spring and early summer.

- Partridgeberry has tiny white flowers in late spring or early summer followed by bright red berries less than ¼-inch wide. It is not a good choice for coastal gardens.

- Periwinkle has five-petaled lavender-blue, purple, or white flowers in spring.

PLANT

ANNUALS

Choose replacement plants carefully. Avoid floppy or stretched-out plants. Ask your garden center manager when the next fresh shipment will arrive. Inspect plants for insects, like whiteflies or spider mites, before purchasing.

Plant zinnia seed. They will sprout in six days and bloom in just a few weeks. Plant dwarf sunflower seed now. Varieties like 'Teddy Bear', 'Sunspot', 'Pacino', and 'Prado Red' take up little space but delight the eyes of humans and birds alike. Plant more caladiums and coleus. They'll look better in fall than the early plants, fading now, that you put out in May.

BULBS

Plant another bed of gladiolus so that you will have blooms all summer and into fall.

If your daffodils are in a spot that is hot and sunny all summer, plant a summer crop of annuals over the bulbs. This will provide them with some shade and the annuals will use up excess moisture, helping the bulbs stay dry.

There are a number of late-summer/fall bloomers that can be planted in the summer as soon as you receive them, including spider lily, *Lycoris radiata*, surprise lily, *L. squamigera*, and autumn daffodil, *Sternbergia lutea*. These bulbs are normally dug and shipped anytime between June and August. Order them now for planting. They may not bloom the first season, but once they are established, they will reward you every year with flowers at a time when few other bulbs are blooming.

EDIBLES

You can root new tomato plants now to keep your garden productive into October:

1. Put the lower 6 inches of a 12-inch-long tomato branch in a jar of water. Keep it in a bright but shady area outdoors.

2. When roots are 1 inch long, the tomato can be transplanted into a pot.

3. In two weeks the plant will be ready to move to your garden.

LAWNS

Too hot for the kids outdoors? Now is a good time to lay sod in the bare areas where the kids have been playing ball.

Remember to dig the soil to a depth of 3 to 6 inches, and rake it smooth before laying sod.

It will be hard to keep children off the lawn when you water the thirsty young sod. Plant sod pieces on half the lawn this month and half next month so the children can at least get some enjoyment from the sprinkler when the first part of the lawn has been repaired.

Can't afford to sod the bare spots in your St. Augustinegrass, zoysiagrass, or bermudagrass lawn? Buy sod pieces at the nursery, and cut them into dozens of plugs with a hatchet or sharp knife. Some garden centers sell special tools that cut sod plugs to the right size. They can be used to dig matching holes as well.

Plant 3-inch-diameter sod plugs 12 inches apart. They will cover the ground by fall. (Zoysiagrass will be the slowest to spread.)

PERENNIALS

If you add any plants to the garden now, keep in mind that they will probably not put out many roots until soil temperatures cool off. Here are a few tips for planting in the summer:

- Start with healthy plants that already have a robust root system.

- Restrict your planting and transplanting to the shade garden during the hot summer months. Minimize planting in sunny areas since root growth is at a minimum in high temperatures.

- Water and mulch immediately after planting.

HERE'S HOW

TO ROOT TOMATOES IN SOIL

If you are conscientious about keeping the soil moist, you can root tomatoes right in the soil. This is how Walter's neighbor Harry does it:

1. Cut a 12-inch branch from your tomato plant. Strip off all the leaves except the two or three around the tip of the branch.

2. Poke a hole in the garden soil deep enough to insert all but the top 3 inches of the branch.

3. Water the soil thoroughly every two days.

4. Make a temporary umbrella for the tender plant using an unneeded branch from a holly or aucuba shrub. Remove the umbrella ten days later. Your new plant is rooted in place and ready to grow!

HERE'S HOW

TO PREPARE A SITE FOR LAYING SOD

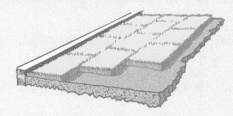

1. Prepare the planting site and soil.

2. Calculate the square footage of the area to be sodded. A roll of sod is usually 1½ feet wide by 6 feet long, covering 9 square feet.

3. Order sod to be delivered or plan on picking it up just prior to installation.

4. Select freshly cut sod with good green color. Be sure it is free of weeds and pests. Use sod that has a blend of several grass varieties and is grown on a soil similar to yours.

5. Keep sod in a cool, shady place to prevent it from overheating and drying out. Lay it as soon as possible.

6. Use a driveway, sidewalk, or curb as your starting point. Lay the first row of sod next to the longest of these straight edges. Butt sod ends together and make sure the roots contact the soil. Stagger the seams as if you were laying bricks. Use a knife to trim the sod to fit.

7. Lay the sod perpendicular to the slope on steep hills. Use wooden stakes to hold it in place.

8. Run an empty lawn roller over the sod to remove air pockets and to ensure good root-to-soil contact. Push it perpendicular to the direction that the sod was laid.

9. Water the sod immediately, moistening it and the top 3 to 4 inches of soil. Keep the sod and soil surface moist until the sod has rooted into the soil below. Continue watering thoroughly but less frequently once this happens. Mow the sod once it is firmly rooted in place and needs cutting.

ROSES

There is no shame in admitting to yourself that a rose has died despite your best efforts. Healthy roses are still available in containers at large nurseries and can be planted now to replace those that fell by the wayside. Three-gallon-sized containers will help the plants survive dry weather.

- Take extra care when digging a new hole for the rose. If the soil is not rich and moist, add plenty of compost or manure.

- Untangle the roots in the container and spread them outwards in the hole.

- Fill the hole with soil while keeping the roots spread.

- Water deeply, and cancel any long vacations you've planned—this new bloomer will need regular weekly watering between now and October.

SHRUBS

This month is generally too hot to add new plants to the garden, as the soil and air temperatures are not ideal for encouraging root growth . . . but if this is the only time you have to plant, get out the shovel! Many of the shrubs that nurseries offer are grown in containers that stay outside all year long. This means that unless the ground is frozen or saturated, plants can be added to your garden throughout the year. This is not true for bare-root plants, which must be dormant when you plant them.

TREES

Wait until fall to plant trees. They won't put out many roots or much branch growth when planted in hot weather.

Gardeners who live on the coast are challenged to find plants that will tolerate constant winds, salt spray, and sandy soils. Here is a list of trees for coastal gardens:

- Japanese cryptomeria, *Cryptomeria japonica*
- Southern magnolia, *Magnolia grandiflora*
- American holly, *Ilex opaca*

- Japanese black pine, *Pinus thunbergiana*
- Live oak, *Quercus virginiana*
- American arborvitae, *Thuja occidentalis*
- Lacebark elm, *Ulmus parvifolia*

VINES AND GROUNDCOVERS

You can plant groundcovers or vines now, but don't expect much growth while the air and soil temperatures are hot. The roots will wait until soil temperatures begin to cool off in the fall before they put on any significant growth.

CARE

ANNUALS

When planting a tall pot with summer annuals, there is no need to fill the entire pot with potting soil. After all, the roots of annual flowers rarely penetrate more than 10 inches into the soil. Fill the pot partially with empty capped plastic soft drink bottles. Add potting soil, and shake the pot vigorously to settle it around the bottles. When the soil no longer recedes below the bottles, fill the pot completely, and plant your annual flowers.

BULBS

Thin bamboo stakes make inconspicuous supports for leaning gladiolus, lilies, or dahlias. Buy stakes long enough to reach at least two-thirds up the plant. Tall lilies may require four-foot-tall stakes.

If you don't replant immediately and want to store your bulbs, make sure you dry them completely.

■ *Specially designed mulching lawn mowers do an excellent job of chopping the clippings so fine they cannot be seen.*

Use mesh bags to store your bulbs like those used to store fruit or onions. Nylon stockings make a good substitute if you don't have a mesh bag. Use a fan to provide good air circulation while you dry the bulbs. Keep them in a cool, dark, dry place until you replant them in fall.

Remove dead flowers from daylilies and dahlias.

EDIBLES

Don't let fruit tree limbs break: prop them up with poles, or remove some fruit to lighten the load.

Pick squash, cucumbers, and okra regularly. A single fruit left to become overmature on the vine will stop bloom production completely.

Prune figs lightly now if needed. Remove the tall shoots in the middle of the bush so they don't grow beyond your reach.

Remove the vertical "water sprouts" that emerge from apple, peach, and pear limbs.

LAWNS

Whether you have sodded or seeded a new lawn, it is important to keep the family and pets off the area until the grass is well established. Compaction from just a few trips across the lawn in one path can prevent good grass growth there for years.

- Sod that is well established cannot be pulled up from the ground. Well-established seeded lawns should appear to be 100 percent covered with grass seedlings.

- Even on a well-established lawn, mowing in the same pattern over and over will result in compaction where the wheels roll. It is best to use a different mowing pattern (vertical, horizontal, or diagonal) each time you mow.

Grasscycling is the practice of leaving grass clippings on the lawn rather than collecting them. Grasscycling saves time and energy, plus it reduces the amount of yard waste that might be taken to the landfill.

- Because clippings contain the nutrient nitrogen, grasscycling allows you to reduce the amount of fertilizer you apply by one-fourth.

HERE'S HOW

TO GET RID OF TREE STUMPS

Fresh tree stumps are a nuisance in the landscape. Chemical removal is totally ineffective. There are two methods for removing stumps.

1. The "natural" method is the slow and inexpensive method. Eventually, Mother Nature will prevail and the stump will rot away. You can speed up the process by drilling several large, deep holes in the top of the stump. Pack the holes with topsoil gathered from under a nearby tree. Thoroughly soak the soil and stump with water. Cover the stump with clear plastic, and let the sun's heat accelerate the decomposition process.

2. The fastest is the "mechanical" method. Rent a stump grinder, or hire a company to grind your stump below the soil surface. Collect the chips, and use them for mulch under shrubs and nearby trees. Avoid mixing the chips into the soil— during decomposition, they will rob nutrients from the grass or plants you use to replace the tree.

- Older, side-discharge mowers can also be used if mowing is done often enough that only one-third of the grass height is removed in one mowing.

PERENNIALS

Prune back by one-third to one-half fall-blooming perennials like asters, chrysanthemums, *Heliopsis*, and *Helianthus*.

This will result in fuller plants that shouldn't require staking, although sometimes the flowers will be a bit smaller. Be sure to do this pruning at least eight weeks before the plants would normally bloom.

Fall-blooming perennials begin blooming in September, with other varieties continuing well into October and November.

Continue to deadhead repeat bloomers like coneflower, black-eyed Susan, coreopsis, scabiosa, stokesia, salvia, and verbena. This will encourage more blooms over a longer period. Plants like yarrow may or may not bloom again but will be much tidier if you cut off the dead flower stalks.

ROSES

Brown jute twine makes a good material for tying rose canes to an arbor. Unlike nylon, the twine will rot after one season and will not cut into plant stems.

■ *Jute twine is the most commonly used type of garden twine because it is strong.*

HERE'S HOW

TO SAVE YOUR BODY

To stay healthy, gardeners should pay attention to these body-saving ideas:

- Alternate movements. If you swap digging, raking, weeding, and pruning, you can avoid repetitive motion injuries.

- Bend from the knees, not from the back. Lift large pots and sacks of fertilizer by first bending your knees, then grasping the object and straightening your knees. Avoid bending over to lift even light items—the lower back is prone to injury and should be spared whenever possible.

Here are some sources of tools for physically challenged gardeners: Walt Nicke Co., www.gardentalk.com; Lee Valley Tools Ltd., www.leevalley.com; A. M. Leonard, Inc., www.amleo.com.

Look for extremely weak or dead limbs every time you walk through your rose garden. Use a sharp pair of pruners to remove any you find.

The broad blades of common hand pruners are sometimes too big to fit easily into tight spots on a rosebush. Look for special rose pruners, such as Felco #6, to make pruning easier—its handles are also smaller and more comfortable for female operators.

It is a good idea to occasionally sterilize your pruners, even if you are not aware of any diseases that are present. Dip them in a bucket containing one part bleach mixed with nine parts water.

SHRUBS

Remove dead branches or blossoms on flowering shrubs once they finish blooming.

Prune and shape hedges of fast-growing species such as privet, glossy abelia, cherry laurel, and holly. The new growth they put out will still have time to harden off before winter.

Removing the dead flower blossoms from your butterfly bush will encourage more blooms; if you're lucky, the shrubs will flower until frost.

TREES

There is still time to prune trees that bloomed in the spring. Cut off seedpods and prune lightly to shape the trees. Prune summer-flowering trees as soon as they finish blooming, if pruning is needed. There are a couple of ways to prune trees:

- **Heading:** Selectively remove the tips of branches at their growing points rather than shearing them back. This selective pruning will leave behind a dormant bud that will eventually grow and fill in empty spaces.

- **Thinning:** This type of pruning removes the branch or stem at its origin. Be sure not to make a flush cut—leave a branch collar. When cutting large limbs, remove a large outer limb first. A section about a foot long should remain; this will make it easier to finish pruning correctly.

VINES AND GROUNDCOVERS

If you have English ivy or Virginia creeper growing on a wall around doors or windows and it threatens to cover the windows, cut it back now. You can root the ivy clippings by sticking them in a soilless mix or wet sand. In four to five weeks you should have rooted cuttings that you can plant directly in the ground.

WATER

ANNUALS

Watering restrictions and, sometimes outright bans, have become a way of life in the metropolitan areas of Georgia. When municipal water is in short supply, there are other sources of water for your plants.

- Water from a dehumidifier or from an air conditioner condensate drain is perfectly safe to use on plants. This water has been condensed from the ambient air—just like rainwater!

- Bathwater can be used to water most plants. The soap, shampoo, and conditioner are so diluted that they will not harm leaves or roots. Avoid using *only* bath water on azaleas and rhododendrons; these shrubs like acidic soil, and soapy water is slightly alkaline.

- If you are lucky enough to live on a lake, it is theoretically possible to pump water from it for your landscape. Before you attempt this, consider: 1) An electrician will be needed to install a 220-volt power line for an electric pump (gasoline pumps are rarely adequate). 2) Irrigation sprinklers demand moderately clean water. How will the lake water be

TO AIR LAYER ROSES

Roses that have limber stems can be propagated by soil layering. Like any plant propagated from a cutting, the new plant will be a genetic duplicate of the rose from which it came. Follow these steps for soil layering:

1. Bend a stem down until it touches the earth. Use a dull knife to gently scrape the bark from the stem in a 1-inch-wide area at the point where it touches the soil.

2. Dust the wounded stem with rooting hormone.

3. Use a trowel to scoop a shallow depression in the soil under the scraped area.

4. Lay the stem in the depression. Cover it with damp soil and place a brick on top to hold it in place. In four months, roots will form underground. You can clip the stem that goes back to the mother plant but do not dig up your new plant.

5. Water the rooted plant regularly until it loses its leaves in winter.

The new, well-rooted plant can be moved next spring.

HERE'S HOW

TO PRUNE LARGE LIMBS

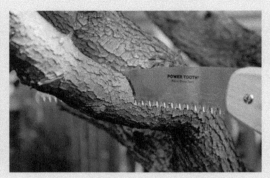

1. Cut upward partway through the branch, and then downward, slightly away from the first cut.

2. Cut off the stub just outside the branch collar (this is the swollen part that comes out from the tree where the branch attaches). The branch collar will gradually close over the wound.

filtered and how often must the filter be cleaned? 3) The initial cost of an irrigation system is substantial. Wouldn't it be less expensive to design a landscape that did not demand so much water?

Avoid pumping water from a nearby creek without considering the effect the lower water level will have downstream. Small fish, frogs, and invertebrates depend on water for their lives. Birds and other predators depend on smaller animals for their food.

BULBS

Stop watering daffodils and other spring-blooming bulbs once they are no longer blooming. Daffodils, especially, require well-drained soils when they are dormant or they will develop rot.

EDIBLES

It is sometimes said that watering vegetable plants on a hot, sunny afternoon will cause spots to be burned in the leaves because the water droplets focus sunlight on the leaves. This is hogwash. Quick afternoon showers are common throughout the summer. Neither vegetables, nor trees, nor flowers, nor any other plants are harmed by water on their leaves on a sunny afternoon.

Water weekly your fruit trees and vines that were planted in the last six months. They need approximately 2 gallons of water per foot of plant height.

LAWNS

Turfgrasses have varying degrees of drought tolerance. Ranked from highest drought tolerance to the lowest are:

First: Bermudagrass

Second: St. Augustinegrass

Third: Centipedegrass, tall fescue, Emerald zoysiagrass, and El Toro zoysiagrass

Fourth: Meyer zoysiagrass

Raise the height of your mower by one notch. It will help the grass withstand hot, dry weather by shading the soil and by raising the humidity at soil level.

It is a shame to discard a perfectly good hose because you accidentally crushed one end with a car tire. Hose repair kits are inexpensive, available at any hardware store, and easy to use. Take the hose with you when you purchase a kit, just to make sure you get the right size. If you can't bring along the hose, look for "universal" kits that work on two or more hose sizes.

PERENNIALS

Water established perennials during a prolonged dry spell (a month or longer without significant rainfall). About 1 inch per week should be enough.

- Attaching a water wand to your hose can make this chore much easier. Not only is

the water more evenly dispersed through the many holes on the end of the breaker, an on/off valve will mean a lot less wasted water.

- Soaker hoses are also an option. Place them in your perennial flowerbeds and cover them with a light coat of mulch. Be sure to inspect them periodically to see how well they are working.

- If you are growing perennials in decorative containers, you can add a granular product designed to absorb and release water in the soil. If you do this, be sure to adjust your watering frequency—you will have to experiment, but if you want to be certain you do not overwater, water only when the top 2-inch depth of the soil is dry.

ROSES

Give roses that were planted last spring at least 2 gallons of water per week.

Check the depth of the mulch under your plants. It should be at least 2 inches thick.

If mulch is touching the stem, pull it back a few inches from the stem of the rose.

If you are forced to dig a hole for a post for a rose arbor this month, first let your water hose trickle moisture into the spot all night long. The water will soften the soil from its concrete-like state. You might have to stop digging after the first foot and allow another night's trickling to soften the soil even deeper.

SHRUBS

This is an important time to check shrubs regularly and make sure they are getting enough water. Shrubs in large containers might need watering at least once a day. When you water containers, whether shrubs, trees, annuals, or perennials, water until it comes out of the holes in the bottom of the pot. If the soil has shrunk away from the sides of the pot, water, let it soak in, and then water again.

When watering shrubs in the ground, too much water can be as harmful as too little. If you're not sure whether to water or not, check the rootball for dampness—don't base your watering decisions solely on the time of year.

New plantings should be watered once a week. Saturate the rootball. If you use the hose, place it near the center of the shrub and leave it on a slow trickle for 15 minutes or more, depending on rootball size.

If you have a problem spot in your garden where the soil stays moist all or most of the time, it's best not to fight it but to select plants that will not only survive but thrive in such an environment. Shrubs that tolerate soils that are constantly moist include:

- Sweet pepperbush, *Clethra alnifolia*
- Winterberry holly, *Ilex verticillata*
- Virginia sweetspire, *Itea virginica*

TREES

Keep newly planted trees watered. Water deeply once a week unless you get 1 or more inches of rain. Drought stress can make your trees more susceptible to insect and disease problems. Consider using plastic water reservoir bags that surround the trunk and allow water to drip into the soil.

VINES AND GROUNDCOVERS

Keep any new plantings well watered. Check containers daily and plants in the ground weekly. Apply 1 to 2 inches of mulch to new plantings. This will help reduce weed infestations, keep soil temperatures cool, and conserve moisture.

■ *Water clematis frequently, especially during the bloom period.*

FERTILIZE

ANNUALS

Continue to fertilize at two- to six-week intervals as discussed in May. When using granular products, be sure to water afterwards to carry the nutrients down to plant roots.

Some gardeners prefer to use "organic" fertilizers like manure, blood meal, and fish emulsion. These products are slightly more expensive but have the advantage of adding plenty of micronutrients to the soil. Research by Dr. Tim Smalley, horticulture professor at the University of Georgia, has shown that composted hen litter continues to release plant food for four years after a 2-inch layer is rototilled into flowerbeds. Apply organic fertilizer at the rate recommended on the container.

BULBS

Fertilize caladiums with a complete water-soluble fertilizer like 20-20-20.

EDIBLES

Continue to fertilize summer vegetables. Don't forget to water the fertilizer into the soil afterwards.

Tomatoes grown in pots on your deck or patio need to be fed regularly because constant watering rinses fertilizer out of the soil. Plan on using water-soluble fertilizer every four weeks.

You can also mix up a large storage container of water-soluble houseplant fertilizer at ¼ strength and simply use it to water the plants each time.

LAWNS

Bermudagrass: Fertilize now (and again in August and September).

Zoysiagrass: Do not fertilize unless a previous feeding was missed.

St. Augustinegrass: Fertilize now.

Tall fescue: To avoid disease and drought problems, do not fertilize tall fescue during the summer. If your tall fescue is more yellow than you prefer, apply a product containing plant-available iron. Follow label directions, typically 1 to 2 pounds per 100 square feet.

PERENNIALS

Don't fertilize now. Hot weather makes plants more susceptible to problems, especially if they are encouraged to put on lots of new growth.

ROSES

Halve your fertilization rate during the hot months of summer. Fertilizer will force a rose to produce new leaves, which will demand water that may be scarce in dry weather.

VINES AND GROUNDCOVERS

Fertilize annual vines, like hyacinth bean and moonvine, with half the recommended rate of a complete liquid fertilizer like 20-20-20. With any luck, many of your vines will bloom until frost. There's no need to fertilize perennial vines or groundcovers now.

PROBLEM-SOLVE

ANNUALS

It may seem contradictory, but the highest incidence of garden root rot problems seems to occur when summer watering restrictions are imposed. Perhaps gardeners fear that since water is limited, they should water all the more! Root rot is caused by soggy soil, which leads to weak root growth and an increase in soil fungi. Symptoms include yellow leaves, wilting, and plant stems that break at ground level.

Prevent root rot by watering annuals deeply once per week and mixing plenty of organic amendments into the soil before planting.

Continue checking for insect damage to your plants. The key to insect control is to identify the insect or other pest responsible. Many can be identified by their characteristic damage, like the lace doily effect of Japanese beetle feeding and the round leaf notches of black vine weevil.

TO MAKE DEFINED EDGES

Another option for making a defined edge where your lawn borders a flowerbed is to dig a trench between grass and bed. This procedure is called trench edging:

- Use a thin shovel or a power tool called an edger to dig a trench 6 inches wide and 2 inches deep along the edge of your grass.

- You can choose whether to leave the trench empty or to mask the bare soil with a shallow layer of pine straw.

- If the trench slants downhill, interrupt the downward flow of water by placing stones or half-bricks in the trench at regular intervals.

BULBS

Pull weeds in your bulb beds when they are young and before they flower and set seed. This will prevent them from spreading freely by seed.

If your dahlias look wilted even after you water them and when you cut open a stem you see brown streaking on the inside it means your dahlias have a fungus called *Verticillium* wilt. This fungus destroys tissues responsible for transporting water throughout the plant. There is no chemical control. Destroy infected plants, and dispose of them in the garbage, not the compost pile. Do not plant dahlias in the same area again or you may have the same problem.

TO CONTROL SLUGS ORGANICALLY

- Use orange or grapefruit rinds or black plastic cell-packs (six- or eight-packs in which annuals or vegetables are sold). Place the overturned rinds or cell-packs under and near the leaves of susceptible plants. Mostly nocturnal, slugs seek dark, moist areas. In the morning, remove the rinds and cell-packs along with the slugs.

- Use a physical barrier like a 1-inch-wide strip of copper around the top edge of containers with susceptible plants.

- Use slug control products that contain iron phosphate. The chemical has very low toxicity.

- Another popular method for controlling slugs is to place a saucer next to the plants that may be attacked. Fill it with beer, and thirsty slugs will drown.

■ *Some gardeners prefer not to kill the hornworm caterpillar. After all, it will eventually turn into a sphinx moth.*

If some of your daylily leaves have yellow and brown streaks or dark brown irregular spots, it could be daylily leaf spot. Remove and destroy any infected leaves. Use drip irrigation or other alternatives to overhead watering. The faster leaves dry, the less chance fungi will have to attack.

Select varieties of daylilies that are recommended for our region. Check with The American Hemerocallis Society (www.daylilies.org).

EDIBLES
Tomato leaves disappearing overnight? Suspect the tomato hornworm, a big green caterpillar camouflaged among the plant stems. Hornworms are easiest to find in late evening, using a flashlight. Look for black excrement pellets on the ground underneath their feeding site.

Tomatoes are susceptible to several diseases, so researchers have bred varieties that are resistant to disease. Look for the letters VFN or VFNT after the variety name. The letters mean the tomato is resistant to:

- Verticillium wilt
- Fusarium wilt
- Nematodes
- Tobacco mosaic virus

There is no defense against tomato bacterial wilt. The plant wilts markedly during the day but may partially recover overnight. After a week of successive wilts, the plant dies. Bacterial wilt remains in the soil for five years. Do not plant tomato, pepper, or eggplant in a bacterial wilt spot; plant beans, peas, or corn instead.

All members of the squash family (watermelon, pumpkin, gourd, cucumber, and squash) form separate male and female flowers on the same vine. Male flowers are first to arrive. They regularly appear for weeks before a

female flower materializes. A healthy vine will eventually produce lots of fruit . . . don't worry if at first you have lots of flowers but nothing to eat!

Bees must be present to pollinate the flowers. If you are getting a few oddly shaped fruit, transfer pollen between male and female flowers. Use a cotton swab or camel hairbrush, shaking it gently inside the flowers three times each day.

LAWNS

Insect damage to lawn grass is difficult to diagnose. Symptoms might include numerous dead patches or grass blades that seem to disappear in an area overnight. One way to check if you have harmful insects is to "float" them out:

1. Mix 2 ounces (4 tablespoons) of lemon-scented dish detergent in 2 gallons of water.

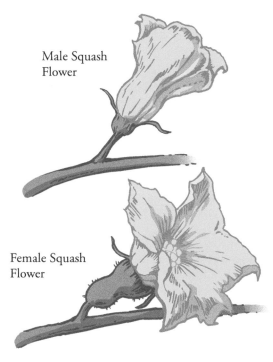

Male Squash
Flower

Female Squash
Flower

■ *Only female flowers grow into fruits, but you need male flowers for pollination.*

TO PRACTICE INTEGRATED PEST MANAGEMENT (IPM)

This approach to pest control is based on the idea of managing insect populations rather than eliminating them. By choosing the right plants for your growing conditions and using good cultural practices, you can minimize potential pest problems.

- Examine your shrubs and other plants on a regular basis. If less than 50 percent of a plant is affected with a pest, use a physical or biological control before you resort to a chemical control.

- Physical controls include traps and barriers like copper strips to keep away slugs and snails.

- Biological controls include the use of beneficial insects like ladybugs that eat aphids and the use of *Bacillus thuringiensis*, a bacterium that kills caterpillars.

2. Pour the mixture over a 2-foot-square area. Insects such as sod webworms and chinchbugs will come wriggling to the surface of the soapy froth.

3. Collect the insects and have them identified by your local Extension office or garden center.

PERENNIALS

Check for aphids, spider mites, and thrips. Sometimes a strong blast of water will get rid of them; insecticidal soaps and horticultural oils can also be effective.

Southern blight is a soilborne fungus that causes stem rot at the soil level and can spread to surrounding plants. Look for white fuzzy balls at the base of plant stems. If plants are infected, remove and destroy them. Leave the area unplanted for six months (if you do plant in the infected area before six months are up, be sure to amend the soil with coarse sand, which will improve drainage). Plants often affected include artemisia, aster, columbine, liatris, phlox, salvia, and Shasta daisy. To reduce this problem:

1. Keep mulch away from plant stems.

2. Avoid overwatering.

3. Good sanitation is also critical. Collect and destroy dead and diseased leaves.

Spot-spray weeds in perennial beds with a nonselective weedkiller. Use extreme caution around desirable plants. Continue to hand-pull weeds.

ROSES

Spider mites are tiny members of the arthropod family that suck sap from rose leaves. They are not insects, because they have eight legs, like spiders. Most insecticides do not control them; instead, the insecticide kills the beneficial insects, which can keep a small mite invasion in check. To identify spider mites, look under leaves for tiny creatures that are about the size of a grain of salt and may be red, yellow, or orange. Damage such as bronzed or stippled yellow leaves may be the first indication

they are active; tiny webs between the base of a leaf and the stem of a plant may be present. To control spider mites:

- Examine leaves weekly during the hot and dry days of summer. If mites are found early, use a stiff spray of water daily to wash them off.

- Spray leaves thoroughly with horticultural oil.

- A miticide can be used if the population is widespread.

- Avoid planting verbena, rosemary, butterfly bush, and foxglove (they're spider mite magnets!) near your roses.

Rose slugs are not true slugs but rather the larvae of small sawflies. They feed from underneath a leaf, consuming the soft tissue between the veins. The damage appears similar to the damage caused by Japanese beetles feeding, but rose slugs eventually chew large holes in leaves rather than leaving them skeletonized. Hit the underside of leaves with a stiff spray of water. Insecticidal soap is very effective on rose slugs.

SHRUBS

Hot weather seems to encourage pests like spider mites and aphids. Examine shrubs regularly for signs of damage; use insecticidal soaps to control these problems before resorting to a chemical pesticide. Sometimes even a blast of cold water from the hose can eradicate a problem like aphids.

Spot-spray weeds around shrubs with a non-selective herbicide. Protect stems and foliage from coming into contact with spray by using a cardboard guard.

If any of your shrubs suffer from powdery mildew, blackspot, or insect problems, make sure to collect and destroy infected leaves as soon as they hit the ground. This will help reduce the spread of diseases and insects.

A good time to hand-weed is the day after a long, gentle rain. Scratching the soil with a cultivator around and between shrubs when weeds are small and before they set seed is a good practice to

■ Bagworms affect pine, spruce, juniper, cedar, and arborvitae trees. The adult moths lay eggs that survive the winter in cocoons that look like pinecones hanging on the trees.

prevent serious infestations of weeds. This is also a good time to apply a light layer of mulch around shrubs. Mulch can reduce weeds and help keep the soil cool.

Check leaves of rhododendrons and large-leaved azaleas for notches. This symptom is characteristic of the black vine weevil, which feeds at night and hides underneath the shrub by day. Use insecticide granules or contact spray under your shrubs.

You may notice a black mold on the leaves of your crapemyrtle. Called sooty mold, this fungus occurs when insects such as aphids and scale secrete a substance called honeydew and the mold grows on top of the honeydew. Simply wash off the leaves and treat the insects with insecticidal soap or insecticide.

TREES

Pick off and destroy bagworms whenever you find them. If you choose to use a contact insecticide, April and May are the months when the moths are most susceptible. Make a calendar note for next year.

VINES AND GROUNDCOVERS

You may see young branch tips on your groundcover junipers turn red or brown, then gray. Once they die, tiny black spots, which are the fruiting bodies of the fungus, may appear on the dead needles and stems. These symptoms mean your juniper suffers from twig blight, a fungus that can enter the plant through both healthy and wounded tissue. Young plants are more susceptible than mature plants. Prune out and destroy infected twigs and branches as soon as you notice them. Spray plants with a fungicide at two-week intervals in the spring when plants begin to put out new growth. Here are some prevention tips:

1. Plant junipers in sites where they will get plenty of sunlight and good air circulation.

2. Avoid overhead watering or watering at night when foliage will stay wet for several hours.

3. Don't overfertilize, and avoid wounding the plant; prune during winter if possible.

HERE'S HOW

TO KILL INVASIVE VINES

You may inherit a garden that has been neglected for a long period of time and has aggressive vines like wisteria, honeysuckle, or kudzu running rampantly through it. Here are some suggestions for controlling or eliminating wisteria:

1. Spray the vine with a nonselective weedkiller when it has lots of foliage. Spray the foliage on the top and undersides until it drips off the plant.

2. Wait ten days to two weeks. Cut off any remaining green foliage.

3. Wait another two weeks, and when a new batch of foliage flushes out, spray it with the weedkiller again. Repeat this until the vine goes dormant in winter.

Another method is to cut the vine down to the ground, and paint the cut surface with a weedkiller containing triclopyr. These techniques can also be used to eliminate English ivy, bittersweet, and grapevines.

August is a good time to evaluate how your garden has fared over the summer and to plan ahead for fall. Are there any gaps where you need to replace a plant that you lost due to disease or old age? Or maybe a plant outgrew its location and you want to replace it. Should you add shrubs, trees, perennials, and bulbs to complement your existing plants? What about adding the element of water? Whether it's a small pond or a large decorative pot converted into a water garden, both will make even the hottest days seem a bit cooler. All you need is a container, a small pump, and a source of water.

Continue regular garden maintenance including weeding and removing dead blossoms and leaf litter. This will make your cleanup later in the fall a manageable task. Don't forget to keep plants well watered, both in containers and those growing in the ground.

The best time to enjoy your garden this month is during the early morning and evening. Subtle garden lighting along paths that also highlight specific plants make the garden more inviting once the sun goes down. There are still late bloomers like the fragrant butterfly ginger and cardinal flower, a bright red beacon in the summer landscape.

You should have received your catalogues for spring bulbs by now, or you can go online and check out the different offerings. Study the inspiring photos as you sip a cold drink inside your air conditioned house and plan what to add to your garden in the fall. It's not too early to order, as most companies will ship your spring-flowering bulbs to you at the best time to plant them, typically October or November.

You may be planning to add some cool-season crops to your garden this month such as lettuce, spinach, and broccoli to name a few. Make sure you have seeds ready to start in cell packs or to sow directly in the ground. And stay cool!

PLAN

ANNUALS

In severe drought, concentrate on maintaining one or two blooming "oases" in your landscape—even if you have to allow the rest of the yard to dry out. Scavenge water from your bathtub or sink to keep your oases beautiful.

BULBS

It's time to begin planning for this fall and next spring. Make a list of bulbs you would like to add to your garden. This is a good time to place your order for spring bulbs. They are usually shipped for fall planting beginning in August and continuing through November.

While there are many spring-blooming bulbs, there are also late summer- and fall-blooming bulbs. Some fall bloomers have foliage that appears in spring and then disappears. When the flowers appear in autumn, it's almost like magic. Plant fall-blooming bulbs with groundcovers like English ivy or pachysandra. The dark green background will help mask the bulb foliage as it ripens and will show off the flowers when they appear in fall. Double your pleasure and plant daffodils in the same spot. This way you will have blooms in spring and fall. Fall-blooming bulbs also complement fall perennials like sedums, asters, and ornamental grasses. The foliage on these bulbs comes up in spring, then dies back in summer, all followed by fall blooms. Here are some fall bloomers:

- Autumn crocus, *Colchicum*—Looking like a giant crocus, these tough bulbs are pest-proof. Flowers are up to 4 inches across in white, lavender, and rose. Plant these bulbs where they will get partial shade in a well-drained soil.

- Crocus, *Crocus* spp.—There are a number of crocus that bloom in autumn. They vary in color and size, from 3 to 6 inches, in shades of white, lilac, and blue. Plant in a sunny location in a well-drained soil.

- Spider lily, *Lycoris radiata*—Has bright red spidery flowers on naked stems that stand out in the early fall garden. This bulb thrives in sun or bright shade with a well-drained soil.

■ *For a natural look, mix several types of bulbs together in a bucket and then scatter them on the ground. Fix the bulbs so the pointy end is up.*

- Autumn daffodil, *Sternbergia lutea*—The flowers of this small bulb look more like a yellow crocus on 4- to 5-inch stems. It produces foliage and flowers at the same time. Plant these bulbs and be patient. Some may take two to three years before they bloom well. Once they are established, wait at least six to eight years before dividing them.

EDIBLES

By now you have likely become tired of harvesting beans, corn, peppers, tomatoes, and squash. You can choose to let the whole garden wither for a few weeks . . . but don't forget to plan a fall garden: you can start buying seeds and finding out when transplants will be available at your nursery.

- Collards, kale, mustard, beets, and turnip are best planted from seed.

- Broccoli, cabbage, cauliflower, and green onion are best grown from transplants.

MAIL-ORDER SOURCES OF BULBS

Brent and Becky's Bulbs
www.brentandbeckybulbs.com

McClure & Zimmerman
www.mzbulb.com

Old House Gardens
www.oldhousegardens.com

LAWNS

August is an excellent month in which to compare your lawn to others in your neighborhood. The stress of drought, heat, disease, and insects will be evident on lawns whose owners have neglected some facet of their care. If yours is the best on the block, congratulations! If yours is not quite on par with the rest, make notes on what practices you can improve in other parts of the year to make your lawn look its best.

PERENNIALS

This is a good month to assess the successes and failures in your perennial garden. Make a list of plants you would like to add to the garden in fall once the weather begins to cool off a bit.

Think about plants that will need to be divided in fall. If plants are healthy and thriving, you don't have to divide them unless they are getting too large for the space they are growing in.

ROSES

Some roses have been developed to spread across the ground, becoming a garden groundcover rather than a shrub or a climber. The blooms may not be huge, but several groundcover roses are very resistant to diseases and insects. Use shears in spring and fall to keep groundcover roses neat and at a uniform height.

PLANTS FOR FALL BLOOMS OR COLORFUL FOLIAGE

FL = colorful foliage
F = flowers

- Amsonia, *Amsonia hubrichtii* **FL**
- Japanese anemone, *Anemone × hybrida* 'Honorine Jobert' **F**
- Aster, *Aster* spp. **F**
- Mum, *Chrysanthemum* 'Apricot Single' **F**
- Joe-pye weed, *Eupatorium purpureum* **F**
- Sneezeweed, *Helenium autumnale* **F**
- Sedum, *Sedum* 'Autumn Joy' **F**

SHRUBS

Larger shrubs provide welcome shade for some annuals and perennials, especially during the dog days of summer. Consider underplanting your shrubs with perennial groundcovers. Fall is a good time to add plants to the garden. Not only will these groundcovers add interest to the garden scene, they will help keep the roots of shrubs cool.

While ivy is a popular groundcover, there are other plants that perform equally well, making good groundcovers or companions to plant under shrubs:

- Dwarf sweet flag, *Acorus gramineus* 'Pusillus', is a diminutive grass that makes a good partner for Virginia sweetspire.

- Bugleweed, *Ajuga reptans*, has numerous cultivars with colorful foliage.

- Green and gold, *Chrysogonum virginianum*, offers yellow flowers in spring and fall.

- Lenten rose, *Helleborus orientalis*, is a great companion for rhododendrons and azaleas or witchhazels.

- Periwinkle, *Vinca minor*, is another good choice for groundcover.

VINES AND GROUNDCOVERS

It's too hot to do much in the garden this month, so plan ahead for fall. If you have areas of groundcovers that need renovating, you can spray with a nonselective weedkiller and then wait until fall to amend the soil and plant.

PLANT

ANNUALS

Few Georgia gardeners manage to keep every plant alive over a hot summer. Remove annuals that have died or become unattractive. Replace them with mature plants of the same size as those in your bed.

BULBS

Plant late-summer/fall-blooming bulbs like spider lilies, surprise lilies, and autumn daffodil.

TO DRY HYDRANGEA FLOWERS

Hydrangea flowers are great to collect and dry for decorative projects in the fall:

1. Collect blooms when they are dry, or they will rot. A good time of day to collect is after 10 a.m. and before noon.

2. If the bloom feels crisp to the touch, it is ready to cut and dry. If it feels soft to the touch, then it is still too early to harvest for drying.

3. Once you cut the flowers, strip all the leaves and remove any brown or damaged parts of the flower.

4. The best place to store the flowers is in a dark, dry, and warm place. Penny McHenry, founder of the American Hydrangea Society, once used the trunk of her car to dry hydrangea flowers. Other methods are to store them in a vase without water or to hang them upside down.

Dried hydrangea blooms will last for months or years, but the colors will fade over time.

■ *Plant ornamental grasses to add movement and flow to the garden.*

Plant spring-blooming bearded iris, and divide those that are overgrown. By doing this now the rhizomes will have plenty of time to acclimate before cold weather sets in. When planting the rhizomes, space them 1 to 2 feet apart, and cover them lightly with soil so the rhizomes are just below the soil surface. Growth is initiated from the end of the rhizome with leaves; point this end in the direction you want the iris to grow.

EDIBLES

If you are not tired of summer vegetables, several can be planted now and still yield a good harvest:

- Bush beans can be grown from seed.

- Tomato, bell pepper, cucumber, and squash can be grown from transplants.

LAWNS

If your lawn is thinning in dense shade, why not replace the sparse grass with a groundcover such as mondo grass, ajuga, pachysandra, or liriope? Even pine straw or wood chip mulch will look better than grass that's struggling along in semi-darkness.

PERENNIALS

Plant container-grown ornamental grasses that bloom in fall or that have colorful autumn foliage.

After they finish blooming, many of the seedheads provide interest well into winter. Grasses with attractive foliage or persistent seedheads include:

- Maiden grass, *Miscanthus sinensis* 'Gracillimus' (5 to 6 feet tall)

- Porcupine grass, *Miscanthus sinensis* var. *strictus* (yellow band on green foliage)

- Switchgrass, *Panicum virgatum* 'Shenandoah' (burgundy-red and green foliage)

- Fountain grass, *Pennisetum* spp. (seedheads look like foxtails and persist into winter)

ROSES

HERE'S HOW

TO TRANSPORT ROSES

If you move from one home to another in August, you might want to carry your favorite roses with you. Although transplanting in the heat of summer is not recommended, it can be done successfully:

1. Prune roses to a manageable size one week before you intend to dig them. Water thoroughly.

2. Collect a sturdy cardboard box for each plant. Line the inside with a plastic garbage bag. Poke drainage holes in the plastic.

3. Dig each rose carefully, remembering that the roots must fit in the box.

4. When the plant is in the box, cover the roots with moist soil. Insert a label with the rose name or description. Place the boxes in the shade near an outdoor faucet at your new home.

5. Inspect the plants daily, water when needed, and plant within two weeks of moving. Although you might have only bare stems left, healthy roses can usually recover their form in a year or two.

SHRUBS FOR COASTAL GARDENERS

Coastal gardeners must often consider salt tolerance and drought resistance when selecting plants for their gardens. Here is a list of shrubs that tolerate salt spray and coastal conditions:

- Groundsel-bush, *Baccharis halimifolia*
- Sea buckthorn, *Hippophae rhamnoides*
- Bigleaf hydrangea, *Hydrangea macrophylla*
- Inkberry holly, *Ilex glabra*
- Yaupon holly, *Ilex vomitoria*
- Shore juniper, *Juniperus conferta*
- Wax myrtle, *Myrica cerifera*
- Oleander, *Nerium oleander*
- Japanese pittosporum, *Pittosporum tobira*
- Rugosa rose, *Rosa rugosa*

CARE

ANNUALS

Mulches such as pine straw or shredded wood chips help conserve moisture by preventing evaporation. Placing about 3 inches of mulch 6 inches back from the base of a tree or shrub is an ideal way to maintain moisture under even the driest conditions. Fine-textured mulches hold moisture better than coarse-textured mulches. Good mulches are pine straw, pine bark mini-nuggets, and shredded hardwood mulch or chips. Avoid large-nugget pine bark, rock, gravel, and marble.

Cut back faded but healthy annual flowers by half, then water, and fertilize lightly with a water-soluble fertilizer. A second season of blooms will begin to appear in two weeks.

BULBS

Rain lilies belong to the genus *Zephyranthes*. There are both native and exotic types of this charming bulb. The autumnal flowers of *Z. candida* are triggered by rain at the end of the summer and continue through fall. The starry white blooms stand out against the dark green rushlike foliage and pop into bloom as soon as it rains. Because the bulbs are so tiny and dry out easily, it is best to purchase them when they are actively growing.

EDIBLES

Look on the ground around your blackberry and raspberry plants. Any canes snaking across the ground should be trained back to their wire arbor.

Regularly harvest squash, okra, and cucumbers. If one fruit gets too big, the plant will stop blooming.

Even though you added organic amendments to the soil when you planted in spring, some of the material has already disappeared, cooked away by the heat and rainfall of the summer. Cover the soil with a 1-inch layer of organic amendment (compost, manure, ground pine bark, and so forth), and rototill it into the earth before planting fall vegetables.

LAWNS

If there is a secret to having an outstanding lawn, it is regular, leisurely observation of the grass and making time to do a little "problem correction" each week. Weed, insect, and disease problems don't appear out of thin air—they develop over time. Even though it is hot and sultry outdoors, take time each week to walk across your lawn, ice-cold drink in hand, noting small problems and planning your response.

How long has it been since your lawn mower blade was sharpened? Cleanly cut grass is healthier and does not look yellow after mowing. Your lawn mower blade should be sharpened once each summer to avoid shredding the grass when you mow.

Often zoysiagrass does not appear to need mowing even though it may be growing higher than the recommended ½ to 1½ inches. Mow your zoysiagrass lawn regularly to avoid thatch buildup.

PERENNIALS

Perennials like salvia will continue to bloom well into fall if you keep them deadheaded; pinch or snip off the faded blossoms so that the plant puts its energy into making more flowers and not setting seed.

Remove yellow or diseased leaves of iris, but leave the seedpods for winter interest.

ROSES

Part of the enjoyment of roses is to recognize different ones by name. If you grow more than one or two roses, it can be difficult to remember which roses you have. Make it a practice to label each as it is planted, using a permanent label.

- White plastic stakes are inexpensive, but they become brittle, breaking easily after one year.

HERE'S HOW

TO PROTECT YOUR SKIN

Intense sunshine may be beneficial to some plants, but it is no friend to a gardener's skin.

- Keep containers of sunscreen in places convenient to the garden so you won't forget to apply it before working in the sun. If you dislike the greasy feel on your fingers, purchase the spray-bottle kind. Products with an SPF greater than 15 are best.

- It might be a good idea to anoint the skin under your shirt as well. A T-shirt has an SPF of only 5.

- Wear a hat to protect your face and neck.

- Long-sleeved, specially made sun-protective clothing is available at camping/hunting/outdoor equipment stores.

Regularly examine your skin for changes in moles and skin pigmentation. An annual appointment with a dermatologist is a good idea if you work in the sun constantly.

HERE'S HOW

TO DIVIDE AN IRIS CLUMP

If you are dividing a clump of iris that is crowded and producing very few flowers, lift the entire clump, and break off the healthy rhizomes. Discard any that are shriveled or leafless. You can break apart rhizomes with your hands, or separate them with a sharp knife. Let the cut ends heal for at least a few hours or up to a day before you replant them. Trim the leaves back to a height of 2 to 3 inches, and replant. The best soil to plant in is one that has been amended with lots of organic material. After planting, water well. Continue watering (check the soil on a weekly basis until frost arrives) as the plant puts down roots.

- Metal labels that stand atop two thick wire legs are durable but can be lost or pulled by accident.

- Thin metal tags that are attached to a rose stem by loose wire aren't likely to be lost but are difficult to read without risking contact with the rose thorns.

Rose blooms are borne on new growth. If you are able to water your roses regularly during this hot season, they can be cut back to stimulate new twigs that will bear flowers in September.

- In the southern half of Georgia, cut back bush roses by one-half.

HERE'S HOW

TO EASILY LIFT YOUR MOWER

The biggest reason lawn mower oil goes unchanged and the blade goes unsharpened is the difficulty of working on the machine while it is on the ground. Removing a blade is particularly difficult. If you have an aluminum extension ladder, a cinderblock, and an outdoor flight of steps, you can lift a mower to make it more accessible:

- Place one end of the ladder on the second or third step. Rest the other end on the ground.

- Position the mower at the lower end of the ladder, facing the steps.

- With a great grunt, push the mower up the slanted ladder. As the wheels leave the ground, the underside of the mower frame will scrape along the ladder frame. Shove the mower up the ladder as far as you can.

- Move the upended cinderblock close to the low end of the ladder. Lift the ladder with one hand and place the end rung on top of the cinderblock set on its end.

- The mower should now be supported 18 inches off the ground by the ladder frame. You can easily reach under it to loosen the blade attachment bolts or the oil drain plug.

Caution: Always disconnect the spark plug when working on a lawn mower.

In the northern half of the state, cut back bush roses by one-third.

Ever-blooming roses such as 'Nearly Wild' and Knock Out™ benefit from a good shearing now, even though they have many flowers.

SHRUBS

Finish any pruning or shearing now so there will be enough time for new growth to harden off before winter arrives.

TREES

After a major thunderstorm, you are probably tempted to get out the saw and clean up! Before you prune, here are some things to think about.

- You may need to hire a professional arborist or tree-removal company if large limbs are hanging or broken and require a chain saw, or if damage to the trees is up so high that an extension ladder is required to reach it.

- Always follow safety precautions. Be aware of any power lines that may be hanging in the tree. Don't touch any wires that may be on the ground.

- Remove broken branches that are still attached to the tree. Remove hanging branches and

HERE'S HOW

TO COLLECT SEEDS

Collect seeds from your favorite perennials as the seedheads dry. Seeds that require no pretreatment, such as cold exposure, can be stored dry in airtight containers or tightly sealed plastic bags. Plants with such seeds are:

- Columbine, *Aquilegia canadensis*
- Butterfly weed, *Asclepias tuberosa*
- Aster, *Aster* spp.
- Blackberry lily, *Belamcanda chinensis* (shown below)
- Blazing star, *Liatris* spp.
- Pincushion flower, *Scabiosa caucasica*

smooth ragged edges with a sharp knife; this will encourage wounds to heal faster and reduce the number of places for insects to hide.

- Don't top your trees. Cutting the main trunk back to stubs will reduce the vigor of the tree. New growth from the stubs tends to be spindly and susceptible to future storm damage.

VINES AND GROUNDCOVERS

Remove and dispose of any dead or diseased stems or twigs of vines and groundcovers. It is best to discard diseased plant material away from your compost pile. Check vines on your arbor or pergola to make sure they are not being girdled, which means the tie cuts into the stem, restricting the flow of water and nutrients. Tie up shoots that you want to train as part of an espalier.

■ *Damaged smaller branches should be pruned back to where they join a larger branch.*

WATER

ANNUALS

Water restrictions or bans make the task of scheduling irrigation in your garden a bit more difficult. Don't make the mistake of watering heavily every time watering is allowed. Many annuals can go for several days between waterings if they are irrigated heavily (by rain or your hose) once per week.

A heavy irrigation is 1 inch or more of rainfall or irrigation or 1 gallon of water per foot of plant height.

Examine plants for signs of water stress (wilting, blue-gray leaves) before you water.

When watering by hand, apply 5 gallons of water per 10 square feet. This is approximately the amount of water delivered by a garden hose operating at medium pressure for one minute.

A soaker hose can effectively water a swath 1 foot wide on either side of the hose. A 50-foot-long hose can water 100 square feet of landscape bed.

Apply 50 gallons of water per 100 square feet when plants show water stress.

Newly purchased soaker hoses are unwieldy at first as you stretch them among plants. Use soil anchor pins made from surplus clothes hangers to hold the hose in place.

Several granular products designed to conserve water have appeared in the last few years. The small granules look like grains of salt when dry; when mixed with water, they absorb the moisture and swell to many times their previous size. Manufacturers claim that by mixing the granules with the soil in a hot, dry flower bed, water can be stored and then released when plants need it. Research has shown these products hold some promise but are not "miracle" substances.

The best way to mix them with your soil is to sprinkle a few tablespoons of crystals in an

Hand-water your annuals during times of watering restrictions.

empty wheelbarrow and add water. Follow the manufacturer's recommended rate. Once the crystals have become like jelly, slowly add garden soil to the wheelbarrow and mix thoroughly. Use the soil to fill your flower bed.

Some of these water-conserving products are diminished by fertilizer; others are consumed by soil organisms. In a few years you'll have to add more of the granules to your soil in order to continue reaping the benefits.

BULBS

Water summer bulbs that are actively growing or blooming. Cannas, elephant ear, caladiums, and ginger lilies should be putting on a show now. There's no need to water spring bulbs that are dormant. Water fall-blooming bulbs when you plant them.

Mulch any new bulb plantings with 1 to 2 inches of mulch. Use buckwheat hulls, cocoa hulls, pine straw, pea gravel, or other products.

EDIBLES

Water figs and apples regularly now as they begin to ripen. Harvest every morning, before the birds can do their damage.

Water vegetables deeply once each week. (Avoid giving them light sprinkles several days in a row.)

LAWNS

Water restrictions are common summer occurrences in metropolitan areas of Georgia. Don't fall into the trap of believing that you should water your lawn whenever allowed. A deep soaking, one per week, is all a lawn needs.

PERENNIALS

Keep perennials watered during the hot dry days, but don't overwater. Feel the soil, and if the top 2-inch depth is dry, it's time to water. A thorough soaking once a week should be adequate if there is no rain. Water plants using a hose at the base of the plant. If you do use a sprinkler, place small cans nearby (tuna fish cans work well), and water until there is ¾- to 1-inch of water in the can.

Avoid overhead watering plants for like phlox or beebalm that are susceptible to powdery mildew. Keeping the foliage dry will minimize this problem.

ROSES

Sometimes rose leaves begin to wilt even though you are watering regularly. Wilting can be caused by too much water (which causes root rot) as well as too little.

- Pull mulch back from the base of the plant before you water. Scrape the soil with a trowel.

- If the soil is moist down to 2 inches deep, no water is needed. Wait until the soil is barely damp at the 2-inch level before watering again.

HERE'S HOW

TO CONTROL KUDZU

Kudzu, although not native to the South, spreads as if it has always lived here. This woody vine is native to China and Japan. Here in Georgia, an established vine can grow to reach 60 feet in one season, with leaves up to 12 inches wide and long. This hardy pest climbs and covers buildings and trees, shades their leaves, and strangles them until they die. If left untended, it keeps growing. Here are some tips for control:

- The key to success is to attack the entire area covered in kudzu at one time. Kudzu plants put out roots all along the vine, and when one section of the vine is killed, this tough plant has the ability to segment itself so that the rest of the vine can keep growing. By the end of August, kudzu plants are exhausted from vigorous summer growth and have expended most of their reserves.

- One approach to eradication is to mow all the foliage before the plant goes dormant each winter and again in spring and summer.

- Another approach is to spray the entire plant with a broadleaf herbicide containing triclopyr or glyphosate. Apply the spray until it drips off the leaves. Since the plants have no reserves, they will not have the energy to sprout many new leaves in spring.

- Watch for signs of growth in early spring. An established kudzu vine can send up sprouts for years before it is substantially weakened. Spray new growth when leaves have expanded but before the plant has a chance to harden off and spread.

- Kudzu is also vulnerable when it flowers, usually in September. The long pendulous purple flowers are fragrant and attractive for such a pesky vine. Spray the flowers and the foliage with triclopyr or glyphosate. It is quickly translocated to the roots where it kills the plant.

- Some people take advantage of these woody vines to make baskets. Collect the vines in winter, and you will have less kudzu to kill in the spring!

- If the plant continues to wilt, dig it up and examine the roots to determine if they are healthy. Healthy roots feel firm, not mushy, when squeezed between your fingers. The soil should smell "musty" but not "stinky." If the roots do seem rotted, remove them, replant the rose, and correct your watering practices.

SHRUBS

Water shrubs planted in the last six months weekly, providing 2 to 3 gallons of water per plant. Water plants growing in pots every day. Water containers until the water rushes out the holes in the bottom and sides of the pot.

TREES

Keep newly planted trees watered. Check them weekly. If you are growing trees in containers, they will need watering more frequently than those planted in the ground.

Trees need watering in summer as do lawns, flowers, and shrubs. A drought-stressed tree is more likely to suffer damage from insects and disease.

- A soaker hose laid under the drip line of the tree and an inexpensive water timer are the best tools.

- Apply 15 gallons of water per inch of trunk diameter once per week to supply a tree's minimum needs during drought. Example: a tree whose trunk is 12 inches thick, 4 feet from the ground, needs 180 gallons of water per week. Attach the water timer to the soaker hose and set it to 180 gallons; it will shut off once 180 gallons has soaked out of the hose. Depending on the length of the hose, this could take two to three hours. For this amount of water the cost is just a few dollars.

- Apply the amount calculated twice each week for optimal tree health.

VINES AND GROUNDCOVERS

Keep new plantings watered. Check them on a weekly basis. Water if the soil is dry when you dig down 2 inches with your finger.

FERTILIZE

ANNUALS

Continue to fertilize at two- to six-week intervals as discussed in May. When using granular products, be sure to water afterwards to carry the nutrients down to plant roots.

■ *Water at the base of plants and keep water off the leaves.*

Granular fertilizer is easy to spread evenly with a spreader, so many homeowners choose it over liquid fertilizer.

BULBS

Fertilize caladiums with a complete water-soluble fertilizer like 20-20-20.

EDIBLES

Fertilize newly planted vegetables with starter solution only. Do not fertilize heavily, since this increases the water needs of your plants.

Do not fertilize established vegetables and fruit now.

LAWNS

- **Tall fescue:** Do not fertilize.

- **Bermudagrass:** Fertilize now (and again in September).

- **Zoysiagrass:** Fertilize now.

- **St. Augustinegrass:** Fertilize now.

- **Centipedegrass:** Do not fertilize. Centipedegrass is naturally a lighter green than other grasses. Fertilizing with an iron sulfate product will make centipedegrass greener.

PERENNIALS

Don't fertilize until fall. Fertilizing now will encourage new growth at a time when plants are under stress from heat and drought, making them more susceptible to pest and disease problems.

Scrape away old mulch and add a new 2- to 3-inch layer; this will dress up your garden and help conserve soil moisture.

ROSES

Fertilize roses with 1 to 2 tablespoons of 10-10-10 per foot of height now, accompanied by the pruning noted below.

For a quick pick-me-up, spray rose leaves directly with a diluted liquid fertilizer. Dilute the fertilizer to one-fourth the rate recommended for soil application. One tablespoon of Epsom salts (magnesium sulfate) per gallon of liquid fertilizer adds magnesium to the soil.

PROBLEM-SOLVE

ANNUALS

The slug and snail population builds and wanes during the year, depending on the weather. The numbers can grow to such heights that most of an annual or perennial plant can be consumed overnight. Symptoms include large, irregular holes chewed in leaves, and silvery slime trails that can be seen on nearby leaves and mulch.

BULBS

Chipmunks and other rodents love to dig up your favorite crocus while it's blooming. When you plant bulbs that critters like, cover the planted area with a wire mesh. The squares should be 1 inch wide, allowing the bulbs room to emerge while discouraging animals from digging them up.

Hand-pull any weeds as soon as you notice them.

Cut fall-blooming bulbs and bring them into the house to enjoy.

EDIBLES

Whiteflies are a common pest of tomatoes and peppers (and gardenias). You can make a trap and catch hundreds of them.

LAWNS

"Brown patch" and "dollar spot" are two common lawn diseases. Both are best controlled by attention to proper watering and fertilization.

Brown patch symptoms are large circular areas of dead grass, in which the edge and center of each area may be dark green. To control brown patch:

- Keep grass as dry as possible between weekly waterings. Water between midnight and noon.

- Follow recommended fertilizer rates. Do not overfertilize.

Dollar spot symptoms appear as dozens of small dead spots. To control dollar spot:

- Water deeply each week. Do not allow the lawn to become drought-stressed.

- Keep grass healthy with a regular fertilization program.

If caught in time, both diseases can be controlled with fungicides. Fungicides are expensive and will not cure an advanced case of either disease.

If you had tremendous numbers of Japanese beetles, you might get some control by poisoning the grubs now. There is no need to use an

insecticide if you find only a few grubs when you dig. Eight to ten grubs per square foot is the threshold at which a poison should be considered.

This is the most effective time to apply grub poisons, but remember to water heavily after application, which will wash the chemical down into the soil where the grubs live. Consider using milky spore disease powder for organic grub control.

Now is also a good time to control broadleaf weeds. Use a selective weedkiller labeled for use on such pests.

PERENNIALS

Continue to check perennials for insect and pest problems. Whenever possible, use insecticidal soaps to control infestations of aphids, mites, whiteflies, and other bugs.

Whether you use organic or chemical controls, apply them only as needed.

If your plants have white powder or black spots on their leaves, they could be suffering from a fungus.

If more than 50 percent of the plant is infected, you may want to throw the plant out and start with a new plant. If only a portion of the plant is infected, there are fungicide sprays you can apply.

Keeping plants groomed will also help reduce problems. Apply any sprays during the coolest part of the day, in early morning or early evening. This way you will avoid a chemical reaction, which can occur when the insecticide reacts with high temperatures and bright sunshine, causing leaf scorch.

Columbine is often affected by leaf miners, which damage the foliage and leave it looking unsightly. Simply cut off the foliage to within an inch of the base and you should get a flush of new growth that will be pest-free.

Groom lamb's ear. Remove leaves that are yellow, brown, or mushy. This will increase air circulation and encourage the plant to put out new growth.

TO TRAP WHITEFLIES

1. Cut out two pieces of cardboard 3 inches by 4 inches in size.

2. Spray-paint the cards bright yellow.

3. Cover the cards with sticky motor oil treatment (STP®, and so forth).

4. Nail the cards to stakes driven on both sides of a plant.

5. When trapped whiteflies cover the card, clean it and reapply the sticky stuff. Or, just start with another fresh card.

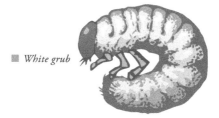

■ *White grub*

Removing weeds while they are in flower and before they set seed will help reduce weed infestations next year.

ROSES

If you read much about roses, you may see mentions of fungicide products with which you are not familiar. If the chemical name is mentioned, write it down exactly so you can take it to your local nursery. If they have never heard of it, call your county Extension office for their expertise—it is possible that the fungicide is only available to professional rose growers or that it is so expensive that the average gardener could not afford it.

SHRUBS

Continue examining plants for insect and disease problems. Sometimes a good blast of water will take care of minor insect pest problems.

TO PREPARE FOR PLANTING FESCUE

If your predominant grass is tall fescue, now is the time to kill other grasses in preparation for planting tall fescue in September.

• Spray any bermudagrass, centipedegrass or zoysiagrass with a nonselective systemic weedkiller.

• Seven days after spraying, irrigate thoroughly to encourage sprouts of the invading grass to emerge.

• Seven days after irrigating, spray the sprouts of weed grasses with nonselective weedkiller.

HERE'S HOW

TO BUILD A "PEANUT BUTTER ELECTRIC FENCE" FOR DEER

Deer can devastate a garden overnight. Many repellents have been tried, but few are effective more than a day or two. Repellents that deter deer with their bitter taste are not good choices for something you intend to eat! Wire mesh fencing is effective but expensive. You might want to try a different kind of fence—an electric fence that does not harm deer but gives them a mild electric shock when they touch it.

1. An electric fence consists of a small wire supported above the ground on insulated stakes. A special electric charger is attached to the wire and to a ground rod that has been driven into the ground. You can buy the materials from a hardware store or home improvement center for less than a hundred dollars. After you string the wire around your garden, it's time to train the deer.

2. Turn off the charger and grab a jar of peanut butter and some aluminum foil.

3. Take a tablespoon-sized wad of peanut butter in your fingers and mold it around the wire at some point.

4. Tear off a strip of aluminum foil 3 inches wide and 12 inches long, and center it over the gob of peanut-butter. Drape the foil strip on both sides of the wire. Crumple the foil where the foil touches the peanut butter. You should now have a wad of aluminum foil protecting the peanut butter from rain and a narrow flag of shiny foil hanging beneath it.

5. Repeat this procedure at 5-foot intervals along the entire circumference of the garden. At night, when hungry deer approach your garden, they will smell the peanut butter and investigate with their nose. *Kazaaap!!!* Those beans don't look quite as inviting when they are accompanied by a side dish of electricity! When the deer wander by the next night, they will be reluctant to come close to any shiny, dangling objects—no matter how good they smell and no matter how inviting the plants inside the wire seem.

6. When you install the electric fence, clear a strip of ground 3 feet wide on either side so you can walk along it every week to keep the wire clear of weeds.

Caution: Do not use an electric fence where children or unknowing visitors might come in contact with it. Post signs identifying your fence at intervals around it.

If needed, spray insecticidal soap to control aphids, spider mites, or whiteflies. You can spray insecticidal soap three to four times a week. Always spray in the early part of the day before temperatures get too hot.

Whether you are using an organic or a chemical spray, good coverage is essential. Spray the tops and undersides of leaves as well as the stems, covering completely, until the spray begins to drip off the plant. When you mix your sprays, never use more than the recommended amounts of product, whether organic or synthetic. More is not better. In fact, you can damage or kill plants by using too much chemical in one application.

Spot-spray weeds in shrub beds with a nonselective herbicide. Spray early in the morning when there are no winds and temperatures are coolest.

TREES

If the foliage on your hemlocks, junipers, or hollies is speckled with brown or red spots, they may have spider mites, tiny sap-sucking creatures that are kin to spiders. Tap a branch over a piece of white paper, and circle any spots. If they move, you will know mites are present and active. To control, first use the hose to blast these critters off the foliage. If this doesn't work, try using insecticidal soap or a miticide. Wait ten to fourteen days after you spray, then try the white paper test again.

■ *Aphids suck sap from plants and secrete honeydew.*

You may need to repeat applications of miticide for effective control.

You may notice the leaves on your mature tulip poplar trees turning yellow and dropping prematurely. Premature leaf drop, leaf scorch, and many other dieback problems are often caused by environmental stresses like pollution, or lack of moisture during hot, dry summers. The best control is to keep established trees watered and stress-free during the hot summer months.

Each week, apply at least 15 gallons of water per inch of trunk diameter.

VINES AND GROUNDCOVERS

If you have a wooded lot, chances are you have poison ivy. Identifying poison ivy is not always easy, but as a rule, avoid "vines with three leaves." Sometimes Virginia creeper, a desirable vine that has five leaflets, is mistaken for poison ivy. If in doubt, leave it alone! Purchase an inexpensive guide to plants that includes color photographs of poison ivy.

As a young vine, poison ivy crawls along the ground and eventually climbs nearby trees. If left untended, these small vines can climb up the trunks of mature trees and develop into huge vines. As a vine matures, the leaves also get larger and in the fall may turn beautiful shades of red, orange, and yellow. Don't be fooled by its autumnal beauty; this vine causes severe allergic reactions in many people. Do not use burning as a method to control poison ivy. Breathing in the fumes can cause a severe reaction in some people. There are several ways to control it. Whichever way you select, be sure to wash your clothes, gloves, and body immediately after contact with the plant.

1. If you decide to be brave and hand-pull poison ivy, be sure to wear heavy-duty gloves and a long-sleeved shirt.

2. You can also use the plastic newspaper bag method to avoid touching the plant. Slip the bag over your hand and arm. Pull the poison ivy, then carefully pull off the bag so it encloses the plant.

■ *Virginia creeper (left) is sometimes mistaken for poison ivy (right)*

September

This month often brings a few breaks from the heat of summer. Nights are occasionally cooler than you expect and daytime temperatures are more moderate. Children are back in school and flowers bloom copiously, as if they realize that winter will get here soon.

Leaves are beginning to change colors. Fall leaf drop will continue for the next few months. Raking is great exercise and you can add the leaves to your compost pile. Within a year you should have rich compost to use in your garden beds. If you don't have a store-bought compost bin, build a simple one with chicken wire and four posts.

Sweet olive shrubs (fragrant tea olive) notice the temperature change and open their tiny, inconspicuous white flowers. They produce one of the most delightful fragrances of any shrub but the leaves are so dense that the blooms are covered completely. It's fun to watch passersby stop, elevate their noses, and look around curiously for the source of the scent.

The Autumnal Equinox happens either on September 22, 23, or 24 every year. The Earth's axis is perpendicular to the sun's rays. On the equinox, night and day are almost exactly the same lengths: 12 hours. The name is derived from Latin, meaning "equal night." Despite the ending days of summer, September is as much about beginning as it is about ending. This is when you can begin plans for planting a fescue lawn with seed. Decide if it makes more sense to wipe out the whole lawn and start from scratch or overseed your struggling turf with fresh seed.

It's also a great time to plan where you'll plant trees in preparation for the actual planting operation in October. During this month you have time to take soil samples and submit them (see the Introduction). You can also call Georgia811 (by dialing 811 on your phone) to have them come out and mark the location of underground utilities on your property.

Do not prune or fertilize trees this month. Both practices can force tender new growth, which will not have time to harden off before the first hard freeze.

ANNUALS

Most large flowerbeds contain several kinds of flowers—some may be perennial, some annual, some brightly colored, and so on. When you plan the layout of the flowers in the bed, a paper sketch might not be as helpful as physically marking where the groups of different flowers will be placed. Use a sharpened stake to draw onto the soil the outline of the different flower groups. When you are satisfied, sprinkle kitchen flour into the lines the stake has made. The white flour contrasts nicely with the soil. If you need to make a change, "erase" the flour with new soil, and draw a new line with flour.

BULBS

There is still time to order your spring bulbs.

Take a soil test. Most bulbs will be happy with a pH that is slightly acidic to neutral (a pH of 7 is neutral, and less than 7 is acidic). If you're not sure about the specific requirements of a particular bulb you're growing, check with your local Extension office (see Resources, pages 221–222).

Prepare the soil in areas where you will be planting bulbs. All bulbs benefit from a soil that is rich in organic matter and well drained. To prepare the soil, spread 3 to 4 inches of organic material evenly over the area you plan to amend. Use composted horse or cow manure, leaf compost, or similar materials. You can also broadcast a complete fertilizer like 10-10-10 (follow the directions on the bag to determine the amount per square foot) evenly over the area, or you can fertilize at the time of planting. Rototill the soil to a depth of 1 foot or deeper. Bulbs need a good 6 to 8 inches of good soil underneath them for their roots. Soils that have a high percentage of organic matter make it easier for nutrients to get to your plants.

Make notes in your garden journal about what bulbs are blooming in your garden now, and how your summer bulbs fared.

EDIBLES

Just because you can find a particular fruit in the grocery store does not mean it will grow in Georgia. Varieties of fruit that do not grow well in our Georgia climate are:

- 'Bing' or any other sweet cherry—winter temperature fluctuations and late frosts kill sweet cherry blooms. (Pie cherries such as 'Montmorency' or 'North Star' produce moderately well in the northern half of Georgia.)

- 'Bartlett' pear—fireblight disease is severe on this variety.

- 'Santa Rosa' plum—late frosts kill blooms, and Pierce's disease causes severe leaf drop. It seems to have a limited life span in south Georgia, although it might grow better in north Georgia.

- Currants, gooseberry—high summer temperatures doom these plants.

- Pomegranate is a fruiting shrub familiar to south Georgia gardeners, but it is not as common in the northern third of Georgia; cold winter temperatures can freeze the plant back to its roots or kill it outright. If you would like the juicy fruit and the colorful foliage of a pomegranate, plant it in a spot protected from cold winter winds.

LAWNS

Whether you're planting seed or spreading fertilizer, an even application of material is important. The best way to accomplish this with a lawn spreader is to use the crisscross method:

1. Apply half your material in two passes going in one direction.

2. Apply the second half in two passes that are at right angles to the first application.

PERENNIALS

This is a good month to refurbish your perennial garden if it is getting overgrown and tired-looking. Decide which plants to add and which to divide or move to another location. Think about the form and texture of individual plants; include types with attractive foliage as well as those with beautiful

■ *Apply seed or fertilizer using a crisscross pattern.*

flowers. Consider all the seasons. Here is a list of plants that offer three to four seasons of interest:

S = sun lover.
SH = shade lover

- Amsonia, *Amsonia hubrichtii* (green feathery foliage in spring, blue flowers, yellow fall color, tawny foliage in winter) **S**

- Artemisia, *Artemisia* 'Powis Castle' (feathery gray-green foliage all year) **S**

- Ginger, *Asarum shuttleworthii* 'Callaway', (glossy green mottled foliage all year) **SH**

- Carex, *Carex hachijoensis* 'Evergold' (green-and-white variegated ornamental evergreen grass) **SH**

- Lenten rose, *Helleborus* × *hybridus* (glossy evergreen foliage and flowers in late winter to early spring) **SH**

- Alumroot, *Heuchera Americana*, cultivars and hybrids (colorful evergreen foliage) **SH**

- Peacock moss, *Selaginella uncinata*, (evergreen blue-green foliage) **SH**

- Lamb's ear, *Stachys* 'Helen Von Stein' (gray-green foliage all year) **S**

ROSES

If you have an informal garden, you might consider incorporating roses into your perennial flower garden. Clematis and roses make happy companions. Vigorous, free-flowering clematis vines can be easily trained to grow through a rose plant. Attach the stems to the canes with jute or string. The rose acts as a living trellis. Plant the clematis at least 2 feet away from the rose, and lead the stems of the clematis to the rose with strings or thin bamboo cane. They can also be fertilized together since they are heavy feeders.

SHRUBS

Fall is an ideal time to plant in the South. Determine now which shrubs you will add to your garden once the temperatures cool off and we get some rain. Make a list before you head out to the nursery. This way you will have an idea of what you want and won't be overwhelmed by all the choices. Plan to include some plants with colorful fall foliage and fruit.

If you haven't taken a soil test in two years, now is the time to do it. Not only will the results provide information about what you need to add to your soil in the way of nitrogen, phosphorus, and potassium (N-P-K), it will give you a reading of the pH. You could have a soil that is rich in nutrients, but if the pH (acidity or alkalinity of the soil) is too low, plants won't absorb the necessary nutrients they require for healthy growth.

Soil pH can range anywhere from 4.0 to 9.0. Most plants are happiest in a soil that has a pH between 6 and 7. Certain plants, however, have particular pH requirements. Knowing what your plants like before you plant will help you determine what to add to your soil.

Fall is a good time to amend your soil too. Organic soil amendments include mushroom compost, cow manure, chicken manure, and cottonseed meal, to name a few. Make sure you mix in plenty of amendments. Spread a 3- to 4-inch layer over the top of the soil before you rototill. Till the soil so that it is mixed in to a depth of 12 to 18 inches. If your soil has a high clay content, mixing in a layer of coarse sand 1 inch thick will help improve drainage.

If you don't have a compost pile, begin one now. Start with all the leaves that you rake up this fall. Chop up these leaves and other materials—this will lead to compost faster than if you leave the leaves whole. Add your grass clippings and kitchen scraps (minus any meats, bones, or animal fats).

To make compost, you need oxygen and moisture. Stir the pile with a garden fork every two weeks and spray it with water. Depending on the weather, you could have "black gold" in as little as six months.

TREES

With fall approaching, it's a good time to start shopping for trees. Check out this list of deciduous trees that display flowers or colorful foliage in the autumn.

- **Japanese maple,** *Acer palmatum* (many selections exhibit leaves of red, yellow, and orange)

- **Red maple,** *Acer rubrum* (many selections with colorful leaves of red, yellow, and orange)

- **Serviceberry,** *Amelanchier* spp. (leaves of red, yellow, and orange)

- **Dogwood,** *Cornus florida* (red fruits and red to purple leaves)

- **Ginkgo,** *Ginkgo biloba* (yellow leaves)

- **Witchhazel,** *Hamamelis virginiana* (fragrant yellow flowers)

- **Witchhazel,** *Hamamelis* × *intermedia* 'Diane' (leaves turn gold)

- **Blackgum,** *Nyssa sylvatica* (leaves of red, yellow, and orange)

- **Ironwood,** *Parrotia persica* (leaves in shades of red, yellow, and orange)

- **Stewartia,** *Stewartia* spp. (orange and red leaves)

VINES AND GROUNDCOVERS

Fall is a great season to add vines and groundcovers to your garden. Plan to plant as soon as the weather cools off a bit. Think about combinations of vines, both annual and perennial. Take a soil test. The results will tell you the quantities of nutrients and lime you need to add to the soil. Prepare the soil, add soil amendments, and till the areas where you will add groundcovers later this fall or next spring.

PLANT

ANNUALS

Though garden centers often have pansies and spring bulbs on hand in September, it is too early to plant them. If a bed of summer annuals is on its last legs, pull out the plants and begin preparing the soil for the cool-season planting that will begin in October.

BULBS

Continue planting fall-blooming bulbs like spider lilies, crocus, and colchicums.

Plant lily bulbs as soon as you receive them, or keep them in a cool, dry place until you plant them.

There are many different types of lilies, differing in size, habit of growth, and time of bloom. Before you plant, treat lilies with a fungicide. This usually comes in the form of a dust. Lily bulbs should be spaced 1 foot apart, but for a mass effect, you can plant them as close as 6 inches apart. Dig a hole to the required depth, and place

HERE'S HOW

TO PLANT A GROUNDCOVER

1. *Prepare your planting area by raking the soil smooth and covering with 3 to 4 inches of organic mulch such as shredded leaves or bark.*

2. *Lay out plants with the proper spacing for their species. This will differ greatly from plant to plant, so carefully read the instructions that came with the plant to avoid overcrowding or isolation. Though not a common groundcover, these pachysandra plants demand a wide berth.*

3. *Spread apart the mulch and dig holes for the plants to the same depth the plants were at in their containers. Space the plants according to the instructions, set them into their holes, and place soil around the bases of the stems.*

4. *Give the entire bed a good soaking. Water as needed the first year to make sure plants receive at least an inch of water each week.*

the bulb in the hole, spreading out the roots. Make sure it is firmly in place.

- Plant small bulbs (1 to 2 inches wide) 2 to 3 inches deep.

- Plant medium-sized bulbs (2 to 3 inches wide) 3 to 4 inches deep.

- Plant larger bulbs (3 inches or wider) 4 to 6 inches deep. One exception is Madonna lily,

Lilium candidum. Never plant them deeper than 1 inch.

Don't worry if you plant your lily bulbs too shallowly—they have special roots that will pull them down to the proper planting depth as long as the soil below is soft.

EDIBLES

In north Georgia, it's time to plant cool-season vegetable seeds and seedlings. Cabbage, lettuce,

■ *Some plants, like this broccoli, are best grown from transplants.*

collards, and broccoli transplants are available at garden centers. Lettuce, beets, turnip, spinach, and radish seeds can be planted. Onion sets (small bulbs) and garlic can be planted now as well. Be sure to soak the soil after planting. Rainfall may not occur as often as you'd like.

Plant parsley, rosemary, sage, and thyme from transplants. Examine the small pots before you buy. Sometimes several plants will be growing in one pot; you can gently separate them just before planting and get several plants for the price of one!

LAWNS

Tall fescue is a common lawn grass in the northern half of the state. Fall is the best time to plant it if you are using seed. The planting can be done successfully until mid-October, but the longer you wait, the cooler the soil becomes and the longer it will take for the seed to germinate.

- Planting a new tall fescue lawn from scratch? Use 6 pounds of seed per 1,000 square feet.

- Overseeding an old lawn? Use 3 to 6 pounds of seed per 1,000 square feet, depending on how much tall fescue already exists.

- Before spreading seed, either aerate thoroughly or scratch the soil hard with a bow rake.

South Georgia lawn-lovers still have time to plant common bermudagrass seed and get acceptable growth before winter.

Bermudagrass sod can still be planted successfully, but it would be better not to plant zoysiagrass, centipedegrass, or St. Augustinegrass sod until spring.

PERENNIALS

If you don't have any perennials that bloom in fall, now is the time to add some—try Joe-pye weed, asters, sedums, and chrysanthemums.

This is also a good season to work on improving the soil by adding organic amendments and rototilling.

A soil test before you add amendments will help you determine the best amendments to add. Then you will be ready to plant this fall or next spring.

■ *Use an aerator to alleviate soil compaction and improve drainage by removing small cores of soil from the lawn.*

A good place to start in understanding your soil is to have it tested by a soil-testing laboratory; check with your local university Extension office for labs in your area. A soil test will provide you with information on existing soil texture, pH, and fertility, along with recommendations on what to add to improve it.

1. Prepare the soil ahead of time. If you are planting a large area, rototill 12 inches deep and add soil amendments to the entire area before you plant.

   If you are planting only a few plants, you can prepare individual holes. Dig down 12 inches, and mix organic material with the existing soil. The planting hole should be twice as wide as the rootball, and the depth should be equal to the depth of the container the perennial is growing in.

2. After you plant, water well.

3. Mulch new plantings with a 2-inch-thick layer of mulch, keeping it away from the crowns of plants.

Pine straw, shredded pine bark, bark nuggets, leaf compost, or products such as ground pine bark are effective mulches that help keep roots cool and reduce weed infestations.

Once temperatures cool off a bit, it is a good time to divide and transplant perennials that have outgrown their spots in the garden or may not be performing as well as they could be. Perennials to divide in the fall include:

- **Bluestar,** *Amsonia* spp.

- **Wild ginger,** *Asarum europaeum*

- **Astilbe,** *Astilbe* spp. (can also be done in spring or summer)

- **False indigo,** *Baptisia australis*

- **False aster,** *Boltonia asteroides*

- **Turtlehead,** *Chelone lyonii*

- **Tickseed,** *Coreopsis verticillata*

- **Barrenwort,** *Epimedium grandiflorum*

- **Ferns** (many different types)

- **Daylily,** *Hemerocallis* spp. and cultivars

- **Alumroot,** *Heuchera americana*

- **Catchfly,** *Lychnis chalcedonica*

- **Iris,** *Iris* spp.

- **Phlox,** *Phlox paniculata*

- **Coneflower,** *Echinacea* or *Rudbeckia* spp.

Minimize transplant shock by cutting back the foliage by one-third to one-half at the time you transplant. This will help compensate for root loss.

SHRUBS

Plant container-grown and balled-and-burlapped shrubs.

1. Dig a hole that is at least three times as wide as the rootball. When planting balled-and-burlapped plants, it is important to loosen the burlap and any twine that is surrounding the trunk. If the material that surrounds the rootball is artificial burlap, carefully place

C. 'Arabella' (integrifolia) blue-mauve, blooms April-Sept., use trailing on the ground

C. 'Betty Corning' (viticella) pale blue, blooms May-August, climber 8-10 feet

C. 'Duchess of Albany' (texensis) bright pink, blooms April-Oct., climber 8-10 feet

C. 'Etoile Violette' (viticella) dark purple, blooms April-Oct., climber 10-13 feet

C. 'Henryi' (early large) white with dark anthers, blooms April-July, climber 10-12 feet

C. 'Josephine' (early large) double pink, blooms April-Sept., climber 8-10 feet

C. 'Madame Julia Correvon' (viticella) red wine, blooms April-Sept., climber 8 feet

C. 'Princess Diana' (texensis) luminous pink, blooms May-Sept., climber 6-8 feet

C. 'Rooguchi' (viticella) purple blooms April-Sept, 3 feet

C. 'Venosa Violacea' (viticella) white with purple veining, blooms May-Oct., climbs 8-10 feet

the plant in the hole and carefully remove as much of the material as possible without disturbing the roots.

2. Apply a 2- to 3-inch layer of mulch around all new plantings, making sure to keep it away from the main stems or trunks. This way you won't create a damp, moist environment that is conducive to potential pest and disease problems.

3. Water all new plantings once a week unless there is adequate rainfall (1 inch a week). Water thoroughly, making sure the root area is saturated. This could take anywhere from ½ to 1 hour, placing the hose at the center of the plant and allowing a pencil-sized trickle.

TREES

Plant container-grown trees this month, but wait until cooler weather to plant balled-and-burlapped trees.

VINES AND GROUNDCOVERS

Add container-grown groundcovers and vines to your garden. This is a good time to add clematis. Whether you are planting or transplanting clematis, experts recommend that you dig a hole 18 inches wide and 24 inches deep, mixing in one part good topsoil and one part composted manure. Clematis is known to put out roots to a depth of 18 to 24 inches—this is the reason for preparing such a deep hole.

Divide established groundcovers if they are crowded, or you want to move some to another area. Here's how:

- Dig up large clumps of liriope or mondo grass with a digging fork or shovel.

- Use a digging spade or straightedge shovel, and chop straight through the clump to break off sections. Shake off loose soil, but remember, the more roots, the better. Make sure each division has roots and shoots.

- Dig up individual pieces or small sections of creeping raspberry and English ivy. They put out roots all along their stems, just about anywhere they touch soil. With these particular vines there is no need to dig a deep bed, as the roots are close to the soil surface.

- Have the new planting area prepared ahead of time so that roots won't dry out.

- Water and mulch transplants.

CARE

ANNUALS

Though the weather is still hot, it's time to plan for saving the seed of some plants and rooting others to hold indoors during the winter.

Reserve a day this month to tidy up plants that have tattered leaves, dead stems, and faded flowers. Even tired plants look better when they are neat.

Take care when weeding your landscape by hand this month. There are several stinging caterpillars that feed on plant leaves; they can make a nasty welt on your skin accompanied by an intense burning sensation.

- The bright green saddleback caterpillar, ¾ to 1 inch long, has a large brown "saddle" in its back and white poisonous bristles at each end of its body.

- The puss caterpillar, 1 to 1½ inches long, has a flattened shape and is covered with brown hair that conceals stinging spines.

Control stinging caterpillars, if you choose to, with a contact insecticide or with a product containing *Bacillus thuringiensis*.

Other caterpillars are dangerous-looking but harmless. Let them go about their business, and you might be rewarded later with a glimpse of a moth or butterfly.

- A hickory horned devil, 4 to 5 inches long and blue-green with orange horns on its head, becomes a regal moth after it pupates.

- A hornworm (which comes in several varieties) has a characteristic horn on one end of its green body; it will become a sphinx moth if allowed to mature.

- Fall webworms form large colonies protected by a large web at the end of tree branches; these caterpillars are covered with white hair but are harmless.

- The spicebush caterpillar has fearsome black eyes at one end of its body; it will become a beautiful spicebush swallowtail butterfly after pupation.

BULBS

If you still have daylilies blooming, pinch off dead blossoms before they form seed unless you want to save the seed. Cut off and save any ripe seedpods from bulbs that you want to grow from seed next year. Once the pods turn from green to brown and they begin to dry out, the seeds inside should be ripe. Store the seed in a dry, cool place. If the foliage on your lilies has turned yellow or brown, it is now safe to cut them back to a height of 2 to 3 inches.

The best time to fertilize your spring-blooming bulbs is in the fall. Often we forget where we planted bulbs until they come up in spring. Use golf tees to mark the location of your bulbs; place them in a circle around a clump of daffodils or

HERE'S HOW

TO TAKE CUTTINGS FOR WINTER

1. Several plants, including coleus, pentas, begonia, and geranium, can be propagated in fall and grown indoors until spring. Use a sharp knife to take 3- to 4-inch cuttings from the ends of vigorous, unflowering branches. Remove all lower leaves; allow just two or three leaves to remain on the cutting tip.

2. Dip the cut end into a rooting hormone.

3. Fill several small pots with a 50:50 mixture of perlite and peat moss. Make a 2-inch-deep hole in the center of the rooting medium. Insert a single cutting 2 inches into a hole. Firm the medium around the cutting. Repeat until all holes are filled. Water the pots, and let drain.

4. Put the pots into clear plastic bags, and seal. Set the pots in a bright east- or north-facing window (not in direct sunlight).

5. Open the bags in three weeks. Remove the plants, and care for each as a houseplant until the weather is warm enough to set them out in April.

HERE'S HOW

TO SAVE SEED

1. As the seedpods on impatiens, cleome, hollyhock, foxglove, and moonvine dry out, collect them, and place each in a separate envelope. In a week or so, the pods will split and release the seeds.

2. Seedheads from perennials like purple coneflower, Shasta daisy, black-eyed Susan, and others can be collected when dry and gently crumbled above a sheet of paper. Separate the seeds from the pods, petals, and chaff as best you can. One way is to purse your lips and blow gently on a mound of seed. Place the cleaned seed in a small envelope, and label it clearly.

3. Insert several envelopes of seed into a pint jar. Enclose 2 tablespoons of dry milk powder in tissue paper, then wrap with a rubber band. Slip this into the jar with the seed.

4. Tighten the jar lid securely, and place it on a back shelf of your refrigerator. A storage temperature between 35 and 45 degrees Fahrenheit plus the drying action of the milk powder makes an excellent environment to keep the seed viable until next spring.

other bulbs. When fall arrives, you will know where to fertilize. You can also use plants to mark where you have bulbs planted. If you plant daffodils in a bed of groundcover, fertilize the groundcover in autumn and the bulbs will be fertilized, too. Because grape hyacinth foliage comes up in the fall, you can plant it to mark where clumps of daffodils are.

EDIBLES

Show your kids how to eat a muscadine: pop it in your mouth, suck the pulp out of the skin, enjoy the juice, then spit out the skin and seeds. What a delicious mess!

Wrap cheesecloth around sunflower heads to keep the birds away. The head is ready to harvest when the back has turned from green to brown.

If your late tomatoes aren't setting fruit, the reason could be poor pollination due to heat and humidity. Use an electric toothbrush to vibrate each flower cluster two to three times a day for three days. Or lightly tap each flower cluster with a pencil four to five times a day for three days.

Remove dead limbs from fruit trees and vines. Remove short stubs that have weak sprouts growing from them.

■ *Muscadine grapes have tough skins but delicious pulp inside.*

LAWNS

After planting tall fescue seed, it must be mulched with wheat straw to protect it from birds and to hold soil moisture. Use no more than one bale of straw per 1,000 square feet.

If you raised your mowing height to help your grass during the summer, lower it to the proper height now.

PERENNIALS

Add some fall bloomers to extend the season in your garden. Here are a few to consider:

- **Aster** (many different species and selections)

- **False aster,** *Boltonia asteroides*

- **Perennial plumbago,** *Ceratostigma plumbaginoides*

- **Chrysanthemum** 'Apricot Single' or 'Hillside Sheffield'

- **Joe-pye weed,** *Eupatorium purpureum*

- **Sneezeweed,** *Helenium autumnale*

- **Jerusalem artichoke,** *Helianthus angustifolius*

- **Mexican bush sage,** *Salvia leucantha* (a tender perennial, it often blooms until frost)

- **Salvia** 'Indigo Spires'

- **Toad lily,** *Tricyrtis hirta*

ROSES

Continue to remove faded flowers from ever-blooming roses. Prune out dead stems. Pull weeds as they appear. Edge your beds using a hand-powered or motorized edger.

Prune hybrid tea and grandiflora roses to remove dead limbs and to shape them for winter.

SHRUBS

Prune only dead, damaged, or diseased branches during this season.

TREES

Remove any dead or diseased branches, but wait until trees are dormant to do any severe pruning. Trees that are pruned now before they are completely dormant could experience cold damage. This damage occurs when new young growth sprouts during mild spells and doesn't have time to harden off before winter sets in.

If your tree has a long dark line running from the top of a branch all the way to the ground and its bark is split open and peeling back from the trunk and branches, you probably have lightning damage. Prune back exploded bark to a healthy strong attachment. Water the tree regularly. Do not fertilize. Only time will tell if the tree will survive.

SHRUBS WITH COLORFUL FALL FOLIAGE OR FRUITS

F = colorful foliage
FR = colorful fruits

- **Bottlebrush buckeye,** *Aesculus parviflora* **F**

- **Chokeberry,** *Aronia arbutifolia* 'Brilliantissima' **FR**

- **American beautyberry,** *Callicarpa americana* **FR**

- **Beautyberry,** *Callicarpa dichotoma* **FR**

- **Sweetshrub,** *Calycanthus floridus* **F**

- **Sweet pepperbush,** *Clethra alnifolia* **F**

- **Fothergilla,** *Fothergilla gardenia* 'Mt. Airy' **F**

- **Oakleaf hydrangea,** *Hydrangea quercifolia* **F**

- **Finetooth holly,** *Ilex serrata* **FR**

- **Winterberry holly,** *Ilex verticillata* **FR**

- **Crapemyrtle,** *Lagerstroemia,* many cultivars **F**

- **Viburnums,** *Viburnum dilatatum* 'Iroquois' **FR** and *Viburnum setigerum* 'Aurantiacum' **FR**

HERE'S HOW

TO PRESERVE HERBS

Herbs can be harvested and preserved throughout the summer and early fall. Here are two methods of keeping them for wintertime use:

Freezing

1. Rinse the herbs quickly in cold water, shake off the excess, then chop coarsely.

2. Place large pinches of herbs in an ice cube tray, cover with water, and freeze.

3. Transfer the cubes to plastic bags or airtight plastic containers. Freeze until needed.

   Do not refreeze herbs after thawing.

Drying

1. If the herbs are clean, do not wet them. Otherwise, rinse the foliage, shake off excess water, and spread the herbs out to dry on paper towels until all surface moisture has evaporated. Remove any dead or damaged foliage.

2. Tie the stems into small bundles with string, and hang them upside down in a warm, dry place out of the sun. Make small, loose bundles, and allow for good air circulation around each bunch.

3. To air-dry herbs with seeds, tie the herbs in small bundles and suspend inside a paper bag with holes punched in the sides. Suspend the bag in a dark area with good air circulation. Collect the seeds when they are dry, and store in dark containers.

Sage, thyme, dill, and parsley are easy to dry. Basil, tarragon, and mint may mold if not dried quickly.

VINES AND GROUNDCOVERS

Limit your pruning to dead or diseased leaves, stems, and twigs on vines.

Prune off dead or diseased leaves on groundcovers, but don't cut them back severely now—wait until they are dormant.

Cut off seedpods as they ripen from annual vines like the purple hyacinth bean, moon vine, and others. Do this on a cool, dry day. Remove the seeds from the pods as soon as possible, carefully cutting away the seedpod. Keep seeds cool and dry until you sow them next spring. If you store them in plastic baggies, like sandwich bags, be sure to include a label with the name of the seed in the bag. Seeds from your garden make great gifts for the holidays.

For gardeners who like edible ornamentals beyond grapes, there are a number of uncommon ornamental vines that also produce tasty fruits.

- **Hardy kiwi,** *Actinidia arguta,* is a heavy bearer of greenish purple edible-skinned fruits the size of grapes.

- **Bitter melon,** *Momordica charantia,* has light green lobed and puckered leaves and bright orange fruits that split open to reveal red interiors.

- **Maypop,** *Passiflora incarnata,* fruit is prized for its juice.

- **Passionflower,** *Passiflora* 'Incense', has egg-shaped fruits.

- **Fern-leaved blackberry,** *Rubus laciniatus,* produces slightly tart berries.

- **Five flavor berry,** *Schisandra chinensis,* has fragrant white flowers and bright red edible fruits.

WATER

ANNUALS

Watch "indicator plants" like impatiens and pentas for signs of drought stress. When these plants are drooping, it's time to water your flowerbeds.

BULBS

Continue to water lily bulbs until the foliage turns yellow and begins to collapse. Adjust the watering to reflect the change in season. Don't let lily bulbs dry out, but don't overwater either. Push your finger into the soil. When the top 2 inches are dry to the touch, water thoroughly. For one plant that is well established, use 1 gallon of water. Let it soak in, then apply another gallon.

EDIBLES

This month is typically dry and hot in all parts of Georgia. Late-maturing vegetables need plenty of water for their fruit to ripen. Water deeply at least once per week.

Check the soil with a trowel after you water. Make sure the moisture has penetrated 6 inches.

Water pecan trees if rainfall is scant. This is a critical month for the nuts—they will not fill out if water is lacking.

LAWNS

After tall fescue seed has been planted, it must be watered regularly until the seeds have established a good root system. If you are under watering restrictions, getting good seed-to-soil contact is very important. Your goal is to keep the top ½-inch of soil moist at all times.

PERENNIALS

Even as the weather begins to cool off, it is important to keep plants watered. If there is no rain, water perennials about once a week, especially transplants and new plantings. Apply 2 gallons of water for a 1-gallon-size perennial.

ROSES

The usual lawn sprinkler system is fine for your turf but bad for roses; wet leaves lead to diseases that are almost impossible to control. Try a drip system or use black rubber soaker hoses instead.

- Drip systems come in kits containing all the parts to water several plants.

- Soaker hoses can be snaked near each plant under the mulch. The soaker hose is attached directly to your water hose.

Black rubber soaker hoses are sold wrapped in a tight circle that is almost impossible to untangle and lay out without help. You can do it single-handedly by slightly pressurizing the hose with water.

- Choose a hot day; wear old clothes and tennis shoes.

Soaker hoses apply water slowly and evenly.

- Lay out the soaker hose near your plants.

- Connect the soaker to your water hose. Turn on the water at full flow for a moment.

- Cut the water flow to a trickle, just enough for a bit of water to weep from the soaker.

- Pull back mulch, put the soaker in place, and re-cover with mulch.

- An inexpensive water timer attached at the faucet makes watering your roses a breeze.

TREES

Continue to check newly planted trees weekly, and water them if you don't get at least 1 inch of rain per week.

VINES AND GROUNDCOVERS

Even as the weather starts to cool off a bit, don't forget to water new plantings. Any groundcovers or vines that have been planted in the last six months should be checked on a weekly basis to see if they need water.

FERTILIZE

ANNUALS

Continue to fertilize at two- to six-week intervals as discussed in May. When using granular products, be sure to water afterwards to carry the nutrients down to plant roots.

BULBS

Fertilize bulbs when you plant them, using a complete fertilizer like 10-10-10 or a specialty bulb fertilizer. This is the key time to fertilize spring-blooming bulbs.

To help improve drainage and make nutrients readily available, add lots of organic material and mix it in with the existing soil.

If you use a complete fertilizer, like 8-8-8 or 10-10-10, it is safer to topdress after you plant the bulbs. If you add it directly to the hole when you plant a bulb, there is the possibility of burning young, tender roots.

EDIBLES

Fertilize newly planted cool-season vegetables. Since the soil is quite warm, water-soluble liquid fertilizers will push the plants off to a fast start.

Apply lime to your garden according to the results of your soil test.

LAWNS

Tall fescue: Fertilize after the middle of the month (and again in November). Use a starter fertilizer (which usually has a high percentage of phosphorus) for the first application if you planted tall fescue seed. Use any brand of turf fertilizer for subsequent feedings.

Bermudagrass: These lawns benefit from a "winterizer" fertilizer application now when growth has slowed but before the grass turns brown. The best date is six weeks before you estimate the first frost will occur in your region. A winterizer fertilizer helps bermudagrass get off to a strong start in spring—this fertilizer contains a moderate percentage of nitrogen and higher-than-usual percentages of phosphorus and potassium.

Zoysiagrass: Do not fertilize at this time.

Centipedegrass: Do not fertilize at this time.

St. Augustinegrass: Do not fertilize in north Georgia. Fertilize in south Georgia only if the August feeding was missed.

PERENNIALS

While it is not necessary to fertilize, you can topdress your perennial plantings with mushroom compost, horse manure, cow manure, or a similar product. (To topdress means to spread a thin layer 1 to 2 inches deep on top of the soil). This will help keep the soil healthy, and plants will respond by developing strong root systems.

ROSES

Fertilize each plant mid-month with 1 to 3 tablespoons of 10-10-10 per foot of plant height, or use a water-soluble fertilizer.

Some rose growers swear by the magical powers of alfalfa pellets (sold at seed and feed stores as animal food). Alfalfa tea is a great fall potion that doesn't interfere with normal rose growth.

1. Add 10 to 12 cups of alfalfa meal or pellets to a 32-gallon plastic garbage can that has a lid.

2. Add water, stir, and steep for four or five days, stirring occasionally; you may also add 2 cups of Epsom salts.

3. The tea will start to smell in about three days, so keep the lid on. Schedule the opening of the barrel for when the rest of the family is away.

4. Use a gallon of brown "tea" on large rosebushes to make strong canes and green leaves late in the growing season.

TREES

Wait until spring to fertilize newly planted trees. As long as they are thriving, established or mature trees don't need to be fertilized. However, if you want to topdress your trees with an organic material such as mushroom compost or horse or chicken manure, now is the time to do so. Topdressing breaks down over time and feeds the soil. This is also a good time to apply a fresh layer of mulch around trees. Scrape away old mulch, and apply 1 to 2 inches of topdressing and 2 to 3 inches of fresh mulch.

VINES AND GROUNDCOVERS

Wait until spring to fertilize perennial vines and groundcovers. If you want to topdress areas where you have vines planted, use mushroom compost or well-rotted horse or cow manure. This will provide good organic material, which will provide nutrients as it breaks down over the winter and next spring.

PROBLEM-SOLVE

ANNUALS

The seeds of winter annual weeds such as chickweed, henbit, and annual bluegrass begin sprouting later this month. You can prevent them in your beds of winter flowers by applying a weed-preventer by mid-month. Read the label on any

■ *Tunneled rhizomes indicate the presence of iris borers. Remove and destroy any infected plants.*

product you are considering to make sure it can be used on flowers. Be sure to irrigate thoroughly after applying the weed-preventer to dissolve the chemical into the soil.

BULBS

Your bearded iris leaves may have turned yellow and have dark streaks. If the leaves pull off easily and the plant dies, you probably have iris borers. Borers can hollow out the rhizomes, which then become infected with a bacterial rot. To prevent this problem, pull off and destroy old brown leaves in the fall and winter. Provide excellent drainage as well.

To prevent unwanted crops of chickweeds and other winter weeds in established beds, apply a granular weed preventer. Note: Read the label carefully before applying any pesticide.

A pre-emergent weed control should be used only if bulbs are established (they have been growing and thriving in the same area for two or three years). Some bulbs may be sensitive to this type of chemical.

EDIBLES

Big green caterpillars on parsley and fennel are the larvae of beautiful swallowtail butterflies. Try not to kill them all. Better yet, plant plenty of parsley and fennel so there is enough for you and the caterpillars.

Fall webworms construct ugly nests at the end of pecan and other tree branches. The webbing protects the caterpillars from weather and predators. The best control is the simplest: poke a long, limber branch into the web and pull it from the tree to expose caterpillars to the elements.

LAWNS

The seaport of Brunswick has the honor of being the introduction point of a destructive lawn pest in south Georgia: the mole cricket. Adult insects tunnel just below the surface of the soil. They feed on grass roots, but the grass suffers great harm just from the drying out of loosened soil. The best first step to mole cricket management is correct watering, fertilizing, and mowing height.

Insecticides are most effective when applied in June, although cricket damage is most noticeable in September.

After applying sprays or granular poisons, irrigate immediately to dissolve the poison in the soil.

The "Georgia Two-Step" fire ant control technique is extremely effective when applied now. The combination of a bait and a mound treatment now can bring fire ants to their knees.

"Winter" weeds germinate in fall but wait to make their appearance the following spring. Chickweed, annual bluegrass, and henbit are common winter weeds.

Mid-September is the best time to apply a pre-emergent winter weed-preventer.

Before planting tall fescue seed, wipe out weeds with a fast-acting but short-lived weedkiller.

■ *This caterpillar will turn into a swallowtail butterfly.*

Use a nonselective weedkiller now, and you can plant grass seed in seven days. Many tough-to-control summer weeds are at their weakest now from summer stress.

Apply a broadleaf weedkiller to violets, wild strawberry, and wild onion in your lawn.

PERENNIALS

Certain poisonous caterpillars and other chewing insects blend in with plant foliage and are difficult to see. Wear gloves that cover you up to your elbows if you are hand-checking leaves for pest problems. The saddleback caterpillar is common now, and the sting is painful like a bee sting. Its name comes from the purplish brown saddle on its green back.

There are also greenish yellow caterpillars with black stripes that run horizontally instead of lengthwise. You don't want to kill these caterpillars even though they eat the plant, because eventually they will turn into beautiful monarch butterflies. This late in the season the monarch larvae won't harm the plant permanently.

You may notice that your *Asclepias tuberosa*, butterfly weed, is covered with yellow aphids. In this case the safest way to get rid of the aphids is to blast them off with the hose.

Cut back flowers when they finish blooming, and remove any foliage that is diseased or dying. This will reduce the number of places for unwanted pests to overwinter.

Leave attractive seedheads, like those of Sedum 'Autumn Joy' or *Baptisia australis*, for winter decorations.

ROSES

Caterpillars are not typically a major rose pest, but September is the month you'll notice them, if at all. Caterpillar damage is usually in the form of irregular holes chewed at leaf edges. Small leaves may have more than half of the leaf consumed. The disease spore *Bacillus thuringiensis*, commonly called B.t., is an excellent caterpillar control. B.t. is not harmful to birds or humans or other

HERE'S HOW

TO CONTROL ARMADILLOS

Armadillos can be a pest on lawns and flowerbeds. They root through the soil looking for grubs to eat. Your landscape will look like a group of small bulldozers visited during the night!

- Use 24-inch-tall fence wire and short wooden stakes to construct a simple funnel trap facing the area from which the animals come each night.

- The mouth of the funnel should be 30 to 50 feet wide.

- The trap sides should taper down to a width of 12 inches—just wide enough to place the opening of a large live trap in the armadillo's path.

- Call your local animal control office for directions on what to do with the captured animal.

mammals. Apply the spray or dust thoroughly to cover your rose leaves.

B.t. is deactivated within a few days, so repeat applications may be necessary.

Replace all the mulch under your roses. This will prevent diseases on next year's leaves.

SHRUBS

Removing diseased leaves from around shrubs will reduce insect and disease problems next year.

If deer are a problem, the best solution is to build a fence. Often this is not possible and gardeners must resort to other tactics. There are organic products reputed to repel deer and discourage other browsing animals because of their taste and smell; look for them in garden centers.

If you have problems with whiteflies on gardenia, try blasting them with a jet of water from the hose.

Spray with insecticidal soaps to control aphids and spider mites. Be sure to get good coverage—spray until it drips off the plant.

To prevent unwanted crops of chickweed in established shrub beds, apply a granular weed preventer. Read labels carefully before using any pesticide.

If you have a weedy area where you want to plant shrubs in the spring, you can use newspaper to smother the weeds. Put down a layer of newspaper, about three to four sheets thick, and then cover it with mulch. Come spring you can rototill the area, add soil amendments, and plant.

One of the advantages of not using chemical sprays to control insect and disease problems in your garden is that beneficial insects that can help control pest problems will not be killed. For example, ladybugs are known to feed on aphids, mites, scale, and many insect eggs. Praying mantises feed on a wide range of insects.

TREES

Fall webworm attacks certain deciduous trees including birch, maple, cherry, linden, willow, honeylocust, and crabapple.

- Unlike the eastern tent caterpillar, which builds its nest in the spring, the fall webworm is not noticeable until late summer or early fall when the nests appear at the end of the branches.

- Since defoliation is minimal and occurs late in the season, at a time when trees naturally begin to drop their leaves, there is generally no cause for alarm.

- Destroy any nests that can be easily reached by pruning them out (if possible, burn the infested branch once you have removed it from the tree), and don't worry about those you can't reach.

Gather fallen leaves, and add them to an existing compost pile or use them to start a compost pile. One way to speed up the process of leaf decomposition is to mow with a mulching mower. The chopped leaves will turn into compost more quickly.

Bamboo is an attractive plant for screening, but it is extremely hard to control. It spreads by aboveground rhizomes and belowground roots. A clump can expand more than 20 feet in just a few years. To control bamboo as it is planted:

- Transplant small clumps in spring, just before growth begins.

- Identify where you want the plant to grow—and where you don't want it. Dig a

■ *To keep deer out of the garden, a fence must be at least 6 feet high.*

▪ A leaf blower can make quick work out of cleaning the lawn of leaves. The blowing action also clears organic debris down to the soil, helping ready the lawn for winter.

trench 18 inches deep around the area. A powered ditching machine is a great help in this endeavor.

• Insert 24-inch-wide aluminum roof flashing edgewise in the trench, leaving 2 inches showing above the soil surface. Lap the ends of the flashing at least 18 inches over each other.

To control bamboo once it has escaped, chop down every cane in the area where you do not wish it to grow. Bamboo shoots will continue to arise each spring where the canes were chopped down. Inspect the spot weekly, and knock down the shoots as they arise. The bamboo roots will eventually starve if you are diligent about removing the shoots.

If the scale-like leaves on your cryptomeria are turning yellow and brown and the plant looks wilted, you may have phytophthora root rot, a secondary problem that occurs in soils that are poorly drained or wet. The best way to avoid this problem in the future is to select the right plant for the right place. If your soil is poorly drained, select tree species that will thrive in this environment.

You may notice caterpillars with spines and barbed horns chewing on the leaves of your oaks, hickories, or maple trees. If you do, you are being visited by the orange striped oakworm, whose eggs were laid on the branch by a moth in June. These caterpillars are about 2 inches long with eight yellow stripes and a row of large yellow spots. It is disturbing to see an entire branch stripped of its foliage, but the damage done by the caterpillar is not serious (the tree is about to lose its leaves anyway this season).

Handpicking is an option; be sure to wear gloves. If the tree is small or newly planted, spray the leaves with *Bacillus thuringiensis*. It is not likely that the caterpillars will return next year, even if you do nothing about them.

VINES AND GROUNDCOVERS

Check vines and groundcovers for signs of dieback or root rot, such as black stems or a group of leaves that are partially black and wilted. If a section of groundcover is suffering because of poor drainage, dig up the plants and add coarse sand (builder's sand or small crushed stone) to the soil. Replant only the healthy portions, and discard those with unhealthy roots or foliage. Sometimes starting over completely with new plants is the most cost-effective control.

Check for insect problems like aphids or mites. The more insects you eradicate this fall, the fewer will overwinter and cause problems next spring. If you notice only a few pests, use a blast of cold water from the hose to control them. If there is a severe infestation, use an insecticidal soap or a synthetic pesticide.

Use a granular weed-preventer in established groundcover beds to prevent winter weeds like chickweed and hairy bittercress.

October

Remember that burst of gardening energy you had back in April? The earth was warming up, the birds were singing, flowers were popping and you had to get out and garden!

Despite that fact that the earth is cooling and birds are departing, this month should be a time of renewed devotion to your landscape.

True, much of what you do won't have immediate results, but the eventual benefit will be enormous.

Did you ever get around to liming your lawn or garden? This is the perfect month! Can you remember how excited you were to see early-blooming bulbs last February? This is a great month to plant them. Want winter color by your mailbox and entryway? It's the best time to plant pansies and ornamental greens. Like saving money? Nurseries put perennials and woody plants on sale now to clear the way for Christmas trees.

If you are dreaming of fresh strawberries for your cereal next spring, plant some now. You can grow them in containers or in the ground.

This is a month of planning, preparing, and planting but make sure you take time to enjoy the garden too. Cooler temperatures and softer light make it easy to overlook any mistakes in the garden. Colorful fall foliage, blooms, and berries abound, both native and cultivated plants. Take note of the berry-bearing shrubs in your garden and if you don't have any, think about adding some that both you and the birds will enjoy. Beautyberry looks good paired with asters and ornamental grasses. And, in the wild, if you're lucky enough to spot it, it grows in combination with our native smoke tree.

Opportunity arrived in spring and it reappears in October. Don't miss it!

PLAN

ANNUALS

This is pansy-planting month throughout the state. Follow these tips in order to have color from their blooms in your landscape in winter.

Timing: In north Georgia, begin planting in early October as daytime temperatures fall into the 70s. In south Georgia, begin planting mid-October or later. Ideal conditions are when the weather is predicted to be cool for the next several days.

Bed preparation: Pansies have fine roots and need very soft soil in order to grow well. They cannot tolerate soggy soil. Rototill a 2-inch layer of organic material into prospective pansy beds.

Spacing: Pansies can be planted at a 6- to 10-inch spacing between plants. The smaller spacing results in a fuller bed but may make pansies more susceptible to disease due to crowding next spring. Use a 10-inch spacing when planting 3- or 4-inch-sized potted plants.

BULBS

Gardeners who live in the warmest parts of the state (coastal gardeners and those who live in zone 8 or 9) need to pre-chill some of the spring-flowering bulbs before they plant them. Although it is possible to purchase bulbs that have already had a pre-chilling treatment, it is easy to do yourself. When purchasing bulbs, be sure to read the fine print. If bulbs are pre-chilled, that should be stated on the package; otherwise, it is safe to assume they are not pre-chilled.

Many of the large tulips require ten weeks of pre-chilling. Place them in a breathable bag in the refrigerator. Keep them away from any ripe fruit that releases ethylene gas, as ethylene gas can interfere with the production of flowers. After this pre-chilling they will be ready to plant in the garden once the soil temperatures are 60 degrees Fahrenheit or cooler.

Some daffodil cultivars require a minimum of fourteen to sixteen weeks of constant cold before they will initiate flower buds. (Check with your local Extension office about the best bulbs for your region. Bulb suppliers should provide specific information about cold requirements for specific bulbs.) Store them in a breathable bag in the refrigerator for six to eight weeks. They will be ready to plant in the garden when the soil temperatures are 60 degrees Fahrenheit or cooler at a depth of 3 to 4 inches.

You can force bulbs to bloom early for blooms indoors, or you can bring them out to the garden and place the pots around for additional color in the spring.

If you want to force bulbs to bloom earlier than they normally would, you can pot them up and store them in the refrigerator or in a room where the temperature can be held below 60 degrees Fahrenheit while the bulbs are rooting for six to eight weeks. After this period, store them at a temperature of 35 to 45 degrees for another six to eight weeks. If it is cold enough outdoors (35 to 45 degrees), you can place the pots under a mulch pile. Daffodil expert Brent Heath recommends using a potting mix that is coarse so that roots will be able to penetrate easily and there will be good drainage. Mixes that contain peat moss, ground pine bark, perlite, and granite sand work well. Water the bulbs when you pot them up, and then only when the soil surface feels dry to the touch.

■ *As temperatures cool down, October is the perfect month to plant pansies.*

When potting up the bulbs, they should just be touching one another, depending on the size of the pot—for example, five bulbs are good for a 6-inch pot.

Once roots begin to emerge from the bottom of the pot, bring it into the house or greenhouse. A temperature of 70 degrees is ideal—the top of the refrigerator is usually this warm or warmer. Give your bulbs the maximum amount of daylight so that they develop strong stems; grow lights can be used to provide supplemental light in the evening.

Check pots regularly now to see if they need water. Water when the soil is dry to the touch, but don't overwater. There is no need to fertilize your bulbs unless you want to plant them in the garden after they finish blooming (be sure the threat of frost has passed). In this case, use a water-soluble fertilizer that is high in phosphorus, potash, and trace elements.

EDIBLES

One of the joys of gardening in Georgia is our long growing season. Gardeners in Minnesota report that their two seasons are "winter and the Fourth of July!" North Georgia gardeners are fortunate to experience 200 to 250 frost-free days per year; south Georgia gardeners may enjoy close to 300 days without freezing temperatures.

The average date of first frost in Atlanta is November 13. Frost has been recorded as early as October 25 and as late as December 6.

The average date of first frost in Tifton is November 21. The earliest recorded frost date occurred October 26, while the latest was December 20.

The most likely date for a last frost in Atlanta is March 27. The earliest date for a last spring frost was February 16, and the latest frost in spring occurred on April 23.

The average date for the last frost in Tifton is March 6. The earliest date a final frost occurred was January 27, while the (surprise!) date for a late spring frost was April 1.

LAWNS

Before you can move into a new home, it must pass a final inspection and receive a "certificate of occupancy." The county housing inspector won't grant a certificate of occupancy if the lawn has not been planted or sodded. The installation of grass is often the last thing done by the builder before the home sale.

- If you have any input into the decision, make sure the appropriate grass has been chosen for your lawn.

- Annual ryegrass is sometimes allowed, but remember that it must be replaced with a permanent grass in spring.

- Ask the builder how the soil was prepared before seed or sod was planted.

- Test the softness of the soil by pressing a pencil into the earth—if it penetrates more than 2 inches easily, grass can grow readily. If the soil seems rock hard, you will have endless problems with your lawn in the future.

- If you are not satisfied that the new lawn will succeed, negotiate appropriate guarantees or concessions at closing.

PERENNIALS

This is an ideal month to add spring-blooming perennials to your garden. Make sure the soil is well prepared and that you have an idea of "what blooms when" before you start adding more plants. Make up a planting list, including information about flower color and the size of the plant and its texture.

Photograph your garden and make notes in your garden journal about plants that offer autumn interest.

ROSES

One of the best ways to succeed with roses is to grow varieties recommended by experts. When you have proven that roses are easy to grow in your landscape, you can branch out to grow varieties about which you know nothing but that intrigue you.

■ *You can plant shrubs, trees, vines with trellises, annuals, and perennials in containers to create gardens where there's little space or no soil.*

TREES

Ginkgo is a handsome large tree whose leaves turn golden in the fall. Its only disadvantage is the messy and offensive-smelling fruit that the female tree produces. To avoid this problem, plant only male cultivars purchased from a reliable source. Male selections grafted or grown from cuttings of other males include 'Autumn Gold', 'Fairmount', and 'Princeton Sentry'.

As trees begin to drop their colorful fall foliage and prepare for winter dormancy, nurseries will begin to dig trees for fall planting. These balled-and-burlapped trees should be planted as soon as you purchase them, to ensure the roots acclimate as quickly as possible. Before planting, loosen the burlap around the main trunks of balled-and-burlapped trees, and take container-grown trees from their containers. To plant a balled-and-burlapped tree:

1. Dig a hole that is at least twice as wide as the rootball and no deeper than the rootball.

2. Cut holes in or remove the burlap that surrounds the rootball. This allows better penetration of water for the roots and helps the tree to become established more quickly.

3. After planting, water thoroughly (water the tree weekly for the first year).

4. Mulch with a good 2- to 3-inch layer of compost, shredded pine bark, pine straw, or other similar materials, being sure to keep it from direct contact with the main trunk. (When the mulch is thick and comes into contact with tree bark, and we have lots of rain, the tree is bound to have insect and disease problems.)

5. Water the tree weekly for the first year.

VINES AND GROUNDCOVERS

Looking at plant combinations in nature is often the best teacher of what can work in your own garden. Deciduous trees provide the perfect living trellis for many vines. The key is selecting those vines that will make good companions for particular trees. A chosen vine should never be so vigorous that it suffocates the tree, and the tree should not be so strong as to overshade the vine.

When planting, keep in mind that the soil near the tree roots may be on the dry side. For this reason it is best to apply a good 2 inches of mulch around the roots of the vine, using caution to keep it away

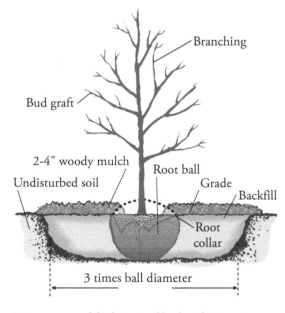

■ *Remove as much burlap as possible when planting a tree.*

from the main stems. If you start with a small vine, in a 1-gallon pot, it will be easier to dig a hole large enough to accommodate the vine. Self-clinging vines like climbing hydrangea and Virginia creeper are well-suited for training on trees, but those that climb by tendrils also make happy companions for many trees. Train vines like Carolina jessamine, American wisteria, trumpet creeper, and crossvine to grow up dead but sturdy small trees. In this way their aggressive nature becomes an asset.

Because the soil near tree roots is often exhausted and shady, certain vines like clematis should be planted a good distance from a mature tree (4 feet).

1. Plant on the sunny side of the tree so the clematis will get a good start.

2. Use bamboo canes or strings to guide the vine into the tree.

3. Once the clematis reaches the tree, it will decide where it wants to grow.

PLANT

ANNUALS

In north Georgia, plant poppy, larkspur, and sweet alyssum seeds now. Lightly scratch the ground around fading perennial flowers using an iron rake. Scatter seeds lightly. Press into place in the soil with the palm of your hand. Do not cover with earth, since these seeds need light to germinate. Do not water; allow nature to nurture the seeds. Little seedlings will germinate by November and they can be thinned. The seedlings will survive the winter without harm and will grow into larger plants next spring.

Pansies are not the only sources of flowers for fall through spring—dianthus, snapdragon, stock, and viola easily withstand winter weather conditions. Ornamental kale and cabbage as well as lettuce and parsley can lend their colorful foliage to your winter landscape.

BULBS

In the middle and northern parts of the state, you can plant spring bulbs provided the soil

temperatures have cooled off to 60 degrees Fahrenheit. Use a soil thermometer to measure the temperature at 3 to 4 inches deep.

Start paperwhites in pots so you will have blooms for Thanksgiving. By staggering the times you plant paperwhites, you can have fragrant blooms indoors from Thanksgiving well into the New Year. Paperwhites do not require a chilling period before they grow and bloom, and some will be in bloom three to four weeks after you pot them up. Keep them in a cool, dark place until they put on a good bit of growth (the foliage should be 3 or more inches tall). At this point, move them gradually into the light.

If you are potting up lots of bulbs for forcing (paperwhites and other types too), use a potting mix that is one part coarse builder's sand, one part perlite, two parts peat moss, and two parts ground pine bark. All pots must have drainage holes. You may place a pot with drainage holes in a decorative pot that doesn't have holes if you like.

Fill the pot three-fourths full with the soil mix. Place the bulbs in the pots, with the sides barely touching, then fill in with small gravel or pebbles to hold the bulbs in place. As the bulbs begin to grow and the stems stretch, stake them so they won't fall over once they begin to bloom. Try placing three attractive bamboo stakes in the pot, at equal distances from one another, and use a natural jute twine or raffia to form a ring around the stakes. Water the bulbs after you pot them up, and then only when the soil is dry to the touch.

EDIBLES

Dream of strawberry shortcake for next June! Plant strawberries in a well-tilled bed. Good strawberry varieties are 'Chandler', 'Florida 90', 'Earliglow', 'Cardinal', and 'Delite'.

- Plant them 12 inches apart, preferably in a raised bed.

- Cover plants lightly with pine straw to protect them for the winter.

In south Georgia, all fall vegetables can still be planted. Cabbage, lettuce, collards, and broccoli transplants are available at garden centers. Lettuce, spinach, and radish seeds can be planted. Onion sets (small bulbs) can be planted now as well. Be sure to soak the soil after planting. October is typically a dry month, and rainfall may not occur as often as you'd like.

Clip out the woody flower stems of mature parsley at ground level, taking care not to damage new leaves that have emerged there. Dig the plants and plant in 6-inch pots to bring indoors to a sunny window.

Although parsley is usually winter hardy outdoors, you'll have fresh parsley handy to use through November if you bring it indoors.

LAWNS

Bermudagrass turns brown and dormant in winter. To avoid this brown look, one can overseed the bermudagrass with annual ryegrass. The ryegrass will be green in winter but will die out in early summer.

1. Mow the bermudagrass as low as possible without your mower blade hitting the ground.

2. Spread ryegrass seed evenly at a rate of 5 to 10 pounds per 1,000 square feet.

3. Fertilize with starter fertilizer.

4. Water thoroughly, then keep the top ½-inch of soil moist thereafter.

Caution: Overseeding with ryegrass may weaken the underlying bermudagrass because it competes for available nutrients during the winter. Follow all bermudagrass maintenance recommendations during the year to help it withstand the stress of being overseeded in the winter. Do not overseed thin or weak bermudagrass lawns.

Tall fescue seed can still be planted, but don't delay. Cold soil causes the seed to germinate unevenly.

PERENNIALS

Amend planting beds with organic materials. Rototill to a depth of 12 inches if possible; add perennials to your garden.

Herbaceous peonies generally love cold weather, but there are a few varieties that perform well in southern gardens. Tips for growing herbaceous peonies in Georgia:

- Plant single or Japanese forms.

- Plant varieties that are early-flowering.

- Provide afternoon shade.

- Provide support for heavy flowers. Stake early with rings they can grow through.

- Some varieties for southern gardens are 'Festiva Maxima', an old-fashioned favorite with double white flowers flecked with red; 'Sarah Bernhardt', with double pink flowers; 'Imperial Red', with single red flowers; and 'Seashell', which has single pink flowers.

Divide plants of Italian arum after the leaves appear. This shade-lover provides handsome foliage in the fall and winter garden.

ROSES

This is an excellent time to transplant roses. As plants lose their leaves, less water is demanded from the roots; the soil is still warm, and root growth can occur in the new bed before winter.

Rose growers can be divided into three classes: lackadaisical, committed, and fanatic. Those in the first class dig a small planting hole, shove the rose in place, and hope it survives. Committed rose growers rototill their soil and add organic amendments. Fanatic rose growers develop their very own special rose soil and use it whenever they plant.

If you are one of the fanatical rose growers, you can take the advice of Pat Henry, the owner of Roses Unlimited. She digs a hole 18 inches deep and wide, fills the hole halfway with the soil mixture described on the facing page, then packs more around her rose roots as she plants it. Pat swears by the results!

SHRUBS

Both soil and air temperatures are cooler now, and with any luck we have had some rain. Plants and people are less stressed now than they were during the hot months of summer when keeping hydrated takes precedence over planting. Now is an ideal time to add new shrubs to your garden or move existing shrubs. Prepare the new location ahead of time so that the rootball will stay out of the ground for the least amount of time. The size of the rootball will be determined in part by the size of the shrub. When transplanting shrubs, be sure to dig a rootball large enough to ensure there are plenty of roots. If you can manage lifting a large rootball, remember that bigger is better.

TRANSPLANTING

- If your shrub is 2 feet tall and wide, start digging out about 12 to 18 inches from the center of the plant.

- Dig at this distance all the way around, loosening the roots as you go.

- Then dig under as far as you can and cut the roots so the rootball is free from the hole.

- With two people and two spades, you have the advantage of working on opposite sides.

■ *When transplanting roses, carefully backfill the hole with loosened soil and water thoroughly so the soil fills in around the roots leaving no air pockets.*

PAT HENRY'S SPECIAL ROSE SOIL

In a wheelbarrow, mix enough of the following ingredients, in the proportions indicated, to fill the hole:

one part compost
one part peat moss
one part good topsoil
one part red clay

Add and mix thoroughly:
1 cup 0-46-0 (superphosphate)
1 cup dolomitic lime
2 cups alfalfa meal or pellets
1 cup gypsum

- Once the rootball is free, take a piece of burlap and slide it under the rootball. This will make it easier to move to its new home.

- When you plant your shrub in its new spot, make the planting area a bit higher than the surrounding soil. Plant the shrub so that the top of the rootball is at the same level as the soil surface in the planting area. This is the best way to provide excellent drainage for the roots.

- Fill in with soil and water in.

- Apply a 2- to 3-inch layer of mulch.

If you have an area that you want to plant next spring, you can prepare the soil now. Spreading 2 to 3 inches of composted manure on top of the soil and tilling it in immediately will result in a soil that is rich in nitrogen and ready to plant in spring.

If possible, perform a soil test before you begin planting this fall. When you plant, you may want to add a cup of garden lime and fertilizer, which can be mixed into the individual planting hole. If you use an organic product like animal manure, make sure it is well composted so it won't burn the roots of plants.

Mulch all new plantings with 2 to 3 inches of mulch.

■ *Gently spread roots wide so they are pointing outward as much as possible.*

Make sure any homemade compost or manure is well rotted (this usually takes about six months) before you use it in the garden. By following this practice you will avoid "burning" tender young growth with ammonia. While most shrubs are not likely to put on new growth in the fall, tender growth in the spring can burn if compost is too fresh.

TREES

October is a great month to plant both evergreen and deciduous trees in Georgia. In the more northern parts of the state they will still have time to establish roots before winter, and in the southern parts of the state, soils will be cooler and less stressful for new plants.

Although it is tempting to transplant small dogwood or magnolia trees from the woods into your landscape, this is usually not a good idea.

VINES AND GROUNDCOVERS

Plant container-grown vines and groundcovers this month. When planting clematis, a 2-foot-deep planting hole is recommended, filled with equal parts of soil and compost. Set the crown at least 1 inch deep (some experts suggest 3 to 4 inches deep). Water generously, and apply 2 inches of an organic mulch. To encourage better branching as well as an abundance of larger

flowers, cut the clematis back by half at the time of planting.

If you are growing ornamental sweet potato vines you can dig the tubers and overwinter them now. They are also edible, but stringy. Some have handsome foliage, like 'Blackie', which has leaves of dark purple brown; 'Margarita', which has chartreuse foliage; and 'Tricolor', which has leaves of pink, white, and green.

CARE

ANNUALS

The magnificent leaves of banana trees and elephant ear tubers will not survive a freeze. Though it is a bit of work, they can be stored for winter and planted outside once again in late spring.

To store banana trees: Cut off all leaves close to the main trunk. Use shovels to excavate a rootball approximately 24 inches in diameter. Wrap the rootball tightly with burlap or sheet plastic. Invite friends to help you move the leafless trunk and its rootball to your basement or to a place where temperatures will not go much below freezing.

■ *Plant the crown of a clematis a few inches below ground level to help keep the roots cool.*

TO OVERWINTER GERANIUMS

Geraniums with an attractive flower color can be removed from the ground and kept indoors for the winter. Although keeping the plants in a sunny window will allow you to observe them daily, a geranium's fleshy stem and roots allow it to survive a few months in darkness.

- Water plants thoroughly a week before frost is predicted.

- Dig individual plants and place in separate paper bags. Medium-sized grocery bags are ideal.

- Place several bags in a cardboard box. Put the box in a cool place, such as a basement or garage.

- Check on the plants at Christmas; moisten the soil with a spray bottle; remove yellow leaves. Repeat in mid-February.

- In late March, bring the plants into a moderately shady, protected spot, and water thoroughly.

- In a week or so, sprouts will emerge from the stems, and the plant can be planted in its spring/summer home (remember to protect from freezing with a covering of pine straw if a late frost threatens).

To store elephant ear tubers: allow frost to kill the leaves. (Use caution when chopping green stems; the sap can damage your eyes.) In the northern third of the state, dig the tubers and allow them to dry in a covered spot. Store in a place where temperatures are between 50 and 70 degrees Fahrenheit. A cool basement is actually not as good as a closet upstairs. In the lower two-thirds of Georgia, elephant ear tubers will usually survive the winter when left in the ground.

Remove summer annuals as they deteriorate. It is usually easier to remove everything all at once from a bed, even though some annuals are still blooming. Rototill the soil, and add organic amendments before planting any winter annuals.

BULBS

Forcing daffodils is fun and rewarding. Below is a list of the best varieties to force as recommended by Brent Heath.

- All paperwhite narcissus
- 'Abba'
- 'Bridal Crown'
- 'Cragford'
- 'Garden Princess'
- 'Ice Follies'
- 'Johann Strauss'
- 'Jumblie'
- 'Kassels Gold'
- 'Little Beauty'
- 'Little Gem'
- *Narcissus obvallaris*
- 'Pipit'
- 'Rijnveld's Early Sensation'
- 'W.P. Milner'

EDIBLES

Prepare your composting area for fall leaves. You can make an inexpensive bin from a piece of wire fence 4 feet wide and 10 feet long:

1. Join the two ends to form a hollow wire barrel.

2. Place a pile of small limbs 6 inches high on the bottom for best air circulation.

3. Pile leaves and other compostables on top of the limbs.

Bring some rosemary inside to dry for winter use.

Dig sweet potatoes, but let them "cure" in a warm place for five days before you store them in a cool basement or unheated garage. Curing changes starches to sugar.

Harvest winter squash and pumpkins before they are damaged by frost. They can be stored in a cool, dry spot for months.

A compost bin can be made out of something as simple as some wire fencing.

Cool weather brings a reminder that tomato vines can't bear freezing temperatures. Follow these tips to store green tomatoes:

- Leave fruit on the vines up to the last week before a frost is imminent.

- After picking, remove stems and dry-wipe to remove dirt.

- Sort out fruit that have a bit of pink showing around the stem. These will ripen quickly in a sunny window.

- Select remaining green fruit that have reached mature size and turned whitish green.

- Wrap individual tomatoes in sheets of newspaper. Place gently in a cardboard box in your basement or a very cool room.

- Green tomatoes will ripen very gradually in storage. Check weekly for rot.

For best flavor, remove from the box and place in a warm window a few days before you need them. If you still have leftover "love apples," look for a good fried green tomato recipe

LAWNS

Moss is a common inhabitant of lawns that are shady or constantly moist. Moss-control chemicals are available, but they are not permanent solutions to the problem. For permanent moss control:

- Loosen the soil deeply to make it drain faster.

- Reduce shade by removing low limbs of nearby trees.

- Correct the waterflow problems that cause the soil to be wet.

Important: Lime does not eliminate moss. Although moss prefers acidic soil, liming will not control the moss unless the environmental conditions mentioned are corrected.

Mow warm-season grasses as needed while the weather cools. You can stop mowing after the first frost.

Mow tall fescue as needed.

PERENNIALS

Cut back spring-blooming perennials now, but wait until early spring to cut back fall-blooming types as well as certain other perennials like artemesia; these overwinter better when you leave them unpruned.

If you add new perennials to the garden this fall, draw a rough sketch indicating where they are in relation to existing plants. This will make it easier to separate the flowers from the weeds next spring when plants begin to sprout. Save the labels for any new plants that you add to the garden. This way you can refer to them if you forget the name of a certain variety once it begins to grow and bloom, and you will be able to match descriptions to names.

Some perennials grown for their foliage look good most of the year, even in winter on a frosty morning:

- Dianthus 'Bath's Pink', *Dianthus gratianopolitanus*

- Epimedium, *Epimedium grandiflorum*

- Alumroot, *Heuchera Americana* (and many selections of this plant)

- Phlomis, *Phlomis fruticosa*

- Lamb's ear, *Stachys* 'Countess Helen von Stein'

- Yucca, *Yucca filamentosa* 'Bright Edge'

ROSES

Prepare for the winter by doing these things:

- Tip back long canes that are in the way as you walk through the garden.

- Re-tie the canes of climbing roses to their support structure. It is easier to do this now than when icy winds are howling through your garden.

- Pull weeds from underneath your plants.

Miniature rose plants are often a temptation when seen at a garden center or on the floral aisle of a grocery store. The plants are small enough to keep indoors and enjoy through the coming winter. Unfortunately, miniature roses kept indoors never seem to prosper. They are susceptible to spider mites, root rot, leaf diseases, and low humidity. To maximize your chances for success, heed the following tips:

- Place miniatures near a very bright window but not touching the glass. Plan to turn the pot halfway around each week to keep the plant symmetrical.

- If you don't have a well-lit window, build a light stand (see February).

- Water only if the soil seems dry to the touch. Do not overwater.

- Keep a sharp eye out for spider mites or mealybugs on the leaves. Control them at once with an insecticide labeled for indoor use.

- Though the blooms are small, a miniature rose planted outdoors will eventually rival in size of some of the larger-blooming types.

Take time to examine each rose plant individually. Prune out any dead branches or weak limbs.

Several rose societies meet regularly in Georgia. To find the group nearest you, write the American Rose Society:

The American Rose Society
PO Box 30000
Shreveport, LA 71130

The society's website (www.ars.org) offers a huge amount of information on rose culture, expert advice, and rose society contacts.

SHRUBS

Prune dead or diseased wood from established shrubs. If there are any wild shoots or suckers, you can also remove them. (Suckers are shoots that arise from roots or underground stems.)

TREES

Wind, humans, and animals can sometimes uproot newly planted trees.

- For small trees, two stakes hammered into the ground near the trunk are adequate. Use a soft rope or cord. Loop a figure eight around the trunk, and tie it to the stake.

- For larger trees, use three stakes placed at equal distances around the tree, outside

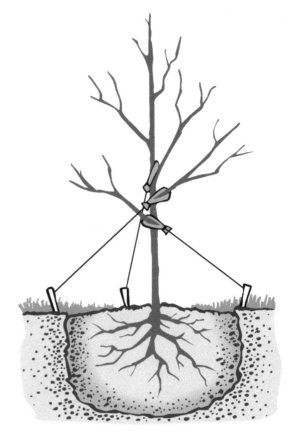

■ *Stake newly planted trees to help prevent high winds from uprooting them.*

the root system. Use cord or wire, covered in rubber hose to protect the trunk. Loop the wire around the trunk, and attach it to the stake. Allow for some slack in the cord or wire. The trunk should be able to move a little as it grows so it will develop strength.

- Stake small trees for six months and larger trees for a year.

VINES AND GROUNDCOVERS

Limit your pruning to removing dead or diseased wood of vines.

There are a number of vines that exhibit colorful leaves or leaves with interesting textures. Here is a list of both annual and perennial types that are noted for their foliage.

SHRUBS FOR FALL AND WINTER INTEREST

E = evergreen
D = deciduous

- **Burning bush,** *Euonymous alatus* (leaves turn fiery red in fall) **D**

- **Fothergilla,** *Fothergilla gardenia* (exhibits red, orange, and yellow foliage in fall) **D**

- **Inkberry holly,** *Ilex glabra* (olive-green leaves) **E**

- **Mountain laurel,** *Kalmia latifolia* (glossy green leaves all year) **E**

- **Drooping leucothoe,** *Leucothoe fontanesiana* (dark green leaves turn purplish bronze in winter) **E**

- **Nandina,** *Nandina domestica* (many selections, some with leaves in intense shades of red) **E**

- **Catawba rhododendron,** *Rhododendron catawbiense* (large green leaves) **E**

- **Himalayan sweet box,** *Sarcococca hookeriana humilis* (glossy dark green foliage) **E**

- **Skimmia,** *Skimmia japonica* (evergreen leaves and brilliant berries) **E**

- **Prague viburnum,** *Viburnum pragense* (glossy green foliage) **E**

- **Variegated Japanese hop vine,** *Humulus japonicas* 'Variegatus' (annual), has handsome variegated leaves that brighten the garden all summer until frost.

- **Climbing hydrangea,** *Hydrangea anomala petiolaris* (perennial), has leaves that turn buttercup yellow in fall.

- **Virginia creeper,** *Parthenocissus quinquefolia* (perennial), has leaves that turn shades of purple, red, and crimson in fall.

- **American wisteria,** *Wisteria frutescens* (perennial), has leaves that turn yellow in autumn.

WATER

ANNUALS

Plants dry out rapidly on sunny days, even when temperatures begin to cool off. Don't wait for plants to wilt; check soil moisture regularly with your fingers.

BULBS

Water your bulbs as soon as you plant them. Give them a good soaking. If you apply 1 inch of water, it should reach roots at a depth of 6 inches in a soil with a moderate amount of clay (30 to 40 percent). Applying double this amount should be enough for bulbs that are planted as deep as 9 to 10 inches.

EDIBLES

Though you may need one hose to keep fall vegetables watered, you won't need all the components you used during the heat of summer. Drain and store water hoses, sprinklers, and soaker hoses to avoid winter damage.

LAWNS

Water newly planted tall fescue lawns regularly.

Water recently sodded lawns deeply so the water penetrates 4 inches into the soil below the sod layer.

Drain your lawn irrigation system before winter arrives:

HERE'S HOW

TO HARVEST AND CURE GOURDS

- Gourds must reach maturity on the vine.

- Once stems turn brown and dry, it is safe to cut and remove gourds.

- To preserve their colors, store gourds in a cool, dry place.

- The American Gourd Society recommends the following recipe to preserve gourds:

Mix 1 cup of borax into 3 cups of hot water. Stir until dissolved. Let the mixture cool to lukewarm. Bring another pot of water to boil. Dip the gourd into the boiling water briefly, then soak it in the borax solution for fifteen minutes. Do not rinse. Hang gourds in a cool place to dry for several weeks. Provide the best air circulation possible. Gourds can be waxed with a good-quality floor wax when they're dry.

1. Turn off the water valve that supplies your system.

2. Allow the system timer to run through all its cycles in its normal manner. Much of the water in your pipes will run out of the lowest irrigation heads. The water that remains will not be under pressure and will not hurt components if it freezes. The system should be fine when you turn it on next year.

An alternative is to purchase a maintenance contract from an irrigation contractor. The workers will check the operation of all of your heads before draining the system in winter. They may also want to shoot compressed air through the pipes to remove all remaining water. They will also check the system again in spring.

Store water hoses where you won't be tempted to move them when they're frozen. A hard-frozen hose is brittle; leaks may result if it is flexed when cold. A hose reel is very handy for hose storage throughout the year.

■ An oscillating sprinkler is a good choice for both small and large lawns because you can control the coverage efficiently by varying the water pressure.

PERENNIALS

Be sure to keep plants well watered, especially new plantings and recent transplants. If you don't get 1 inch of rain, set out sprinklers, and water until there is ¾ inch of water in a nearby tuna fish can.

ROSES

One way to minimize watering and weeds at the same time is to use landscape fabric under your roses. Landscape fabric is a porous plastic material that allows water and fertilizer to come through but does not allow weeds to grow up through it.

1. Spread the fabric over your well-tilled rose bed before planting.

2. Cut an "X" with a razor knife where you wish to plant a rose.

3. Plant through the fabric. Tuck the fabric around the stem when finished. (If you decide to use the fabric after your roses are established, cut the fabric into strips that can be placed between and alongside individual plants. Avoid arranging the fabric more than two layers thick.)

4. Cover the landscape fabric with mulch.

5. Remove and renew the mulch every two years. As it decomposes, weed seeds will sprout in it, which is the situation you're trying to avoid.

SHRUBS

Keep all new plantings well watered. Check them weekly and water as needed if there has not been a good rain (1 to 2 inches is a good rain). Don't let the cooler weather fool you. Wind can also cause plants to dry out more quickly.

TREES

Keep newly planted deciduous trees or conifers well-watered (newly planted trees are those planted within the past six months). Conifers will survive the winter much better if their needles or scales are filled with water when they go into winter dormancy—they will be less likely to dry out from winter winds.

VINES AND GROUNDCOVERS

Water plants that have been planted within the last six months, unless they receive at least 1 inch per week of rainwater. Check weekly to see if they need water.

FERTILIZE

ANNUALS

Pansies and other cool-season plants bloom wonderfully during the winter as long as they receive proper nutrients. Fertilizing cool-season plants is different from fertilizing summertime annuals because the soil is cold while they are growing and blooming. Soil organisms that help release fertilizer nutrients in warm soil are not very active in chilly soil.

- Immediately after planting, fertilize with a water-soluble fertilizer.

- Repeat two weeks later if daytime temperatures are still in the 70s.

- Every four weeks, while the soil is cold, fertilize with a product that contains a high percentage of nitrate nitrogen. Nitrate nitrogen does not rely on soil organisms to convert it to a form the plant can use. (Fertilizer products that do not contain nitrate nitrogen do very little for pansies that are growing in cold soil.) Continue to fertilize according to label directions until March 15.

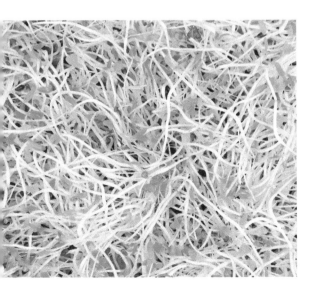

■ *Alfalfa makes a good cover crop when planted in the fall.*

- Resume fertilizing, with a water-soluble fertilizer, in late March. Fertilize every two weeks until you replace cool-season plants with summer annuals.

BULBS

If you plant spring bulbs now, you can topdress with a complete fertilizer like 10-10-10 or specialty bulb fertilizer. If you mixed fertilizer into the soil when you tilled it, there is no need to fertilize again.

EDIBLES

If parts of your garden will not be used until next spring, you can improve the soil and prevent erosion by planting a cover crop now. Plants can be tilled into the soil just before you plant next spring. Good cover crops are:

COVER CROP	SEEDING RATE PER 1,000 SQUARE FEET
Crimson clover	3.3 ounces
Winter wheat	40 ounces
Annual ryegrass	½ to 1 pound
Alfalfa	80 ounces

If you decide not to plant a cover crop over your garden for the winter, at least mulch the garden with wheat straw to prevent erosion. The straw will be almost completely decomposed by spring.

LAWNS

Tall fescue: There's still time to give tall fescue lawns that first fall feeding. Use any turf fertilizer. Use a starter fertilizer for the first application if you planted seed.

Bermudagrass: May be fertilized with a low nitrogen, high potassium product in south Georgia.

Zoysiagrass: Do not fertilize at this time.

Centipedegrass: Do not fertilize at this time.

St. Augustinegrass: Do not fertilize at this time.

Fireplace ashes can be scattered over your lawn rather than disposing of them. They provide a bit of phosphorus and potassium, plus they counteract acidity, just like garden lime. Spread no more than 10 pounds per 1,000 square feet per month. Caution: Never store ashes in a flammable container; always place them in a covered metal pail.

PERENNIALS

Topdress perennials with 2 inches of organic materials like composted manure (cow or horse), mushroom compost, or composted leaves. Take care to keep compost away from the stems and crowns.

Fertilize established herbaceous peonies with 8-8-8 and bonemeal. Read the product label for recommended amounts.

ROSES

Do not fertilize now. The nitrogen in the fertilizer could cause your roses to be less cold tolerant.

SHRUBS

You can use a starter fertilizer when planting your new shrubs. Starter fertilizers have a high percentage of phosphorus to help plants establish roots quickly. A 10-52-17 ratio is fine. You can also fertilize shrubs with a balanced fertilizer such as 10-10-10. Read the label carefully before applying any fertilizers.

TREES

If your trees are growing well, there's no reason to fertilize. If you decide to fertilize, first get a soil test—it will help you determine which nutrients you need to add in the spring

VINES AND GROUNDCOVERS

There is no need to fertilize groundcovers or vines now, but it is a good idea to prepare the soil in new beds, adding organic material before you plant, whether you will plant later this fall or next spring.

PROBLEM-SOLVE

ANNUALS

Before the first frost, newly planted pansies are sometimes devoured by caterpillars of the fritillary butterfly. Symptoms are leaves that have been consumed back to the mid-vein. Look for small black droppings on the soil under the plant. Spray affected plants immediately with *Bacillus thuringiensis* (B.t.).

If you plant in early October, or if you've had caterpillar problems before, consider applying a preventative spray of B.t. or a contact insecticide just after planting.

BULBS

Clean up any dead or diseased leaves on your summer bulbs. Dispose of these in the garbage. This will reduce the spread of potential insect or disease problems that might otherwise overwinter.

EDIBLES

Use a hoe or rake to remove sprouts of chickweed in your garden. The plants may be small now, but they will cause a big problem if left unattended until spring. Rake out and replace all the mulch and dead leaves under peach, pear, apple, and crabapple trees. You'll prevent diseases on next year's leaves.

Clean all the old vines from tomato cages before putting them in storage. Many pests overwinter in plant debris such as vines, stems, and leaves.

Pull out withered plants and put them on your compost pile or rototill them into the soil.

LAWNS

Don't forget to spread a weed-preventer as soon as possible on established lawns to suppress weeds such as chickweed, annual bluegrass, and hairy bittercress next spring.

Remember that weed-control chemicals can harm germinating seed as well as grass that is going dormant:

- Do not apply a weed-preventer to newly seeded tall fescue lawns.

- Do not use "weed and feed" products or a broadcast application of broadleaf weedkiller on any turfgrass at this transitional time.

■ *Apply fire ant treatment to individual mounds.*

- Spot-spray broadleaf weeds that pop up this fall.

The effectiveness of the "Georgia Two-Step" fire ant control depends on doing it while ants are actively foraging for food:

- In south Georgia, you can use the Two-Step technique until the weather becomes chilly.

- In north Georgia, treat individual mounds with contact insecticide.

PERENNIALS

Keep beds free of diseased or dead leaves. This helps eliminate conditions that encourage insects to overwinter.

Use insecticidal soap for minor insect problems.

ROSES

Rose mosaic virus is a common rose disease that seems to do little harm. It appears as a bright yellow mottling on individual rose leaves or small branches. The disease is not fatal to plants, but it may reduce flowering and cause early autumn leaf drop. The disease is not spread by insects, by water splash, or by pruning tools. Amateur rosarians simply prune off the affected leaves.

Professionals seek out roses from reputable growers who can guarantee that their plants are disease-free. These roses will remain healthy unless accidentally infected.

SHRUBS

There should be fewer insect problems as the weather cools off, but continue to check for signs of damage. Use an Integrated Pest Management (IPM) approach. This includes selecting varieties of plants that are best suited to grow in your environment and eliminating those that have proved to be in constant need of spraying just to keep them healthy. Check euonymous for scale, azaleas for lace bug, and rhododendrons for black vine weevil.

TREES

Rake up any diseased leaves, and dispose of them separately from the compost pile. This will cut down on the possibilities for spreading pest and disease problems in the future.

Prune out any dead or diseased wood from newly planted trees.

VINES AND GROUNDCOVERS

During mild weather, certain insects may still be active. Check for evidence of aphids or scale. Signs may include distorted leaves or shoots, or brown hard spots on the undersides of leaves. If there is a mild infestation, spray with insecticidal soap or horticultural oil.

Rake up leaves that cover your groundcovers. The better the light and air circulation, the happier they will be. Add these leaves to your compost pile, or use the lawn mower to chop them up. Finely chopped leaves can be put back on your flowerbeds as mulch.

November

November is a month of drastic change. One day your majestic ginkgo has all of its yellowing green leaves. On the next day the leaves have all turned butter yellow and dropped precipitously to the ground, making a golden carpet.

There are also unexpected surprises like Japanese maples that seem to color up overnight, showing off fiery shades of red, orange, and yellow. When the autumn is mild you may even have a few roses that brave the weather. Look for lingering blooms from salvia and chrysanthemums. If you grew gourds in your garden, they are ideal to use for Thanksgiving decorations. Pumpkins left in the garden will give you a chance to make delicious pies. Don't forget to roast the seeds too!

There is still plenty of time to plant spring-flowering bulbs. If you add daffodils, hellebores make great companions. Look for varieties like 'Ivory Princess', 'Pink Frost', and the upright bear's foot hellebore.

Frost has nipped the leaves from Shasta daisy, and the brown flower scapes of your daylilies stand forlornly, waiting to be removed. Bermudagrass lawns that were a vibrant green in summer have quickly gone buff brown.

Underground, change happens as well. White grubs burrow deeper to escape winter cold. Brown leaves begin to break into smaller pieces and become enmeshed with the upper soil layer, where earthworms consume them and excrete them as castings.

With your landscape "undressed," you can cast a critical eye toward the structure of your trees. The most important thing to look for is co-dominant trunks. When two tree trunks both head for the sky, parallel to each other, nothing good can result. Inevitably one will press the other out of place and the weaker will come crashing to the ground. This is particularly evident in maple, poplar and flowering pear trees. Once the leaves have dropped, pruning can commence. Remove or shorten by half the smaller of two co-dominant trunks.

And most of all, remember to give thanks for your glorious garden.

PLAN

ANNUALS

Many gardeners dream of having a greenhouse in which they can putter with their plants throughout the weekend. Greenhouse kits can be purchased from home improvement centers or through special garden catalogs. Before you invest a great deal of money, consider the following questions:

Do I have a proper site and enough room?
The greenhouse should be in full sun to avoid high winter heating bills. Siting it near trees invites frequent damage to the glazing. Municipal building codes often limit how close you can build next to a property line. Check with your local zoning office.

How will I provide heat to the greenhouse?
Solar heating will not keep it warm on cold winter days. A natural gas or electric heater will be required.

How will I provide electricity?
The cost of running an electric line from your home to the greenhouse can be substantial. Installation should only be performed by a licensed electrician.

■ *A wood frame greenhouse with sheet-plastic cover is an inexpensive, semipermanent gardening structure that can be used as a potting area as well as a protective greenhouse.*

How will I provide water?
Extending a water line can be accomplished by a handy gardener, but a trench must be dug at least 12 inches deep in which to place the pipe.

BULBS

If you don't have any daffodils in your garden, consider adding some this fall. Daffodils are among the most satisfying of bulbs to grow because they thrive with just a minimum of care once they are established. Knowing the best varieties for our Georgia climate will help ensure your success. Prepare the soil where bulbs will be planted.

EDIBLES

One of the most important practices of a smart gardener is to keep notes on what happened in the garden during the year. The notes can be kept formally in a journal, or informally in a shirt pocket-sized spiral notepad or on a smartphone. Now that the growing season is all but over, take time to jot down anything you would change for next year.

- Did your tomatoes perform as you expected?

- Was brown rot a problem on your fruit? How (and when) can it be prevented next year?

- Were the rows spaced properly, or should you make adjustments next year?

- Were you able to harvest something almost every month? Were some months heavier than others? Did this overload your ability to use the produce? Should more or less of some items be planted?

- How well did your weed- and insect-control measures work? Should your prevention methods be put into action earlier?

LAWNS

On a warm day, walk across your lawn and note any problems that could be cured during the next growing season.

- Does the grass grow evenly in all areas?

- Are particular spots prone to weed and disease problems?

- Was it easy to mow all areas?

- Could the size of your lawn be reduced to save water and maintenance time?

It is a common practice of builders to install bermudagrass sod in the front lawn and to plant tall fescue in the back. Remember that if you have two different grasses, they will have two different management schedules:

- Tall fescue is fertilized and mowed in the cool months but not in summer.

- Bermudagrass is fertilized and mowed in summer but not in winter.

If the backyard is sunny, consider converting to bermudagrass or zoysiagrass.

PERENNIALS
In all but the most northern parts of the state, this is a good month to add container-grown perennials to your garden before the ground freezes.

ROSES
More than a few gardeners avoid roses because of their thorns. Though most roses have thorns of varying ferocity, some are known to be quite amiable.

SHRUBS
Once leaves fall, examine the structure of your shrubs and determine if they need pruning. Wait until they are dormant in winter or early spring before you do any drastic pruning. If two branches are rubbing or crossing, remove one of them.

TREES
This is an ideal month to plant trees in Georgia, provided the ground is not too wet. To determine the ground's wetness, dig up a shovelful of soil. If you can form a loose, crumbly ball that holds together briefly but still breaks apart easily, then the soil is just moist enough for planting. If you can't get the shovel out of the ground easily, then it is too wet.

Redbud flowers

Evergreen trees provide interest in the landscape all year long, serving as focal points, wind barriers, screening, and hedges, while large deciduous trees provide welcome shade in the summer. Once you have large key trees sited, it is a good time to think about adding understory trees that will grow happily under the canopy of the larger trees such as oak, hickory, and ash. Some good understory trees are:

- **Southern sugar maple,** *Acer barbatum* (25 to 30 feet, good choice for wet coastal areas)

- **Trident maple,** *Acer buergeranum* (20 to 25 feet, colorful fall foliage, handsome bark)

- **Chalk maple,** *Acer leucoderme* (25 to 30 feet)

- **Juneberry,** *Amelanchier arborea* (20 to 30 feet, flowers in spring, berries in summer)

- **Eastern redbud,** *Cercis canadensis* (20 to 30 feet, pink flowers in spring, flowers appear before leaves)

- **Chinese fringe tree,** *Chionanthus retusus* (20 feet, white flowers in spring)

- **Grancy graybeard,** *Chionanthus virginicus* (20 to 30 feet, white flowers in spring)

- **Franklin tree,** *Franklinia alatamaha* (20 to 30 feet, white flowers in summer)

- **Carolina silverbell,** *Halesia carolinia* (30 to 40 feet, white bell-shaped flowers in spring)

- **Tall stewartia,** *Stewartia monadelpha* (20 to 30 feet, white flowers in summer)

- **Japanese stewartia,** *Stewartia pseudocamellia* (20 to 40 feet, white flowers in spring and summer)

- **Japanese snowbell,** *Styrax japonicus* (20 to 30 feet, white bell-shaped flowers in spring)

- **Fragrant snowbell,** *Styrax obassia* (20 to 30 feet, fragrant white bell-shaped flowers in spring)

VINES AND GROUNDCOVERS

This is a good month to look at the garden and see where you can use vines and groundcovers to help solve problems. If you have a chain-link fence in an area that is mostly shady and want to cover it quickly, vines like Carolina jessamine or English ivy are ideal. Both are evergreen and easy to train. You can tuck new growth up and through the links of the fence. The yellow flowers of Carolina jessamine in spring are an added bonus. If you want to have late-season color in the garden with vines, the climbing aster, *Aster carolinianus*, produces masses of lavender daisies in November. It has a lax habit and the long stems must be tied up. An open brick wall is ideal, because you can weave the stems in and out of the openings.

Sometimes an area where a patch of lawn is required is simply too shady to grow turf with any success. In all but the northern parts of the state, there is an alternative: Dwarf mondo grass can make a rich green carpet that looks good all year long and requires only a minimum of care. It will thrive even with a moderate amount of foot traffic. The ultimate height of dwarf mondo grass is 3 to 4 inches. When planting, you will probably want to space individual

plants 6 to 8 inches apart to get a thick covering in a short amount of time. Once your new lawn is established you can use a broom to sweep off leaves that accumulate. The more air, light, and moisture your mondo lawn receives, the happier it will be.

PLANT

ANNUALS

Winter annuals, especially pansies, that are not growing vigorously by this time will not survive a severe winter. Replace weak plants with new ones. Examine the root systems of the replacements to make sure they are healthy. Roots should be white and numerous, and spread uniformly in the potting soil.

In north Georgia, look for already-sprouted seedlings of foxglove, hollyhock, money plant, and flowering tobacco; they should be no closer than 6 inches apart. Unless they are already in a favorable place, move the small plants to a "nurse bed" where they can grow for the winter. Next spring you can move them from the nursery to their appointed spots.

Plant poppy, larkspur, and sweet alyssum seed now.

BULBS

Plant spring-flowering bulbs. Don't forget to replant any spring-flowering bulbs that you dug during the summer. Early-flowering types can be planted under deciduous trees since they will be going dormant by the time trees leaf out fully and create heavy shade.

Most spring-flowering bulbs thrive if they are planted in full sun or part shade, but the flowers will last longer if they are protected from the hot midday sun.

If you have elephant ear that you want to save, you can dig up the tuberous roots and keep them cool and dry over the winter. The roots can be as big as a softball. If you grow them in containers, cut back the foliage after there is a hard frost (to about 12 inches high). Use caution when you cut back the foliage, as the sap contains microscopic crystals of oxalic acid, which can be very dangerous to your

HERE'S HOW

TO DIG AND STORE TENDER BULBS

In the middle and northern parts of the state (zone 7 or colder), summer bulbs like dahlias, cannas, elephant ear, and caladiums should be dug up and stored for the winter. Here are some tips for digging up dahlia tubers and other summer-blooming bulbs like caladiums.

- Wait until a frost kills back the foliage. Cut back the stem to a height of 12 inches.

- Use a digging fork, and carefully dig around and under the clumps. Lift them out of the ground.

- Follow this technique if you divide the clumps long after you dig them. Use a sharp knife, making sure each tuber has a stalk about 1 inch and an eye (this is where new growth will initiate).

- Dust dahlia tubers with sulfur, and then cover them with sawdust, sand, or vermiculite. Store them over the winter in a dry, cool (40- to 50-degree-Fahrenheit) place.

If you decide to store the clumps whole and divide them in the spring, cover them with sawdust, sand, perlite, peat moss, or vermiculite, and keep them in a cool, dry place. Separate the tubers two to four weeks before you plant them, using the method described above.

eyes. Cover the stems with an old cloth as you prune off the leaves. Keep the container in a cool, dark space, and provide a minimum of moisture to keep the plant alive until spring when you can bring it back outside.

EDIBLES

You can have a winter garden even if you don't own a plot of land. Plant winter container gardens on your sunny patio or porch. Utilize the same large pots that contained your summer annuals.

- Use greens such as arugula, parsley, mustard, lettuce, and spinach. Even green onion bulbs will grow very well if you have plenty of sunshine.

- Don't be afraid to mix pansies and snapdragons with your edible plants.

- Fertilize with houseplant fertilizer according to label directions.

- Move the container(s) to a sheltered spot if frigid or windy weather threatens.

This is a great time to plant bare-root fruit and nut trees—but be sure to plant varieties that grow well in your area!

Brambles are highly productive and have few pests. Plant blackberries and raspberries now, in the sunniest spot possible.

TO PLANT A SALAD BOWL

This is a fun project that gives you lettuce longer. The bowl is portable, so you can move it around on colder or warmer days to give the lettuce the conditions it needs to grow.

1. Purchase wide, shallow pots to plant salad bowls, or, if you have an old plastic salad bowl, you can drill holes in the bottom and plant it. Fill the bowl about halfway with potting soil.

2. Plant the lettuce bowl with lettuce transplants. For extra taste, plant some bunching onions in the center of the bowl and a dill plant or two on the edges. Fill in around the plants with potting soil and water the plants. On hot days, move the bowl into some shade. On cool days, move the bowl into the sun. If temperatures are forecast to drop below freezing, bring the bowl into the garage.

In south Georgia, plant carrots now. They can also be planted in north Georgia, but some winter injury may occur. 'Nantes', 'Danvers', and 'Chantenay' are good varieties. Do not fertilize carrots; splitting will result. Let them absorb nutrients left over from your summer garden.

LAWNS

It is very late to be planting tall fescue seed in the northern half of Georgia except in the area south of Atlanta and north of Macon. In areas north of Atlanta, you can do it, but germination will take weeks.

Tall fescue sod should be available now. It can be installed anytime between now and next summer.

There's still time to plant annual ryegrass for erosion control, or just to use as a green spot in a brown landscape.

Do not plant zoysiagrass, centipedegrass, or St. Augustinegrass sod in the northern half of Georgia now. These grasses do not have enough time to grow good roots before cold weather sets in.

In the southern half of the state, all sod can be planted, but use caution. Avoid planting in sunny or windy weather. Remember to water new sod regularly until it is well established.

Bermudagrass sod can be planted now if you are certain you can water it regularly during the winter to keep the roots moist.

This is an excellent month to plant liriope or mondo grass in shady spots where grass refuses to grow:

- The easiest way to get plants is to divide a clump already growing in your yard or that of a friend. Ask your neighbors if they have an area where one of these groundcovers is growing.

- Dig the clump, wash it off, and divide it into individual plants.

- Replant some of the sprouts where they grew originally. Take the rest to your landscape and install 6 inches apart.

- Water twice, at three-day intervals. No further care should be required.

PERENNIALS

Hardy ferns add color and texture to the shade garden. Here is a selection of hardy ferns for Georgia gardens:

- **Lady fern,** *Athyrium felix-femina* (dies back in winter, upright habit, 2 to 3 feet)

- **Japanese painted fern,** *Athyrium nipponicum* 'Pictum' (deciduous, wonderful variegated grayish red-silver foliage, grows 1 to 2 feet)

- **Japanese holly fern,** *Cyrtomium falcatum* (glossy evergreen, 2 to 3 feet tall)

- **Autumn fern,** *Dryopteris erythrosora* (evergreen, new foliage is a coppery color, grows to 3 feet)

- **Cinnamon fern,** *Osmunda cinnamomea* (deciduous, large upright fronds, grows 3 to 5 feet)

- **Royal fern,** *Osmunda regalis* (deciduous, 4 to 6 feet, native to swamps and wet areas)

- **Christmas fern,** *Polystichum acrostichoides* (evergreen, 12 to 18 inches, has a prostrate habit)

- **Southern shield fern,** *Thelypteris kunthii* (deciduous, 2 to 3 feet, tolerates more sun than most ferns)

Plant hellebores now for late winter/early spring bloom. Perfect for the shade garden, these evergreen plants look good twelve months of the year.

- Bearsfoot hellebore, *Helleborus foetidus* (light green flowers, blooms from February to June)

- Lenten rose, *Helleborus × hybridus* (flowers range from white to purple, February to May—the plant tolerates drought and a half-day of full sun, although it will thrive in a moist woodland)

Sow seed of perennial poppies, including the scarlet *Papaver orientale,* which is best grown in the more northern parts of the state:

1. Prepare the soil by adding soil amendments and rototilling. Rake out the area where you will sow seeds.

2. Sow seeds; barely cover them—poppy seeds need light to germinate.

3. Water until the soil is wet 1 inch deep.

Sow seed of butterfly weed. These spring bloomers produce a range of flower colors from yellow to orange to scarlet. Germination rate is low, so plant thickly. Cover seed lightly with soil.

Propagate perennials once they are dormant: anemone by root cuttings; perennial geranium by division; daylilies by division into plantlets, each with a single fan; and alumroot by division.

ROSES

Roses can still be planted or transplanted in the southern part of the state.

SHRUBS

This is an ideal time to plant balled-and-burlapped and container-grown shrubs. The sooner you get them into the ground, the better. This will give them time to acclimate before the weather turns cold. Guidelines for planting shrubs:

1. Dig a hole that is at least twice as wide as the container the plant is growing in or the width of the rootball.

2. The depth of the hole should be no deeper than the depth of the container or the rootball.

3. Use the soil you dug out of the hole and fill in around the rootball, tamping it down to minimize air pockets.

4. Water well and apply a 2- to 3-inch layer of mulch.

HERE'S HOW

TO PROPAGATE SHRUBS FROM CUTTINGS

Propagate azaleas, hollies, and other broad-leafed evergreens from cuttings. Here is Walter's preferred method for propagating favorite shrubs:

1. Fill a plastic shoebox half-way (6 to 8 inches deep) with a 50:50 mix of peat moss and perlite. Make sure the mix is barely moist.

2. Take your cuttings. They should be 4 to 6 inches long. Strip off most of the leaves except for the top three or four.

3. Dip the end of the cutting in a rooting hormone and insert it into the rooting medium.

4. Label each variety. Cover the box with clear plastic wrap and place in a sunny window. Check on it weekly to make sure the medium has not dried out.

5. In one month, tug gently to see if any roots have developed. If the cutting does not resist, press it back into the mix and check again in a few weeks. You should have roots in six to eight weeks.

6. Once you have roots, pot up the cuttings in small pots. Overwinter them indoors or in a cold frame until spring, when you can plant them outside.

TREES

If you have cracked and heaved sidewalks, the common culprits are tree roots. The damage occurs when a root grows under the concrete and then swells to a much greater diameter as the years pass.

- Avoid planting trees within 15 feet of a sidewalk or drive.

- If the cracking has just begun, you might find relief by trenching beside the sidewalk and removing the offending root. Next, install 12-inch-wide aluminum flashing edgewise in the trench to prevent other roots from growing under the concrete.

Tree roots depend on a network of soil organisms, called mycorrhizae, to do much of the work involved to absorb water and nutrients. Research has shown that in poor soils, adding mycorrhizae to the soil when a tree is planted can help it become established faster.

Although any tree can be valuable in some situations, a few seem to have so many problems that they are rarely appropriate for a home landscape.

- Silver maples are prone to weak limbs, which crash down unexpectedly in windstorms. The roots often swell aboveground, making lawn mowing a hazardous experience.

- Lombardy poplar trees are sold for quick screening. They grow tall quickly, but they typically survive only a few years in the Georgia climate.

- Norway maple has invasive roots and is usually short-lived in our summer heat.

CARE

ANNUALS

On a warm weekend, make a final cleanup of your landscape:

1. Clip the dried stalks of annuals (and perennials) 3 to 4 inches from the ground.

2. Tuck pine straw around newly planted annuals.

3. Gently brush fallen tree leaves off flower beds. Use them for mulch under trees and shrubs.

Spend a warm afternoon clipping and removing the brown stems of annuals killed by frost. Accumulate your clippings in one spot and transport them to the compost pile when finished. Vacant beds can be covered with pine straw and left for the winter, or you can plant winter annuals. Remove faded flowers from the pansies you planted in October.

Collect the bags of leaves (especially pine straw) that your neighbors stack so helpfully at the curb. Use the leaves to build several compost piles. Use the pine straw immediately for mulch, or pile it under a plastic tarp to use later in the winter.

BULBS

If there are any seeds you want to save, cut off the pods while they are still brown and before they turn mushy.

EDIBLES

Blackberry and raspberry plants should be grown on a wire trellis. You can build a sturdy trellis easily in an afternoon:

1. Set 4 × 4 pressure-treated posts 10 feet apart. The posts should be 5 feet tall after installing in the ground.

2. Stretch three heavy-gauge wires between the posts, at 24, 42, and 60 inches from the ground.

3. Plant brambles 24 inches apart.

4. Tie the canes to the wires as they grow longer.

A cold frame offers the opportunity to enjoy fresh cool-season vegetables for much longer than might be possible with a normal garden. Construct several, if you like. To simplify management, you

■ *Mulch helps keep plant roots cool and moist and adds organic matter to the soil.*

TO BUILD A COLD FRAME

A cold frame is a smaller, unheated version of a greenhouse. In it you can protect half-hardy annuals from brief freezes and can toughen annual seedlings before planting in beds next spring. Many cold frame designs have been tried. Here is one you can make yourself from a double-hung storm window and some 2 × 6 lumber.

1. Purchase the storm window first. A large one (approx. 36 × 75 inches) is best. Make sure both sashes slide easily.

2. Using the storm window dimensions and the 2 × 6 lumber, construct a bottomless and topless box onto which the storm window can be mounted. Attach the storm window to the box frame with screws.

3. Using the same dimensions as the first one, construct two or three more bottomless/topless boxes.

4. Place a bottomless/topless box on the ground in a sunny, sheltered spot. Stack one or two boxes on top—use two if you need the additional height. (Whether you use two or three boxes in the stack, the one to which the storm window is mounted should be the very top one.)

5. Seal the joints between the boxes with duct tape on the inside and outside.

6. Open one of the storm window sashes, and place your plants inside. Leave it open on sunny days (so it does not overheat), and close it at night. Your plants will enjoy the mini-greenhouse in fall and spring even though you can't be in there with them!

can devote each frame to a different crop: lettuce, spinach, beets, turnip greens, and so forth.

Remove the foliage of asparagus plants now, before the red berries fall off. Otherwise, seeds will sprout, and the asparagus bed will become too crowded.

Once the leaves fall from fruit and nut trees, examine the trees' form. Make plans to prune them during the winter.

LAWNS

Are your neighbors raking up pine straw and putting it in bags for the garbage man? If they can't use it in their landscape, ask if you can have some

for yours. If you have the space, stockpile bags under a tarp so you'll have plenty of mulch next year.

Keep the leaves raked (or blown) off your newly planted tall fescue lawn.

Fall leaves are much easier to handle when they have been shredded. If you have a bagging mower,

■ *Using a mulching mower will cut the clippings finely, ensuring they break down and disintegrate as quickly as possible.*

HERE'S HOW

TO CLEAN A SPRAYER

This is a good month to clean tools and pots. Items that might be contaminated with disease spores or pesticides should be thoroughly cleaned. Clean your pesticide sprayers thoroughly with a 1:10 mixture of bleach and water:

1. Disassemble the wand; clean the nozzle.

2. Pressurize the tank and shoot some of the cleaning mixture through the nozzle.

3. Partially fill the tank with clean water and circulate it through the wand and nozzle.

4. Turn the tank upside down to drain. Afterwards, reassemble loosely and store in a covered spot.

Empty any caked potting soil from pots. Dump it on an empty garden bed for rototilling next spring.

Rinse out any remaining soil with a hose.

Soak clay and plastic pots, seed trays, and seed-starting items in a bucket filled with a 1:10 mixture of bleach and water.

Allow them to dry afterwards and stack them neatly where you can find them when you need them.

HERE'S HOW

TO PLANT FESCUE IN COLD WEATHER

If you have a tall fescue lawn spot that simply must be planted in cold weather, here is a trick that can be used to extend the season:

- Rake the area with a hard-tined garden rake (a bow rake).

- Scatter seed lightly and evenly over the spot. Water and cover very thinly with wheat straw.

- Cover the whole area with clear plastic sheeting; anchor it loosely with stones or large limbs.

- Sunshine will warm the soil and encourage the seed to sprout quickly.

- Lift the plastic when the grass is green underneath.

Caution: Do not attempt this technique if the weather is unusually warm or sunny. Your seed may overheat and die under the plastic.

COMPANION PLANTS FOR POPPIES

When poppies finish blooming by mid- to late summer, they will disappear, leaving a bare spot in the garden. These perennials bloom at different times and can help fill the gaps:

- White boltonia, *Boltonia asteroides*
- Calamint, *Calamintha nepeta* subsp. *nepeta*
- Russian sage, *Perovskia atriplicifolia*

simply rake up a pile of leaves and mow through them until you fill the bag. Shredded leaves can be used as mulch under trees and shrubs or can be added to your compost pile. High-performance mulching mowers can shred leaves so finely they won't be noticed on your lawn; the particles simply add organic material to your soil.

PERENNIALS

Once there is a frost, prune back dead stalks and leaves of perennials such as asters, chrysanthemums, salvias, Russian sage, and other late-blooming plants. Don't cut stems all the way back—leave 3 to 4 inches to help protect the crowns. This will also help you keep track of where perennials are planted so you won't accidentally dig them up when they are dormant.

Prune off the stems and leaves of herbaceous peonies to minimize the chances of fungus spores overwintering.

ROSES

Here's some good news for gardeners who have grown roses in the colder parts of the United States. Temperatures in Georgia do not usually drop low enough to permanently harm roses. While a late spring frost can eliminate rose blooms for the season, cold rarely kills Georgia roses. You can put away your rose hoops, bales of straw, and snow shelters.

Tie down the canes of climbing roses so they can't whip against their arbor in the wind.

HERE'S HOW

TO MAKE POTPOURRI

Though your roses have faded, you can still remember their fragrance by making potpourri. Use ingredients you find at a craft shop for your first experiments. Next year you can collect fragrant rose petals and fragrant leaves, blooms, and colorful berries from other plants. A typical potpourri consists of:

- Flower buds, blooms, or petals
- Differing textures added by leaves, peels, or berries
- A fixative to hold the scent of the various components
- Essential oils to add strong scents (such as cinnamon or citrus) to the mix

Once you have gained confidence making potpourri, you can spend next November making personalized mixtures as gifts for your friends during the upcoming holidays.

Prune out any dead branches or "in-the-way" limbs.

SHRUBS

Limit your pruning to dead or damaged wood. If you want to prune evergreens, wait until they are dormant, usually in December, January, and February.

Here is a list of shrubs that bloom on old wood. Wait until after they flower to prune these shrubs:

- Flowering quince, *Chaenomeles japonica*
- Forsythia, *Forsythia* species and cultivars
- Fothergilla, *Fothergilla gardenii*
- Hydrangea, *Hydrangea macrophylla*
- Oak leaf hydrangea, *Hydrangea quercifolia*
- Mock orange, *Philadelphus coronarius*
- *Rhododendron calendulaceum*
- *Rhododendron catawbiense*
- *Rhododendron maximum*
- Spirea, *Spiraea prunifolia*
- Viburnum (most species and cultivars)

MOLES AND VOLES

Moles may be mistakenly blamed for eating the roots of plants, but it is more likely that voles are the problem. Moles prefer insects. They tunnel through the soil, causing havoc as they go when plants are uprooted. Trapping is the most effective control for moles. Voles burrow under mulch and eat roots and stems as they go. To discourage them, try these techniques:

1. Pull leaves and mulch away from trunks and stems of plants (voles).

2. Put a shovelful of sharp gravel or expanded shale in the planting hole (moles).

3. Use some castor oil in each planting hole (voles). For small plants, a tablespoon should be adequate; for larger plants, use several tablespoons.

■ *When mulching trees, keep the mulch away from the tree trunk so voles and other small animals won't make nests close to the tree.*

TREES

Older trees often develop hollows in the trunk due to damage from previous years. It is not recommended that you fill these hollows. Concrete, foam, or other materials will eventually crack, making an excellent hiding place for borers and disease fungi.

VINES AND GROUNDCOVERS

Before or when you pull up annual vines that were killed by frost, collect any remaining seedpods, and save the seed for next year. Prune to remove any dead, diseased, or broken branches of vines.

Cut away and dispose of any leaves or stems on groundcovers that are damaged by insects or fungus. You can usually recognize fungus because the leaves and stems are black and look rotten.

Color in the winter garden comes from foliage, fruits, flowers, and bark. Below is a list of groundcovers and vines that hold their own in the winter garden:

- **Sweet flag,** *Acorus gramineus* 'Ogon' (groundcover)

- **Wild ginger,** *Asarum shuttleworthii* 'Callaway' (groundcover)

- **Cyclamen,** *Cyclamen hederifolium* (groundcover)

- **Carolina Jessamine,** *Gelsemium sempervirens* (vine)

- **Persian ivy,** *Hedera colchia* 'Sulphur Heart' (vine)

HERE'S HOW

TO SELECT AND CARE FOR CAMELLIAS

Camellias are a staple for many Southern gardens. By growing a range of types you can have blooms from early fall through spring. Mulch them with 2 to 3 inches of mulch. The mulch is especially important to conserve moisture and keep the camellia roots cool since they are close to the surface of the soil. Plants do not thrive in soils with a high pH. Water regularly for at least the first two years.

Camellia japonica. This is the camellia that most people think of when they refer to camellias. They grow 10 to 15 feet tall and 6 to 10 feet wide.

Camellia sasanqua. This species is more refined with smaller leaves and flowers. It may grow 6 to 10 feet tall. This species flowers from September into December. Many selections will tolerate full sun and drought but the better the growing conditions, the better the performance of your shrubs in general.

■ *Lenten rose*

- **English ivy,** *Hedera helix* cultivars (vine or groundcover)

- **Lenten rose,** *Helleborus* hybrids and cultivars (groundcover)

- **Groundcover juniper,** *Juniperus* species and cultivars (groundcover)

- **Monkey grass,** *Liriope muscari* (groundcover)

- **Mondo grass,** *Ophiopogon japonicus* (groundcover)

- **Creeping raspberry,** *Rubus calycinoides* (groundcover)

- **Periwinkle vine,** *Vinca minor* (groundcover)

The ancient art of topiary is defined as the practice of training shrubs and small trees into ornamental or fantastic shapes such as animals, letters, and geometric forms. One way to create topiary is to train vines on forms. Usually metal, these forms can be placed in the ground or in a large decorative pot.

Many types of English ivy and Asian star jasmine are easy to train on topiary forms.

1. Start with many small plants (in 2- to 4-inch pots) that have long trailing stems.

2. Tuck the stems up and through the form, covering as much area as possible.

3. Clip new growth on a regular basis to encourage stems to branch.

4. Tuck stems as they develop, and clip as needed to define the shape of the topiary. (This can be as often as once every two weeks during the growing season.)

WATER

ANNUALS
Water pansies and other flowers that you have recently planted if no rainfall occurs. All these plants need to be growing vigorously as colder weather nears; make sure the soil is moist to 6 inches deep.

BULBS
Water bulbs after you plant them. Apply 2 to 3 inches of mulch on top of newly planted bulb areas.

EDIBLES
Fall is an excellent time to plant fruiting trees, vines, or shrubs, but even though air temperatures are cool, the soil may be dry. Give newly installed plants at least 5 gallons of water each week unless rain occurs.

At full pressure, most hoses deliver 5 gallons of water in one minute.

LAWNS
Drain your irrigation system and outdoor faucets. If the faucets can't be drained, cover them with insulation for the winter. Hardware stores stock foam pipe wrap and faucet covers that are easy to install.

PERENNIALS
Water new plantings and transplants weekly unless there is adequate rainfall (1 inch per week). If you use a sprinkler, use tuna fish cans to measure the amount of water plants receive. Once the can has ¾ to 1 inch of water, you have watered long enough.

Once the ground freezes, apply a fresh layer of mulch (about 2 inches, keeping it away from stems and crowns) to perennial beds. This will help conserve moisture and reduce weed infestations.

ROSES

Roses need at least twelve months to establish or to reestablish a root system.

Water regularly any roses that have been planted or transplanted in the last six months.

SHRUBS

Water all new plantings as well as existing plantings so that they are well prepared to go into winter.

TREES

Conifers can dry out quickly in winter winds. Be sure to keep them watered even during the colder months, unless the ground is frozen.

VINES AND GROUNDCOVERS

Keep up with watering new plantings on a weekly basis if there is no regular rainfall, at least 1 inch per week. Fall weather may be cooler, but it can also be dry.

FERTILIZE

ANNUALS

Fertilize cool-season flowers with a water-soluble fertilizer like 20-20-20.

BULBS

Fertilize bulbs when you plant them with a complete fertilizer like 8-8-8 or 10-10-10.

Topdress bulbs that you planted last fall.

EDIBLES

It is not necessary to fertilize fruits, vegetables, or herbs during the cold season.

Make sure your fertilizers are stored where they will not get wet during the winter.

LAWNS

Lawn fertilizer does not "go bad," even when it becomes lumpy and breaks through the bottom of the bag. If it can be pulverized enough to flow through your spreader, apply it to your lawn on the usual schedule. If the lumps are too hard to break, throw them, in moderate amounts (½ cup per plant), under your woodland trees and

shrubs in spring. Fertilize tall fescue, preferably in the early part of the month. Do not fertilize bermudagrass, zoysiagrass, centipedegrass, or St. Augustinegrass.

ROSES

Organic fertilizers such as cottonseed meal, bloodmeal, or bonemeal that have been stored for the winter are attractive food for opossums, rats, and raccoons. Store organic products such as these in a metal trash can that has a tightly fitting lid.

SHRUBS

You can apply fertilizer lightly once shrubs are dormant. Use a balanced fertilizer like 10-10-10, applying ½ pound per 100 square feet of shrub bed. The fertilizer will be available to plants in early spring once they start actively growing again. As a general rule when using a granular l0-10-10, apply ½ tablespoon of fertilizer per foot of shrub height.

VINES AND GROUNDCOVERS

There is no need to fertilize established vines and groundcovers now. If you plant a large area of groundcovers and use small rooted plugs, prepare the soil before you plant, being sure to incorporate generous amounts of organic material. When the soil is friable and rich in organic materials, it will be easier for roots to establish.

PROBLEM-SOLVE

ANNUALS

Pull weeds like chickweed and henbit now, before they have time to mature and drop seed. Dig out the roots of wild violet, wild onion, and dandelion; simply pulling off the leaves will not control these perennial weeds.

BULBS

Clean up any remaining leaf litter. It should be safe to put most leaves on the compost pile even if they were affected by insects or disease, unless the disease is a virus, such as mosaic virus. Any bulbs or plant parts infected with a virus should be disposed of in the garbage.

EDIBLES

When leaves have fallen, thoroughly spray fruit trees with dormant oil. Dormant oils are heavier than other horticultural oils; the oil suffocates insects that hide on and under the bark.

LAWNS

Squirrels may dig holes in your lawn in order to hide acorns. The holes are unsightly, but little can be done to deter the rodents. If the holes bother you greatly, use a live trap, baited with peanut butter, to capture a few of the creatures and give them a nice trip out of town.

PERENNIALS

Pull weeds when they are young.

SHRUBS

Remove leaf litter that may harbor overwintering insects or diseases from the ground around shrubs.

TREES

English ivy is an attractive and hardy groundcover that spreads rapidly, but when the ivy climbs up trees, it is damaging. As it grows into the treetop, the ivy foliage shades lower branches. In addition, the ivy collects additional ice and rain, and the tree may be damaged by the additional weight. English ivy is not a parasite—its aerial roots simply cling to the tree bark for support. Here's how to get rid of it:

- Use a heavy screwdriver to pull the vine from the bark so your pruners can grip the vine enough to clip it in two.

Dandelions are best controlled by digging out the roots.

Remove the entire root system or rhizome of a weed, but be careful not to uproot neighboring plants. Use a weeding tool to get leverage if needed.

- Pull the vine from the tree trunk as high as you can reach.

- Remove the ivy from an area 6 feet from the tree trunk in all directions.

- The ivy in the tree will gradually wither over the next year.

Protect newly planted young trees from damage caused by rodents and lawnmowers. Build a simple wire cylinder. Use ¼-inch hardware cloth that is 18 to 24 inches high. Wrap it very loosely around the tree trunk.

Trees purchased from a nursery may have tree wrap covering the lower trunk. Tree wrap makes a great hiding place for boring insects. The string or wire used to attach a stake to the tree will eventually girdle the trunk. Remove the wrap and any stakes attached to the trunk soon after planting.

VINES AND GROUNDCOVERS

Once there has been a hard freeze, pull down annual vines and dispose of them. This will help reduce the number of places in which insects can overwinter. Rake up leaves in groundcover beds, and add them to the compost pile.

Weed groundcover beds. Whenever possible, pull weeds before they flower and set seed. This will reduce future infestations of weeds.

Check vines and groundcovers for insects like scale, aphids, or spider mites. Spray with horticultural oil.

December

December temperatures range from "jacket weather" in the northern half of the state to "shirt sleeves, mostly" in the southern half. Only a few times will you need to really bundle up when you go outdoors.

It's easy to go on a garden walkabout as you fill bird feeders and pick up fallen limbs. Few things are blooming, save pansies, but this is a great time to appreciate to contribution of colorful foliage and contrasting textures. For annuals with ornamental foliage, look at the purple leaves of ornamental kale and cabbage. Some cabbages have white centers that really stand out against surrounding green leaves. The last few years have seen the introduction of "frilly leaf" cabbages, which add even more interest.

Notable shrubs include the gold speckles on evergreen aucuba leaves. Make a note to return in March to catch their purple flowers, which few gardeners notice. If your aucuba has red berries, it's a female. Male plants have differently shaped flowers and no red fruit.

'Goshiki' osmanthus is another variegated foliage shrub that really stands out, particularly in large containers. Variegated pittosporum is less a container plant but makes a nice gray/green shrub wall in the lower half of Georgia. Though it's considered not winter hardy in north Georgia, most plants survived some recent bitter cold. Another "you can't grow it here" plant that failed to read the label: fatsia. Looking like a philodendron on steroids, this coarse shrub gives great contrast to finer-leaved companions. Plus, the white Sputnik flowers on tall stalks this month will have everyone asking, "What the heck is that?"

December is not typically as frigid as January but you can prepare your plants for later winter cold now. This mostly involves avoiding water stress. Be sure annuals such as pansies and ornamental cabbages are mulched. Water newly planted evergreen trees and shrubs (magnolia, Leyland cypress, arborvitae, azalea, and so forth) so the roots can find moisture and rehydrate after a cold night. For just-in-case emergencies, keep black plastic handy so you can quickly cover marginally hardy plants if a severe cold front approaches.

Wishing you "Happy Holidays" with your friends, family, and plants!

PLAN

ANNUALS

December is a time for slow walks through your landscape, coffee in hand, to reflect on what has pleased you in the last year and what can be improved. If you have taken photographs regularly, you can spread them on the kitchen table to follow the progress of your flowers during the growing season. Were there times when nothing was blooming?

Research the peak bloom time for different annuals. Make notes in your garden journal or smartphone on what to plant in the bare spots next year. Don't forget that some selections of the same annual plant bloom before or after the variety you commonly use. If you are always successful with a particular annual, look for other selections that bloom at the time you need flowers. Why mess with success?

Did some plants grow larger than expected? Make notes of where to plant or move them next spring so they won't overshadow their neighbors.

Was the backdrop for your flowers always effective? Refer to the lists of good trees, shrubs, and grasses in other chapters of this book for ideas. Consult *Georgia Getting Started Garden Guide* for our recommendations of the best plants for Georgia's conditions.

BULBS

While all daffodils belong to the genus *Narcissus*, not all *Narcissus* are daffodils. Daffodils belong to the genus *Narcissus*, most of whose members have the familiar six flat flower petals surrounding a central cup. Daffodil is the common name for all members of the *Narcissus* family.

You can use either "daffodil" or "narcissus" correctly when referring to any of this familiar family of bulbs.

Older Southern gardeners would commonly refer to any early, yellow, fragrant narcissus as a jonquil. However, "jonquil" is properly used only as the common name for the Jonquilla group of daffodils. Daffodil is the proper common name for all thirteen groups of these bulbs.

EDIBLES

If space is limited, you'll find that several raised beds produce more vegetables than an equivalent amount of flat ground. Choose a warm weekend to construct your beds. Treated or untreated wood, stones, or concrete blocks can be used to line the bed.

- The sides of a bed should be at least 8 inches tall.

- Beds can be any convenient length, but it is easier to weed and maintain beds that are 30 to 40 inches wide.

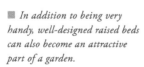 *In addition to being very handy, well-designed raised beds can also become an attractive part of a garden.*

With some landscaping creativity, you can have a yard filled with colorful plants—and no lawn.

- Dig and loosen the soil inside the bed, rototilling in a 2-inch-thick layer of soil amendment.

- Fill the remainder of the bed completely with good-quality planting soil. Mix it deeply with the undersoil. Buy extra—after a few weeks the bed will settle and will need refilling.

LAWNS

No law says you have to have a lawn (although neighborhood covenants may require one). It is possible to have a very attractive front yard without enduring the work and management a lawn requires.

On a warm December day, walk across your lawn and envision what it would look like if it were filled with beds of flowers or shrubs or tree islands.

PERENNIALS

It's time to begin thinking about next year's spring and what you will plant.

Sketch a plan that shows which perennials you want to include in your garden, paying attention to placement, color schemes, time of bloom, and ultimate size. If you're not sure where to begin when designing your perennial garden, try this technique:

- While the perennials are still in their pots, place the pots in the spot where individual plants will grow. Move them around until you are pleased with the design, keeping in mind what plants will look like when they're blooming and during the rest of the year, including the dormant season.

- Once you plant your perennials, if you think two colors clash or if one variety turns out to be too aggressive for the spot you've planted it in, you can move plants to another location— perennials are resilient and forgiving.

ROSES

Some gardeners plan their rose beds so they will be as attractive when the blooms are absent as when the plants are covered with blossoms. Rose hips are the fruit (seed container) of a rose bloom. As they age in fall, many hips turn vivid shades of yellow, orange, and red. They are edible and are an excellent source of vitamin C. Do not remove flowers after they fade or the hips will not form. Roses with attractive hips include:

- 'Dortmund'
- 'Frau Dagmar Hartopp'
- Old Blush'
- *Rosa rugosa* 'Alba'
- *Rosa rugosa* 'Rubra'

Before removing plants from their containers, place them in the prepared garden to see how they will look together. Experiment with different groupings until you find an arrangement that pleases you.

SHRUBS

Make notes in your garden journal about shrubs that look good in the winter. Don't limit yourself to evergreens. Deciduous shrubs with colorful berries, beautiful bark, or fragrant flowers also look good in winter. Plan to add some of these to your garden in the spring, or even now, provided the ground is not frozen.

Evergreen shrubs effective for screening or hedging in the shade:

- **Glossy abelia,** *Abelia grandiflora* (5 to 7 feet)

- **Inkberry holly,** *Ilex glabra* (8 to 10 feet)

- **Anise,** *Illicium* spp. (6 to 10 feet, fragrant foliage)

- **Leucothoe,** *Leucothoe populifolia* (*Agarista populifolia*) (8 to 12 feet)

- **Holly tea olive,** *Osmanthus heterophyllus* (10 to 20 feet)

- **Prague viburnum,** *Viburnum pragense* (10 feet)

TREES

Deciduous trees in the winter landscape become studies in shape and form. Some display striking bark or interesting flowers. Visit botanical gardens and arboreta, and take note of the trees that stand out in the winter garden.

Evergreens serve a multitude of roles as specimen plants, hedges, screens, and windbreaks. Hemlocks, pines, holly, and arborvitae withstand pruning and can be maintained as large hedges. Pines for Georgia vary in their rate of growth, habit, and ultimate size; they thrive with little or no fertilizer and can survive a good bit of drought. Most pines develop a large taproot; therefore, with the exception of small seedlings, they are best purchased as balled-and-burlapped or container-grown plants. Consider these pines:

- **Pitch pine,** *Pinus rigida* (40 to 60 feet in height by 30 to 50 feet)

- **White pine,** *Pinus strobus* (best for north Georgia)

- **Loblolly pine,** *Pinus taeda* (60 to 90 feet tall)

- **Japanese black pine,** *Pinus thunbergiana* (20 to 80 feet by 20 to 40 feet; tolerates salt spray)

- **Virginia pine,** *Pinus virginiana* (15 to 40 feet by 10 to 30 feet)

VINES AND GROUNDCOVERS

As winter approaches, take time to review the gardening year and examine your successes and failures. If you tried certain vines for the first time, did you grow them in the best manner? While many vines make good garden companions for roses, shrubs, or trees, some are best grown alone. Take, for example, the moon vine. This aggressive vine will quickly cover a structure or plant. If paired with another aggressive grower like the 'New Dawn' rose, it can create a maintenance headache. When the moon vine dies at the end of the growing season, it is nearly impossible to extricate it from amongst the canes of a rose without incurring bodily harm. For this reason, moon vine and other aggressive annual vines like morning glories are best grown on their own structures where they won't damage other plants.

PLANT

ANNUALS

Cool-season annuals make great companions in a pot. Find a decorative container (or several!), and plant arrangements of pansies, parsley, and snapdragons. Keep the pots outdoors (by your front door, on your deck, and so forth) for most of the winter, but bring them indoors for a few days at a time to decorate your home during the holiday season.

BULBS

If you haven't planted them yet, get those spring-flowering bulbs in the ground.

In coastal areas, there is still time to plant spring-flowering bulbs this month and next month. If you have a large area and you want to grow spring-flowering bulbs, naturalizing or mass planting might be a good technique to try. Prepare the soil ahead of time.

Dig out large areas to the depth required by whatever type bulb you are planting. If you are planting crocus in the lawn, you won't need to dig as deeply as you will if you plant large daffodils. After you dig out an area, set aside the soil. Place the bulbs in the planting space, which can be an irregular shape. This will result in a more natural-looking planting when the bulbs bloom in the spring. If you want a more formal look, plant in rows or a definite geometric shape, and space the bulbs at a regular distance from one another. A cluster of 100 in one spot will make for a more dramatic effect. If you use the same variety, it will also have more of an impact than having a scattering of types blooming at all different times. You can do this easily with crocus, daffodils, snowdrops, and snowflakes.

If you want to force paperwhites for the New Year, plant some today. You can plant them in soil and top off the pot with pebbles. Another method that works well is to use a decorative container: Use pebbles to hold the bulbs in place. Fill up the pot with water, but don't cover the top one-fourth of the bulb. Keep the bulbs in a cool spot with dim light until they put up 3 to 4 inches of stems and leaves. At this point, move them into a bright room; as they grow, move them to the sunniest window you have.

EDIBLES

After leaves have been nipped off by frost you can transplant any of your small fruit trees to new sites.

- Don't try to transplant fruit trees larger than 8 feet tall. You'll be more successful buying a new tree rather than waiting for a transplanted tree to start growing again. If the tree is 8 to 12 feet tall, you can reduce its height to 6 to 8 feet by pruning.

- Dig a 6-foot-wide hole into which the tree will be planted.

- No need to fertilize now. Wait until next summer, when the tree has fully leafed out.

LAWNS

Tall fescue sod can be planted anytime it is available. Bermudagrass sod can be successfully installed in the northern half of the state throughout the winter as long as it is kept from drying. Do not plant zoysiagrass or centipedegrass sod. In the southern half of the state, all types of sod can be planted, but use caution. Avoid planting in sunny or windy weather. Remember to water new sod regularly until it is well established.

PERENNIALS

In the southernmost parts of the state you can add perennials to your garden throughout the year. In areas where the ground freezes, wait until spring to add new plants.

Sow seed that requires a cold treatment (columbine, turtlehead, purple coneflower, and garden phlox). Start them in pots, and leave them outside through the winter, in areas where the temperature stays cool, next to the house in the shade.

Prepare your soil now for spring planting. Wait until a warm, sunny day when the soil is dry. Rent a small rototiller, and till the soil, adding amendments as you go—remember, the better the soil, the better the gardening results. Mix one-third organic material, one-third coarse sand, and one-third existing soil. After you mix all the ingredients together, mulch the bed with a good 2 to 3 inches of mulch, and let it sit until spring when you can turn it under and begin to plant.

ROSES

Roses need not always be planted in the ground. They grow quite nicely in containers if given the sunshine, water, and shade they need.

CONTAINER GROWING PROS

- You can determine the exact flower color before planting in a permanent location.

- You can evaluate if the rose will grow in a semi-shaded spot.

HERE'S HOW

TO PLANT A BED OF BULBS

1. *Remove the soil to the proper depth so that the bottom of the bulbs will be three to four times as deep as the width of the bulbs. Incorporate any needed soil amendments, including organic matter, fertilizer, and bone meal.*

2. *Toss the bulbs into the garden.*

3. *Even out spacing as needed but avoid straight planting lines. Make sure the bulbs have their basal plate facing down, pointed side up.*

4. *Cover the bulbs with soil and water well.*

- The rose does not have to compete with its neighbors for sun, moisture, and nutrients.

- There are no worries about soil problems if you use a premium potting soil.

- Maintenance (pruning, fertilizing, spraying, and so forth) is easier.

CONTAINER GROWING CONS

- Water management is imperative throughout the year.

- Large containers (at least 5-gallon-size or larger) will be needed for large plants.

- A rose plant must grow in a new container for at least a year before it can be moved to a bed.

TO PLANT A CONTAINER-GROWN TREE

1. Remove the tree from the container. Examine the roots to be sure they are healthy.

2. Use a hand cultivator to loosen the roots. If roots are wrapped around the rootball many times, use a sharp spade or pair of pruners and make four vertical cuts, evenly spaced around the rootball. Gently tease the roots at the bottom of the rootball so that they spread out. Make sure there are no large roots at the top of the rootball that could girdle the trunk.

3. Place the tree in the hole on top of a solid mound of soil. Fill in the hole around the tree, about halfway, using your shovel handle or foot to firm the soil and eliminate air pockets. Water the tree and add the rest of the soil, being careful not to compact it.

4. Mulch the area around the tree with a 2- to 3-inch layer of material, keeping it away from the trunk of the tree (mulch piled up against the trunk of the tree can cause it to rot).

5. Once it is planted, water the tree thoroughly. Thereafter, water the tree regularly, weekly for the first six months or so, and then once a month for the next year, if there is not adequate rainfall.

• Containers may overheat.

TREES

In the southernmost parts of the state, you can plant container-grown trees.

CARE

ANNUALS

Overenthusiastic gardeners may find there is not enough room in their home to carry over the plants that would normally reside outdoors.

Rooted cuttings on windowsills, patio plants stacked by the sliding glass door, and normal houseplants may all vie for space.

Consider "lending" your plants to a school's lobby or an assisted-living home. Both plants and people will benefit from the change of scenery.

A product called "floating row cover" is underappreciated for its usefulness in the garden. Made of very lightweight, translucent, woven plastic, a sheet of row cover can be spread over newly planted annuals to protect them from frost. Since the row cover is not opaque, it can be left on the plants for a few days until they are hardened off. Row cover is also useful for protecting annuals from unexpected frost in the spring.

You can make soil anchors for the row cover from surplus wire clothes hangers. Use tin snips to make three cuts: in the center of the long, straight part and on both sides of the hook, under the twisted wire. Pliers may be needed to

TO CARE FOR TOOL HANDLES

Hoes, rakes, and shovels are expensive. It is easy to prolong their life by following a few good garden habits:

1. Rinse tools with fresh water to remove dirt as soon as you are finished using them. Soil left on wooden handles causes them to deteriorate quickly.

2. Paint boiled (not raw) linseed oil on wooden handles three times a year. Let it soak in overnight, then wipe off with a rag.

3. Use sandpaper on wooden handles that have become rough. They will feel much better to your touch. After sanding, give the handle a linseed oil treatment.

4. Spray a lubricant like WD-40 on the blades to protect them.

A floating row cover helps protect tender plants from frost damage.

straighten the wire slightly so it slides into the soil easily.

Good stocking stuffers: a water timer, solid aluminum trowel, indoor-outdoor thermometer, hand pruners, indoor plant food, rain gauge, a garden book, and garden magazine subscriptions.

BULBS

If you want to force spring-flowering bulbs to bloom, there is still time. Below is a list of bulbs that are relatively easy to force. While some bulbs like paperwhites and hyacinths can be forced in water with pebbles, most spring bulbs need oxygen and should be potted up in a pot with soil and drainage holes. You can force these bulbs to enjoy indoors or to bring out into the garden after the danger of frost has passed in early spring.

- Crocus
- Hyacinth
- Daffodil
- Siberian squill
- Dwarf iris
- *Tulipa* 'Apricot Beauty'
- Glory of the snow

EDIBLES

If you still have beets, collards, mustard, or turnip greens in your garden, don't be afraid to eat them. Old-timers say they have the best taste when the leaves have endured a frost or two. A thin layer of pine straw will protect them from temperatures below freezing.

A good pair of handpruners and long-handled loppers are essential for maintaining fruit trees and vines. When purchasing pruning tools, the motto "You get what you pay for" is quite true. While inexpensive pruners may cost less than $10, they become dull quickly and are difficult to maintain. Here are some buying, sharpening, and care tips:

- Plan to spend $25 to $40 for good pruners. The best models can be disassembled easily and have a replaceable blade. (Felco® #2 is a favorite of many gardeners.)

- In general, anvil-type pruners are less versatile than bypass (scissor-type) pruners.

- Brightly colored handles are a plus if you tend to misplace your tools.

Store all your garden tools (shovel, spading fork, trowels, and so forth) neatly for the winter—don't pile them in a heap. Spray metal surfaces with a lubricating spray to thwart rust.

- Firmly attach an 8-foot-long 2 × 4 to the wall of your storage building.

- Hammer twelve-penny (12d) finishing nails into the 2 × 4 at 12-inch intervals.

- Drill ¼-inch-diameter holes in the handles of wooden tools and hang them from the nails.

LAWNS

Rake the last of the fall leaves from your lawn. A pile of wet, matted leaves now can lead to big dead spots next spring. Use them for mulch under shrubs and trees.

Mow tall fescue and ryegrass regularly, removing only one-third of the height each time.

Mowers are tough machines, but a little maintenance now will make them much easier to operate:

- Don't leave your lawn mower out in the rain. Water can get in the gas tank and prevent starting next spring. It is best to drain the tank completely, or run the mower until it is out of gas.

- Flip your mower on its side and clean the underside of the mower with a sturdy stick.

HERE'S HOW

TO SHARPEN PRUNERS

Handpruners and loppers can be sharpened after hard use.

1. Disassemble the pruner and place the handle in a vise. The blade should be upwards and easily accessible from all sides.

2. Use a whetstone (available at hardware stores) lubricated with oil. Some whetstones have a "fine" side and a "coarse" side for more versatility. Shine a light on the blade so you can see the manufacturer's original bevel.

3. Holding it at the original bevel angle, slide the whetstone up the blade from the base to the tip of the blade. Use many light strokes. Strive for a uniformly bright and sharpened edge.

4. Slide the stone against the flat backside of the blade once or twice to break off the tiny metal curls that were formed when the beveled side was sharpened.

5. Use oil or a lubricating spray to lubricate your pruners after each use.

6. Examine the blade regularly for nicks and chips. Replace if badly damaged.

Never use a pruner to cut wire unless it has a special notch designed for that purpose.

Remove caked grass. Check the mower shaft for string or wire wrapped around it.

- Use a spray lubricant to protect and lubricate wheel axles, control cables, and blade height adjusters. A five-minute task today can save hours of frustration next spring.

- This is a fine time to have the blade sharpened if this was not done earlier in the year.

Caution: Always disconnect the spark plug before maintaining a lawn mower.

PERENNIALS

If you haven't cleaned up the perennial garden yet, do it now. Prune dead stalks and leaves—remember to leave 3 to 4 inches of stem as a marker (you will cut down the remaining dead stalks in early spring once new growth begins to emerge). Discard any diseased leaves or plants.

Cut back 'Miss Huff' lantana to 6 inches above the ground. Though some gardeners say waiting until spring is best, our experience has shown this not to be true.

ROSES

Roses growing in pots may need protection if winter temperatures threaten to go lower than 20 degrees Fahrenheit. Here's how to keep them safe:

- Move the pot close to the house, preferably against a north- or east-facing wall.

- Wrap the entire plant and pot with burlap or an old sheet. Remove when temperatures warm up.

SHRUBS

You can do a little selective pruning of evergreens like holly, nandina, and camellia if you want to use them for holiday decorations, but wait until early spring, just before they begin to actively grow, to do any substantial pruning.

TREES

Prune out any dead, diseased, or broken branches from trees planted in the past six months.

HERE'S HOW

TO SHARPEN A MOWER BLADE

1. *Remove the spark plug or battery from the mower or otherwise disable it so that it cannot accidentally start. Tip the mower on its side, so that the entire underdeck area is accessible. Tip: If your fuel tank contains gasoline, remove the cap, cover the opening with foil or plastic wrap (inset), and then replace the cap. This prevents gas from dripping out of the vent hole in the cap.*

2. *Wedge a wood scrap piece between the blade and the mower deck to stabilize the blade so it doesn't spin while you remove the bolt holding it in place. You can also purchase a special device for this purpose from yard and garden centers.*

3. *Remove the blade. Use a closed-end wrench to loosen the bolt that secures the blade to the mower motor. If the bolt is stuck, try spraying it with penetrating lubricant and letting it soak in for a few minutes before retrying.*

4. *Secure the blade in a vise. Inspect the entire blade for damage, and then file along the cutting edge, using smooth, even strokes at an angle that matches the existing bevel. Use the same number of strokes on each edge.*

If you have deciduous trees that require major pruning, schedule the work to be done in the next few months while trees are still dormant. Be sure you hire or consult with an arborist if you are not sure which branches are alive and which are dead.

CHOOSING A "CUT-YOUR-OWN" CHRISTMAS TREE

- Contact the Georgia Farmers and Consumers Market Bulletin (http://agr. georgia.gov/market-bulletin.aspx) in early November and ask for their yearly Christmas tree farm issue.

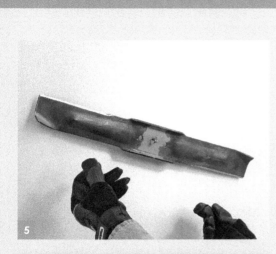

5　Check the blade's balance by hanging it on a nail that has been driven into the wall. The blade should hang level. If the blade is not balanced, file metal off the heavier end until it is.

6　Reattach the blade to the mower's motor following the manufacturer's instructions and cut a small strip of grass as a test. Inspect the tops of the cuttings to make sure they have been sliced cleanly, indicating that the blade is sharp.

- To investigate other farms, visit the Georgia Christmas Tree Growers Association (www.gachristmastree.com).

- Another good resource is the Georgia Farm Bureau Certified Markets list (www.gfb.org/commodities/cfm/default.html)

- Plan to bring the whole family on the outing. Many farms have wagon rides, a petting zoo, or other activities.

- Bring a big piece of sheet plastic to cover the tree on the way back. Otherwise, the tree needles will be as dry as toast after a frigid and windy ride on top of your car.

CHOOSING A CUT CHRISTMAS TREE FROM A LOT

- Good varieties are Fraser fir, Scots pine, Noble fir, white pine, Virginia pine, and Leyland cypress.

- Shake the tree or pull your fingers lightly down a branch—few needles should drop out.

- Remember to cut at least ½ inch off the base of the tree before standing it in water.

CARING FOR A LIVE CHRISTMAS TREE

- Good varieties are cryptomeria, hemlock, Hinoki cypress, umbrella pine, arborvitae, Leyland cypress, and Virginia pine. Not recommended: Colorado blue spruce, Alberta spruce, and white pine.

- Plan to have the tree indoors for no more than seven days so it will have a better chance of surviving when you plant it outside.

- Keep the rootball moist. Ice cubes wrapped in a cloth and placed on top of the ball will slowly trickle water to the roots.

- If you cannot plant the tree on your property, offer to plant the tree at a local school or house of worship.

VINES AND GROUNDCOVERS

Once vines are dormant, you can prune to shape them, but be sure not to prune off flower buds for next spring.

If your luffa gourds have turned brown on the stem, you may think it is too late to harvest them—but it's not. Luffa gourds should be left on the vine until the stem is completely dry and the gourd is beginning to turn brown at both ends or the gourd is completely dry. Once they are harvested, they can be peeled. If the shell has dried completely, you can peel it away bit by bit. You can also soak the gourd for fifteen minutes to two hours, softening the shell and making it easier to peel. The interior sponge will have forty to eighty seeds.

Soak the sponge in warm water, and then hang to dry. Adding a small amount of bleach to the water will make for a bright luffa sponge. Save any seeds from desirable luffa sponges for next year's crop. Luffa sponges make good gifts.

WATER

ANNUALS

Water winter annuals if rain has not fallen in the last seven days. Do not allow their roots to become dry.

An overlooked benefit of winter mulch is that it retains soil heat. Pine straw, in particular, traps an insulating layer of air close to the earth. Keep an extra couple of bales of pine straw in a sheltered spot so dry straw will be handy if needed.

EDIBLES

Be sure to turn off the water supply valve and drain your watering system before hard freezes arrive. Wrap with insulating foam outdoor faucets that cannot be drained. Coil up soaker hoses and water hoses, and store them in an out-of-the-way spot so you can work in your garden easily next spring.

LAWNS

Water newly planted fescue sod to keep it moist.

ROSES

Summer sunshine in Georgia can heat the soil in black plastic containers enough to kill plant roots. If you choose plastic pots, use the clay-colored type rather than the dark green or black. Group plants close enough so that each shades the other. Use potted foliage perennials to screen the outermost pots. Place a 1-inch layer of small pine nuggets on top of the soil to insulate it.

TREES

Water new plantings, especially evergreens, like magnolia or Leyland cypress, once per week in the absence of rain. Drain the hose after use.

FERTILIZE

ANNUALS

Fertilize cool-season flowers again.

EDIBLES

Have a bag of lumpy fertilizer?

It doesn't go bad . . . and your plants will appreciate it next year:

1. Spread a sheet of plastic on your garage floor and place the fertilizer in the middle.

2. Use a hammer to break up the lumps into pieces no larger than ½-inch in diameter.

3. Scoop the fertilizer into a lidded 5-gallon plastic bucket. Seal the lid tightly.

4. Use a permanent marker to label the bucket's contents.

5. Scatter as needed in spring

LAWNS

Fescue: Fertilize only if the November feeding was missed.

Bermudagrass: Do not fertilize at this time.

Zoysiagrass: Do not fertilize at this time.

Centipedegrass: Do not fertilize at this time.

St. Augustinegrass: Do not fertilize at this time.

PERENNIALS

You can still topdress with composted manure or mushroom compost. Apply 2 inches of the organic material, then apply a fresh layer of mulch. Don't pile it up around stems where insect or disease problems could develop.

PROBLEM-SOLVE

ANNUALS

Rabbits are often unfairly accused of eating the leaves of annuals in winter. It is more likely that the leaves wither due to insufficient roots during windy, cold days or to root rot. Visit your beds after a rain and note if water stands there for more than a few minutes. If so, the bed is not well drained.

Consider redirecting the source of the water (moving gutter drains, trenching around the bed, and so forth). Examine the roots of plants whose leaves have disappeared. If they are almost nonexistent, re-dig the bed, and add more soil amendments to raise it farther above the surrounding soil.

BULBS

If you haven't cleaned up the garden yet, now is the time to remove leaf litter from summer bulbs and other perennials. A clean garden means fewer places for pest and disease problems to overwinter.

EDIBLES

Much can be done now to prevent pests and diseases next year in your fruit and vegetable garden. Fruit that didn't get picked during the summer may still be hanging on your trees— these "mummies" should not be left on the tree. Pick them off and remove them completely from your garden to prevent potential disease problems. Rake dead leaves under fruit trees, vines, and shrubs; replace them with fresh mulch. Spray trees with dormant horticultural oil to kill overwintering insects.

LAWNS

Watch for the bright green leaves of chickweed in your lawn. Spot-spray with a broad-leaf weedkiller.

Spray for wild onions in your lawn. Do this a second time in February, and another time in April. If you'd rather not use a herbicide, a stiff dandelion fork can be used to dig out the underground bulbs.

Tall fescue lawns that were planted in fall may appear slightly yellow after a December cold snap.

This minor frost damage will disappear in just a few days. It will not reoccur once the grass has become well established.

PERENNIALS

Pull any weeds that are left in the garden.

ROSES

Make sure all your pesticides are stored in a relatively inaccessible spot, preferably a locked cabinet.

If you have pesticides that have lost their label, contact the Georgia Department of Natural Resources, Environmental Protection Division for disposal options. While you clean and straighten your pesticide storage area, take time to reread the label on each product. Note the Caution, Warning, or Danger signal words, and double-check your application practices.

SHRUBS

Keep removing dead and diseased leaves from shrub beds. This will reduce the chances of insect and disease problems in the spring.

TREES

Rake up any leaf litter that you missed in the autumn; this will reduce the number of places for insects to overwinter.

VINES AND GROUNDCOVERS

Pull weeds out of groundcover beds and from the bases of vines. If you see signs of scale or spider mites, treat plants with horticultural oil.

■ *Pull out chickweed before it sets seed.*

Bibliography

No good gardening book can be completed without references. The following books have been invaluable to us, and we invite you to discover the tremendous amount of horticultural information contained in them.

Armitage, Allan. 2008. *Herbaceous Perennial Plants: A Treatise on Their Identification, Culture and Garden Attributes.* Stipes Publishing, Champaign, IL

Armitage, Allan. 2000. *Armitage's Garden Perennials: A Color Encyclopedia.* Timber Press, Portland, OR.

Armitage, Allan. 2001. *Armitage's Manual of Annuals, Biennials, and Half-hardy Perennials.* Stipes Publishing, Champaign, IL

Armitage, Allan. 2010. *Armitage's Vines and Climbers.* Timber Press. Portland, OR.

Brooklyn Botanic Garden. *Plants and Gardens Handbooks,* many different subjects. List available from Brooklyn Botanic Garden, 1000 Washington Ave., Brooklyn, NY.

Copeland, Linda and Allan Armitage. 2001. *Legends in the Garden: Who in the World is Nellie Stevens.* Cool Springs Press. Minneapolis, MN.

Darke, Rick. 2004. *Timber Press Pocket Guide to Ornamental Grasses.* Timber Press. Portland, OR.

Dirr, Michael, 2011, *Dirr's Encylopedia of Trees and Shrubs.* Timber Press. Portland,OR.

Dirr, Michael. 2009. *Manual of Woody Landscape Plants.* Stipes Publishing. Champaign, IL.

Gardiner, J.M. 1989. *Magnolias.* Globe Pequot Press. Chester, PA.

Gates, Galen et al. 1994. *Shrubs and Vines.* Pantheon Books. New York, NY.

Halfacre, R. Gordon and Anne R. Shawcroft. 1979. *Landscape Plants of the Southeast.* Sparks Press. Raleigh, NC.

Harper, Pamela. 2000. *Time-Tested Plants: Thirty Years in a Four-Season Garden.* Timber Press. Portland, OR.

Hipps, Carol Bishop. 1994. *In a Southern Garden.* Macmillan Publishing. New York, NY.

Lawrence, Elizabeth. 1991. *A Southern Garden.* The University of North Carolina Press. Chapel Hill, NC.

Lawson-Hall, Toni and Brian Rothera. 1996. *Hydrangeas.* Timber Press. Portland, OR.

Loewer, Peter. 1992. *Tough Plants for Tough Places.* Rodale Press. Emmaus, PA.

MacKenzie, David. 1997. *Perennial Groundcovers.* Timber Press. Portland, OR

Mikel, John. 1994. *Ferns for American Gardens.* Macmillan Publishing. New York, NY.

Ogden, Scott. 1994. *Garden Bulbs for the South.* Taylor Publishing. Dallas, TX.

Still, Steven. 1994. *Manual of Herbaceous Ornamental Plants, 4th edition.* Stipes Publishing. Champaign, IL.

Wilson, Jim. 1999. *Bullet-Proof Flowers for the South.* Taylor Publishing. Dallas, TX

Georgia Gardening Resources

Botanical Gardens

Atlanta Botanical Garden
Piedmont Park at The Prado
Atlanta, Georgia 30357
www.atlantabotanicalgarden.org

The Atlanta Botanical Garden is a lush oasis in the heart of Midtown Atlanta. The ABG features 15 acres of landscaped gardens, a conservatory that houses endangered tropical and desert plants from around the world, and a 15-acre hardwood forest with walking trails. This is an easily accessible gardening resource in the midst of urban Atlanta.

Atlanta History Center
130 West Paces Ferry Road NW
Atlanta, Georgia 30305
www.atlhist.org

On the grounds of the Atlanta History Center, visitors can experience 32 acres of gardens, woodlands, and nature trails that show the horticultural history of the Atlanta region. Seven distinct gardens feature a variety of gardening styles from native plantings to formal landscaping with boxwoods and classical statuary. A Garden for Peace has been installed as part of an international effort to promote world peace.

Callaway Gardens
Pine Mountain, Georgia 31822-2000
www.callawaygardens.com

Located 70 miles southwest of Atlanta and 30 miles north of Columbus, Callaway Gardens is a manmade landscape in a unique natural setting. It was conceived by its creators Cason Callaway and his wife Virginia as a place for visitors to discover natural beauty. Today, Callaway Gardens features the largest glass-enclosed butterfly conservatory in North America, and Mr. Cason's Vegetable Garden showcases Southern vegetables and annual flower trial gardens. In addition, the Sibley Horticulture Center showcases a year-round floral display that integrates indoor and outdoor plant settings. More than a million people visit the 1,500 acres of Callaway Gardens each year.

Fernbank Museum of Natural History
67 Clifton Road, NE
Atlanta, Georgia 30307

Fernbank Science Center
156 Heaton Park Drive, NE
Atlanta, Georgia 30307-1398
fsc.fernbank.edu

The grounds of the Fernbank Museum of Natural History and Fernbank Science Center feature two distinct garden areas. Adjacent to the Fernbank Science Center is the Fernbank Forest. For many years visitors have walked through the 65-acre woodland, a primeval Piedmont forest containing 1½ miles of paved trail lined with signs identifying various specimens. The grounds of the Fernbank Museum of Natural History feature the Stanton Rose Garden. Visitors there will see 1,300 roses, including All-America Rose Selections test plants.

Georgia Southern Botanical Garden
Georgia Southern University
1211 Fair Road (State Highway 67)
Statesboro, Georgia 30460
www2.gasou.edu/garden

The Georgia Southern Botanical Garden is a 10-acre site located two blocks from the campus of Georgia Southern University. The garden features native plants of Georgia, particularly those of the Coastal Plain. Various gardens include a Magnolia/Holly allee, a butterfly border, and an arboretum. Also within the botanical garden are a children's vegetable garden, nature trails, and seven original farm structures.

Massee Lane Gardens
One Massee Lane
Fort Valley, Georgia 31030
www.peach.public.lib.ga.us/ACS

Beginning with the planting of one camellia plant in 1936, Massee Lane Gardens now serves as the headquarters for the American Camellia Society. Located on the site of a former peach farm dating from the early 1900s, the garden also features an education museum, a rose garden, and a Japanese garden.

Perimeter College Botanical Garden
3251 Panthersville Road
Decatur, Georgia 30034
www.gpcnativegarden.org

The Perimeter College Botanical Garden focuses exclusively on Georgia native plants, and includes the largest collection of native plants in the state. Dozens of native ferns are featured along a shaded forest path. Approximately 1,500 sun- and shade-loving native plants can be seen at the Perimeter College South Campus.

State Botanical Garden of Georgia
2450 South Milledge Avenue
Athens, Georgia 30602
www.uga.edu/~botgarden

The State Botanical Garden of Georgia is a 313-acre preserve under the direction of The University of Georgia. The garden has 5 miles of nature trails, an International Garden, and a three-story tropical conservatory. The State Botanical Garden holds educational programs all year long and has a growing and active patrons organization.

Educational and Professional Organizations
Extension Service
800-ASKUGA1
www.gaurbanag.org

Local phone numbers can be found under your county government phone listings. The University of Georgia Cooperative Extension Service is an educational organization sponsored by the University of Georgia and local county governments. All Extension Service offices have staff members who specialize in agriculture/horticulture, home environment, and youth development. Offices offer free educational pamphlets and advice, and many publications are available for download at the Extension Service Web site.

The Garden Club of Georgia
www.uga.edu/gardenclub

A statewide organization of gardeners dedicated to inspiring beautification, conservation, and gardening education in Georgia.

Georgia Environmental Monitoring Network
www.georgiaweather.net

This unit of The University of Georgia maintains dozens of weather monitoring sites scattered throughout the state. Data from each site is uploaded daily to the Internet, where visitors can track historical and current rainfall amounts, soil temperatures, air temperatures, and other climatic conditions. Very handy for settling arguments about how "bad" the weather was in the past.

Georgia Forestry Commission
(800) GA-TREES
www.gfc.state.gas.us

Educates citizens about the importance of Georgia timber and forests. Supplies tree seedlings in bulk at low cost to citizens.

Georgia Green Industry Association
(888) GET-GGIA
www.ggia.org

A statewide organization of landscape and nursery companies that promotes professionalism in the industry. Sponsor of the Georgia Certified Landscape Professional and Georgia Certified Nursery Professional programs.

Georgia Native Plant Society
www.gnps.org

An organization of gardeners interested in learning more about the care and culture of native plants. Monthly meetings are free and open to the public.

Georgia Organics
www.georgiaorganics.org

An organization dedicated to promoting organic gardening and farming practices plus the sale of organic produce.

Georgia Perennial Plant Association
www.georgiaperennial.org

An organization of gardeners interested in learning more about the care and culture of perennial plants. Monthly meetings are free and open to the public.

Georgia Urban Ag Council
www.georgialandscapepro.com

An organization of metro Atlanta landscape companies and associated professionals. Sponsors "The Landscape Source," a listing of member companies and their areas of expertise.

Southeastern Flower Show
www.flowershow.org

The Southeastern Flower Show benefits the Atlanta Botanical Garden as well as amateur and expert gardeners throughout the South. Held in the latter part of February every year, the show features dozens of gardens presented by top garden designers, judged horticultural classes, and an extensive vendors market. Seminars and workshops by gardening experts make this a must-attend event for Georgia gardeners.

Glossary

Acidic soil: On a soil pH scale of 0 to 14, acidic soil has a pH lower than 5.5. Most garden plants prefer a soil a bit on the acidic side.

Afternoon sun: A garden receiving afternoon sun typically has full sun from 1:00 to 5:00 p.m. daily, with more shade during the morning hours.

Alkaline soil: On a soil pH scale of 0 to 14, alkaline soil has a pH higher than 7.0. Many desert plants thrive in slightly alkaline soils.

Annual: A plant that germinates (sprouts), flowers, and dies within one year or season (spring, summer, winter, or fall) is an annual.

***Bacillus thuringiensis* (B.t.):** B.t. is an organic pest control based on naturally occurring soil bacteria, often used to control harmful caterpillars such as cutworms, leaf rollers, and webworms.

Balled and burlapped (B&B): This phrase describes plants that have been grown in field nursery rows, dug up with their soil intact, wrapped with burlap, and tied with twine. Most of the plants sold balled and burlapped are large evergreen plants and deciduous trees.

Bare root: Bare-root plants are those that are shipped dormant, without being planted in soil or having soil around their roots. Roses are often shipped bare root.

Beneficial insects: These insects perform valuable services such as pollination and pest control. Ladybugs, soldier beetles, and some bees are examples.

Biennial: A plant that blooms during its second year and then dies is a biennial.

Bolting: This is a process when a plant switches from leaf growth to producing flowers and seeds. Bolting often occurs quite suddenly and is usually undesirable, because the plant usually dies shortly after bolting.

Brown materials: A part of a well-balanced compost pile, brown materials include high-carbon materials such as brown leaves and grass, woody plant stems, dryer lint, and sawdust.

Bud: The bud is an undeveloped shoot nestled between the leaf and the stem that will eventually produce a flower or plant branch.

Bulb: A bulb is a plant with a large, rounded underground storage organ formed by the plant stem and leaves. Examples are tulips, daffodils, and hyacinths. Bulbs that flower in spring are typically planted in fall.

Bush: See **shrub.**

Cane: A stem on a fruit shrub; usually blackberry or raspberry stems are called canes, but blueberry stems can also be referred to as canes.

Central leader: The term for the center trunk of a fruit tree.

Chilling hours: Hours when the air temperature is below 45°F; chilling hours are related to fruit production.

Common name: A name that is generally used to identify a plant in a particular region, as opposed to its botanical name, which is standard throughout the world; for example, the common name for Echinacea purpurea is "purple coneflower."

Contact herbicide: This type of herbicide kills only the part of the plant that it touches, such as the leaves or the stems.

Container: Any pot or vessel that is used for planting; containers can be ceramic, clay, steel, or plastic—or a teacup, bucket, or barrel.

Container garden: This describes a garden that is created primarily by growing plants in containers instead of in the ground.

Container grown: This describes a plant that is grown, sold, and shipped while in a pot.

Cool-season annual: This is a flowering plant, such as snapdragon or pansy, that thrives during cooler months.

Cool-season vegetable: This is a vegetable, such as spinach, broccoli, or peas, that thrives during cooler months.

Cover crop: These plants are grown specifically to enrich the soil, prevent erosion, suppress weeds, and control pests and diseases.

Cross-pollinate: This describes the transfer of pollen from one plant to another plant.

Dappled shade: This is bright shade created by high tree branches or tree foliage, where patches of sunlight and shade intermingle.

Day-neutral plant: A plant that flowers when it reaches a certain size, regardless of the day length, is a day-neutral plant.

Deadhead: To remove dead flowers in order to encourage further bloom and prevent the plant from going to seed.

Deciduous plant: A plant that loses its leaves seasonally, typically in fall or early winter.

Diatomaceous earth: A natural control for snails, slugs, flea beetles, and other garden pests, diatomaceous earth consists of ground-up fossilized remains of sea creatures.

Dibber: A tool consisting of a pointed wooden stick with a handle. Used for poking holes in the ground so seedlings, seeds, and small bulbs can be planted.

Divide: Technique consisting of digging up clumping perennials, separating the roots, and replanting. Dividing plants encourages vigorous growth and is typically performed in the spring or fall.

Dormancy: The period when plants stop growing in order to conserve energy, this happens naturally and seasonally, usually in winter.

Drip line: The ground area under the outer circumference of tree branches, this is where most of the tree's roots that absorb water and nutrients are found.

Dwarf: In the context of fruit gardening, a dwarf fruit tree is a tree that grows no taller than 10 feet tall and is usually a dwarf as a result of the rootstock of the tree.

Evergreen: A plant that keeps its leaves year-round, instead of dropping them seasonally.

Floating row covers: Lightweight fabric that can be used to protect plants from pests. Usually white in color.

Floricane: A second-year cane on a blackberry or raspberry shrub; floricanes are fruit bearing.

Flower stalk: The stem that supports the flower and elevates it so that insects can reach the flower and pollinate it is the flower stalk.

Four-inch pot: The 4-inch × 4-inch pots that many annuals and small perennials are sold in. Four-inch pots can also be sold in flats of 18 or 20.

Four-tine claw: Also called a cultivator, this hand tool typically has three to four curved tines and is used to break up soil clods or lumps before planting and to rake soil amendments into garden beds.

Frost: Ice crystals that form when the temperature falls below freezing (32°F) create frost.

Full sun: Areas of the garden that receive direct sunlight for six to eight hours a day or more, with no shade, are in full sun.

Fungicide: This describes a chemical compound used to control fungal diseases.

Gallon container: A standard nursery-sized container for plants, a gallon container is roughly equivalent to a gallon container of milk.

Garden fork: A garden implement with a long handle and short tines, use a garden fork for loosening and turning soil.

Garden lime: This soil amendment lowers soil acidity and raises the pH.

Garden soil: The existing soil in a garden bed; it is generally evaluated by its nutrient content and texture. Garden soil is also sold as a bagged item at garden centers and home improvement stores.

Germination: This is the process by which a plant emerges from a seed or a spore.

Grafted tree: This is a tree composed of two parts: the top, or scion, which bears fruit, and the bottom, or rootstock.

Graft union: This is the place on a fruit tree trunk where the rootstock and the scion have been joined.

Granular fertilizer: This type of fertilizer comes in a dry, pellet-like form rather than a liquid or powder.

Grass clippings: The parts of grass that are removed when mowing, clippings are a valuable source of nitrogen for the lawn or the compost pile.

Green materials: An essential element in composting that includes grass clippings, kitchen scraps, and manure and provides valuable nitrogen in the pile; green materials are high in nitrogen.

Hand pruners: An important hand tool that consists of two sharp blades that perform a scissoring motion, these are used for light pruning, clipping, and cutting.

Hardening off: This is the process of slowly acclimating seedlings and young plants grown in an indoor environment to the outdoors.

Hardiness zone map: This map lists average annual minimum temperature ranges of a particular area. This information is helpful in determining appropriate plants for the garden. North America is divided into eleven separate hardiness zones.

Hard rake: This tool has a long handle and rigid tines at the bottom. It is great for moving a variety of garden debris, such as soil, mulch, leaves, and pebbles.

Hedging: This is the practice of trimming a line of plants to create a solid mass for privacy or garden definition.

Heirloom: A plant that was more commonly grown pre-World War II.

Hoe: A long-handled garden tool with a short, narrow, flat steel blade, it is used for breaking up hard soil and removing weeds.

Hose breaker: This device screws onto the end of a garden hose to disperse the flow of water from the hose.

Host plant: A plant grown to feed caterpillars that will eventually morph into butterflies is called a host plant.

Hybrid: Plants produced by crossing two genetically different plants, hybrids often have desirable characteristics such as disease resistance.

Insecticide: This substance is used for destroying or controlling insects that are harmful to plants. Insecticides are available in organic and synthetic forms.

Irrigation: A system of watering the landscape, irrigation can be an in-ground automatic system, soaker or drip hoses, or hand-held hoses with nozzles.

Jute twine: A natural-fiber twine, jute is used for gently staking plants or tying them to plant supports.

Kneeling pad: A padded, weather-resistant cushion used for protecting knees while performing garden tasks such as weeding and planting.

Landscape fabric: A synthetic material that is laid on the soil surface to control weeds and prevent erosion.

Larva: The immature stage of an insect that goes through complete metamorphosis; caterpillars are butterfly or moth larvae.

Larvae: This is the plural of larva.

Leaf rake: A long-handled rake with flexible tines on the head, a leaf rake is used for easily and efficiently raking leaves into piles.

Liquid fertilizer: Plant fertilizer in a liquid form, some types need to be mixed with water, and some types are ready to use from the bottle.

Long-day plant: Plants that flower when the days are longer than their critical photoperiod, long-day plants typically flower in early summer, when the days are still getting longer.

Loppers: One of the largest manual gardening tools, use loppers for pruning branches of 1 to 3 inches in diameter with a scissoring motion.

Morning sun: Areas of the garden that have an eastern exposure and receive direct sun in the morning hours.

Mulch: Any type of material that is spread over the soil surface around the base of plants to suppress weeds and retain soil moisture is mulch.

Nematode: Microscopic, wormlike organisms that live in the soil, some nematodes are beneficial, while others are harmful.

Naturalized: Plants that are introduced into an area, as opposed to being native to it, are said to be naturalized.

Nectar plant: Flowers that produce nectar that attract and feed butterflies, encouraging a succession of blooms throughout the season.

New wood (new growth): The new growth on plants, it is characterized by a greener, more tender form than older, woodier growth.

Nozzle: A device that attaches to the end of a hose and disperses water through a number of small holes; the resulting spray covers a wider area.

Old wood: Old wood is growth that is more than one year old. Some fruit plants produce on old wood. If you prune these plants in spring before they flower and fruit, you will cut off the wood that will produce fruit.

Organic: This term describes products derived from naturally occurring materials instead of materials synthesized in a lab.

Part shade: Areas of the garden that receive three to six hours of sun a day are in part shade. Plants requiring part shade will often require protection from the more intense afternoon sun, either from tree leaves or from a building.

Part sun: Areas of the garden that receive three to six hours of sun a day. Although the term is often used interchangeably with "part shade," a "part sun" designation places greater emphasis on the minimal sun requirements.

Perennial: A plant that lives for more than two years. Examples include trees, shrubs, and some flowering plants.

Pesticide: A substance used for destroying or controlling insects that are harmful to plants. Pesticides are available in organic and synthetic forms.

pH: A figure designating the acidity or the alkalinity of garden soil, pH is measured on a scale of 1 to 14, with 7.0 being neutral.

Pinch: This is a method to remove unwanted plant growth with your fingers, promoting bushier growth and increased blooming.

Pitchfork: A hand tool with a long handle and sharp metal prongs, a pitchfork is typically used for moving loose material such as mulch or hay.

Plant label: This label or sticker on a plant container provides a description of the plant and information on its care and growth habits.

Pollination: The transfer of pollen for fertilization from the male pollen-bearing structure (stamen) to the female structure (pistil), usually by wind, bees, butterflies, moths, or hummingbirds; this process is required for fruit production.

Potting soil: A mixture used to grow flowers, herbs, and vegetables in containers, potting soil provides proper drainage and extra nutrients for healthy growth.

Powdery mildew: A fungal disease characterized by white powdery spots on plant leaves and stems, this disease is worse during times of drought or when plants have poor air circulation.

Power edger: This electric or gasoline-powered edger removes grass along flower beds and walkways for a neat appearance.

Pre-emergent herbicide: This weedkiller works by preventing weed seeds from sprouting.

Primocane: A first-year cane on a blackberry shrub, a primocane doesn't produce fruit.

Pruning: This is a garden task in which a variety of hand tools are used to remove dead or overgrown branches to increase plant fullness and health.

Pruning saw: This hand tool for pruning smaller branches and limbs features a long, serrated blade with an elongated handle.

Push mower: A lawn mower that is propelled by the user rather than a motor, typically having between five to eight steel blades that turn and cut as the mower is pushed.

Reel mower: A mower in which the blades spin vertically with a scissoring motion to cut grass blades.

Rhizome: An underground horizontal stem that grows side shoots, a rhizome is similar to a bulb.

Rootball: The network of roots and soil clinging to a plant when it is lifted out of the ground is the rootball.

Rootstock: The bottom part of a grafted fruit tree, rootstocks are often used to create dwarf fruit trees, impart pest or disease resistance, or make a plant more cold hardy.

Rotary spreader: A garden tool that distributes seed and herbicides in a pattern wider than the base of the spreader.

Runner: A stem sprouting from the center of a strawberry plant, a runner produces fruit in its second year.

Scaffold branch: This horizontal branch emerges almost perpendicular to the trunk.

Scientific name: This two-word identification system consists of the genus and species of a plant, such as *Ilex opaca*.

Scion: The top, fruit-bearing part of a grafted fruit tree is the scion.

Scissors: A two-bladed hand tool great for cutting cloth, paper, twine, and other lightweight materials, scissors are a basic garden tool.

Seed packet: The package in which vegetable and flower seeds are sold, it typically includes growing instructions, a planting chart, and harvesting information.

Seed-starting mix: Typically a soilless blend of perlite, vermiculite, peat moss, and other ingredients, seed-starting mix is specifically formulated for growing plants from seed.

Self-fertile: A plant that does not require cross-pollination from another plant in order to produce fruit.

Semidwarf: A fruit tree grafted onto a rootstock that restricts growth of the tree to one-half to two-thirds of its natural size.

Shade: Garden shade is the absence of any direct sunlight in a given area, usually due to tree foliage or building shadows.

Shop broom: A long-handled broom with a wide base used for efficiently sweeping a variety of fine to medium debris.

Short-day plant: Flowering when the length of day is shorter than its critical photoperiod, short-day plants typically bloom during fall, winter, or early spring.

Shovel: A handled tool with a broad, flat blade and slightly upturned sides, used for moving soil and other garden materials, a shovel is a basic garden tool.

Shredded hardwood mulch: A mulch consisting of shredded wood that interlocks, resisting washout and suppressing weeds, hardwood mulch can change soil pH.

Shrub: This woody plant is distinguished from a tree by its multiple trunks and branches and its shorter height of less than 15 feet tall.

Shrub rake: This long-handled rake with a narrow head fits easily into tight spaces between plants.

Sidedress: To sprinkle slow-release fertilizer along the side of a plant row or plant stem is to sidedress.

Slow-release fertilizer: This form of fertilizer releases nutrients at a slower rate throughout the season, requiring less-frequent applications.

Snips: This hand tool, used for snipping small plants and flowers, is perfect for harvesting fruits, vegetables, and flowers.

Soaker hose: This is an efficient watering system in which a porous hose, usually made from recycled rubber, allows water to seep out around plant roots.

Soil knife: This garden knife with a sharp, serrated edge, is used for cutting twine, plant roots, turf, and other garden materials.

Soil test: An analysis of a soil sample, this determines the level of nutrients (to identify deficiencies) and detects pH.

Spade: This short-handled tool with a sharp, rectangular metal blade is used for cutting and digging soil or turf.

Spur: This is a small, compressed, fruit-bearing branch on a fruit tree.

Standard: A fruit tree grown on its own seedling rootstock or a nondwarfing rootstock, this is the largest of the three sizes of fruit trees.

String trimmer: A hand-held tool that uses monofilament line instead of a blade to trim grass.

Succulent: A type of plant that stores water in its leaves, stems, and roots and is acclimated for arid climates and soil conditions.

Sucker: The odd growth from the base of a tree or a woody plant, often caused by stress, this also refers to sprouts from below the graft of a rose or fruit tree. Suckers divert energy away from the desirable tree growth and should be removed.

Summer annual: Annuals that thrive during the warmer months of the growing season.

Systemic herbicide: This type of weedkiller is absorbed by the plant's roots and taken into the roots to destroy all parts of the plant.

Taproot: This is an enlarged, tapered plant root that grows vertically downward.

Thinning: This is the practice of removing excess vegetables (root crops) to leave more room for the remaining vegetables to grow; also refers to the practice of removing fruits when still small from fruit trees so that the remaining fruits can grow larger.

Topdress: To spread fertilizer on top of the soil (usually around fruit trees or vegetables) is to topdress.

Transplants: Plants that are grown in one location and then moved to and replanted in another, seeds started indoors and nursery plants are two examples.

Tree: This woody perennial plant typically consists of a single trunk with multiple lateral branches.

Tree canopy: This is the upper layer of growth, consisting of the tree's branches and leaves.

Tropical plant: This is a plant that is native to a tropical region of the world, and thus acclimated to a warm, humid climate and not hardy to frost.

Trowel: This shovel-like hand tool is used for digging or moving small amounts of soil.

Turf: Grass and the surface layer of soil that is held together by its roots.

Variegated: The appearance of differently colored areas on plant leaves, usually white, yellow, or a brighter green.

Vegetable: A plant or part of a plant that is used for food.

Warm-season vegetable: A vegetable that thrives during the warmer months. Examples are tomatoes, okra, and peppers. These vegetables do not tolerate frost.

Watering wand: This hose attachment features a longer handle for watering plants beyond reach.

Water sprout: This vertical shoot emerges from a scaffold branch. It is usually nonfruiting and undesirable.

Weed and feed: A product containing both an herbicide for weed control and a fertilizer for grass growth.

Weeping: A growth habit in plants that features drooping or downward curving branches.

Wheat straw: These dry stalks of wheat, which are used for mulch, retain soil moisture and suppress weeds.

Wood chips: Small pieces of wood made by cutting or chipping, wood chips are used as mulch in the garden.

Index

Meet Erica Glasener

ERICA GLASENER

Erica Glasener, horticulturist, author, lecturer, and award-winning host of HGTV's *A Gardener's Diary* for fourteen years. As the host for this popular TV show, she introduced her audience to gardeners, horticulture professionals, specialty plant growers, landscape architects, and more from across the country. In July of 2011 she received a Garden Media Award from the Perennial Plant Association for her promotion of perennials through writing and lectures. Currently she provides online content for the Southern Living Plant Collection (southernlivingplants.com/) and for Fiskars where she is a garden expert (www2.fiskars.com/Activities/Gardening/Gardening-Experts). She also writes a bimonthly blog for Gibbs Gardens, located in Ball Ground, Georgia.

For over ten years she wrote a column on plants and garden design for the *Atlanta Journal-Constitution.* She has also written about gardening for *Southern Lady Magazine* and served as a contributing editor for *Fine Gardening.* Her articles have appeared in *The New York Times, The Farmer's Almanac,* and *The Green Guide.* A frequent guest on regional and national lifestyle radio programs, she enjoys helping people solve garden problems. A popular speaker, she presents lectures at garden shows across the country from Seattle to Epcot. In 2010 she was invited to Homer, Alaska, as a speaker. The author of several books, her latest is *Proven Plants: Southern Gardens.* She lives with her family in Atlanta,

Georgia, where her garden serves as a test site for many of the plants she writes about. To keep up with her garden activities, you can subscribe for free updates at www.ericaglasener.com or follow her on Twitter @ericaglasener.

Meet Walter Reeves

WALTER REEVES

Walter Reeves is retired from the University of Georgia Cooperative Extension, where he worked for twenty-nine years. He grew up on a farm in rural Fayette County, Georgia, where he learned to garden from his parents and his grandmother, Bubber.

He hosts *The Lawn and Garden Show* radio call-in show on NewsTalk WSB every Saturday morning and has hosted gardening radio shows for twenty-five years.

Walter also writes a weekly column of garden questions and answers for the Thursday Living section of the *Atlanta Journal-Constitution* and has just completed his twentieth year of this effort. He hosted *Your Southern Garden* on Georgia Public Television for ten years.

In his spare time, Walter manages www.walterreeves.com, which contains over 6,000 articles and answers to garden questions. He also edits and publishes *The Georgia Gardener,* a bi-weekly email newsletter.

He's the author of *Month by Month Gardening in Georgia; Georgia Gardener's Guide; Georgia Vegetables, Fruits, Herbs, and Nuts;* and *501 Garden Questions and Answers for Georgia,* all published by Cool Springs Press.

Walter has served on the board of Southface, the sustainability organization, for sixteen years. He is an honorary Master Gardener and an enthusiastic promoter of environmentally responsible landscaping.

Photo Credits

Cool Springs Press: pp. 8 (all), 11, 12, 26, 43, 53 (all), 56, 71 (all), 73 (all), 74, 76, 81, 85, 90, 92, 104, 111 (both), 112, 122, 128, 129, 143, 157 (all), 158 (right), 159, 167, 171, 179, 180 (both), 182, 186, 192, 195 (all), 200, 202, 205 (top), 208, 209 (bottom), 212 (all), 216 (all), 217 (both)

Katie Elzer-Peters: pp. 39, 72, 83 (both), 106, 109, 113, 118, 124, 126 (all), 130 (left), 133, 136, 138 (right), 144, 146, 147, 151 (top), 158 (left), 166, 168, 174, 176, 196 (both), 199, 203

Erica Glasener: pp. 18, 20, 21, 22, 23, 36, 46, 49, 62, 64, 65, 67, 70, 75, 84, 86, 93, 102, 134

iStock: pp. 44, 99

Troy Marden: pp. 162

Walter Reeves: pp. 138 (left), 142, 151 (bottom), 193, 205, 214, 219

Shutterstock: pp. 6, 32, 35, 60, 95, 107, 114, 116, 119, 130 (right), 152, 164 (both), 172, 187, 190, 206, 209 (top)

Neil Soderstrom: p. 141 (all), 170

Wikimedia: pp. 123